Libya, the Responsibility to Protect and the Future of Humanitarian Intervention

Edited by

Aidan Hehir
University of Westminster, UK

and

Robert Murray
University of Alberta, Canada

palgrave
macmillan

First published 2013 by
PALGRAVE MACMILLAN

Palgrave Macmillan in the UK is an imprint of Macmillan Publishers Limited, registered in England, company number 785998, of Houndmills, Basingstoke, Hampshire RG21 6XS.

Palgrave Macmillan in the US is a division of St Martin's Press LLC, 175 Fifth Avenue, New York, NY 10010.

Palgrave Macmillan is the global academic imprint of the above companies and has companies and representatives throughout the world.

Palgrave® and Macmillan® are registered trademarks in the United States, the United Kingdom, Europe and other countries.

ISBN 978–1–137–27394–9

This book is printed on paper suitable for recycling and made from fully managed and sustained forest sources. Logging, pulping and manufacturing processes are expected to conform to the environmental regulations of the country of origin.

A catalogue record for this book is available from the British Library.

A catalog record for this book is available from the Library of Congress.

Typeset by MPS Limited, Chennai, India.

Libya, the Responsibility to Protect and the Future of Humanitarian Intervention

Also by Aidan Hehir

Humanitarian Intervention: An Introduction, 2nd edition
(Palgrave Macmillan, 2013)

The Responsibility to Protect: Rhetoric, Reality and the Future of Humanitarian Intervention (Palgrave Macmillan, 2012)

International Law, Security and Ethics (co-editor, Routledge, 2011)

Humanitarian Intervention: An Introduction (Palgrave Macmillan, 2010)

Kosovo, Intervention and Statebuilding (editor, Routledge, 2010)

Humanitarian Intervention after Kosovo (Palgrave Macmillan, 2008)

Statebuilding: Theory and Practice (co-editor, Routledge, 2007)

Also by Robert W. Murray

International Security and the Arctic (co-editor, Cambria Press, 2014)

System, Society and the World: Exploring the English School of International Relations (editor, e-International Relations, 2013)

Aidan would like to dedicate this book to Mary Hehir

Robert would like to dedicate this book to the four most patient people he knows – Mark Spencer, Pierre Lizée, Andy Knight and Tom Keating

Contents

Tables and Figures

Tables

Figures

Acknowledgements

We would like to thank everyone at Palgrave Macmillan who helped bring this project to fruition and each of the contributors to this book.

Aidan would like to thank his colleagues at the Department of Politics and International Relations at the University of Westminster and all his friends and family, especially his wife Sarah and daughters, Esmé, Elsie and Iris.

Robert would like to thank his family, his friends, the feedback and support of Dr Matthew Weinert (University of Delaware), his colleagues at the University of Alberta, and to express gratitude for the tireless work and dedication of his co-editor Aidan.

Notes on Contributors

Aidan Hehir is Director of the Security and International Relations Programme at the University of Westminster, UK. He researches and writes on the laws governing the use of force, and humanitarian intervention in particular. He has published a number of books including *The Responsibility to Protect: Rhetoric, Reality and the Future of Humanitarian Intervention* (Palgrave Macmillan, 2012); *Humanitarian Intervention: An Introduction* (Palgrave Macmillan, 2010; 2nd edition 2013); *Humanitarian Intervention after Kosovo* (Palgrave Macmillan, 2008).

Eric A. Heinze is Associate Professor of Political Science and International Studies at the University of Oklahoma, USA. His research deals with the ethics and law of armed conflict, human rights, and international intervention. He is the author of *Waging Humanitarian War: The Ethics, Law and Politics of Humanitarian Intervention* (SUNY, 2009); co-editor of *Ethics, Authority, and War: Non-State Actors and the Just War Tradition* (Palgrave Macmillan, 2010); and editor of *Justice, Sustainability, and Security: Global Ethics for the 21st Century* (Palgrave Macmillan, forthcoming).

Tom Keating is a Professor and former Chair of the Department of Political Science at the University of Alberta, Canada, where he has also served as former Vice-Dean in the Faculty of Arts. He is the author of *Canada and World Order* (Oxford University Press, 2013) and also of *Global Politics, Emerging Networks, Trends, and Challenges*, co-authored with Andy Knight (Oxford University Press, 2010). His primary areas of expertise are Canadian foreign policy, international relations and international ethics.

Alan J. Kuperman is Associate Professor at the LBJ School of Public Affairs, University of Texas at Austin, USA. He is author of *The Limits of Humanitarian Intervention: Genocide in Rwanda* (Brookings, 2001) and co-editor of *Gambling on Humanitarian Intervention: Moral Hazard, Rebellion and Civil War* (Routledge, 2006). He currently leads a five-year research project on Constitutional Design and Conflict Management in Africa, funded by a Minerva grant from the US government. He holds a PhD in political science from MIT.

Robert W. Murray is an Adjunct Professor of Political Science at the University of Alberta, Canada. He also serves as a blogger for e-International Relations and is a Contributor for Troy Media. His work has focused primarily on issues of international security theory and foreign policy analysis.

Kim Richard Nossal is Professor of Political Studies and Director of the Centre for International and Defence Policy at Queen's University, Kingston, Ontario, Canada. His latest book, with Stéphane Roussel and Stéphane Paquin, is *International Policy and Politics in Canada* (Pearson, 2011).

Theresa Reinold is a postdoctoral research fellow at the Social Science Research Center, Berlin. Her current research focuses on the diffusion of rule of law scripts in a world of legal and cultural pluralism. Her articles have appeared in *The American Journal of International Law*, the *Review of International Studies*, the *Journal of Intervention and Statebuilding*, the *International Journal of Constitutional Law*, and *Global Responsibility to Protect*, among others. She has also written a monograph titled *Sovereignty and the Responsibility to Protect: The Power of Norms and the Norms of the Powerful* (Routledge, 2012).

Brent J. Steele is an Associate Professor of Political Science and International Relations, and Director of Faculty Programs for the Office of International Programs at the University of Kansas, USA. He is the author of a number of articles, and three books, *Ontological Security in International Relations* (Routledge, 2008), *Defacing Power: the Aesthetics of Insecurity in Global Politics* (University of Michigan Press, 2010) and *Alternative Accountabilities in Global Politics: the Scars of Violence* (Routledge, 2013). He is also the co-editor of two volumes, *Ethics, Authority and War: Non-state Actors and the Just War Tradition* (Palgrave Macmillan, 2009, with Eric Heinze), and *Theory and Application of the 'Generation' in International Relations and Politics* (Palgrave Macmillan, 2012, with Jonathan Acuff).

Alex de Waal is executive director of the World Peace Foundation at the Fletcher School, Tufts University, USA. He has written widely on Sudan and the Horn of Africa, including humanitarian crisis and response, human rights, HIV/AIDS and governance in Africa, and conflict and peacebuilding. During 2009–12 he served as adviser to the African Union on Sudan. Among a number of books, he is the author of *Famine Crimes: Politics and the Disaster Relief Industry in Africa* (James Currey, 1997) and co-author, with Julie Flint, of *Darfur: A New History of a Long War* (Zed Books, 2008).

1
Introduction: Libya and the Responsibility to Protect

Aidan Hehir

Introduction

Resolution 1973 authorising the imposition of a no-fly zone over Libya was passed – on 17 March 2011 – on the third day of the International Studies Association's (ISA) Annual Convention. The crisis in Libya erupted after the call for papers had closed and thus it was not the subject of any conference papers. Prior to the Resolution being passed, however, Libya and the Responsibility to Protect (R2P) did feature prominently in many of the panel discussions. Prior to 17 March, no-one, at least to my knowledge, predicted that the UN Security Council would sanction measures as robust as those contained in Resolution 1973. At the 2012 ISA convention there was a proliferation of papers, panels and roundtables discussing the significance of the intervention; the only thing academics seemed to agree on was that Resolution 1973 was a surprise.

International Relations (IR) academics were certainly not alone in failing to anticipate the dramatic convulsions of February and March 2011, and the intervention in Libya joins a long list of 'unforeseen events'. In defence of the utility of IR, this oft-proven inability to accurately anticipate events is arguably mitigated by a capacity to retrospectively analyse motivations and catalysts and, most importantly, situate superficially unique case studies in a broader narrative and identify their likely future implications. Yet events such as the intervention in Libya, while mobilizing sudden collective interest, invariably spark division and heated debate. Of course, the contestation that characterizes academia, particularly within IR, is arguably one of its strengths. This book seeks to engage with the ongoing debate and aims to temper the more effusive exhortations that greeted Resolution 1973. We do not purport to offer 'the definitive' explanation as to why events in Libya unfolded as they did, but rather to analyse this case study's significance for R2P and the future of humanitarian intervention more generally. One prediction which is surely incontrovertible is that Libya will join the long list of 'seminal' post-Cold War case studies – Somalia, Bosnia, Rwanda, Kosovo, Iraq, Darfur and others – and thus continue to be the subject of debate for many years.

This introductory chapter initially provides a brief overview of events in Libya from February to October 2011 to serve as a basic contextual foundation. I then discuss R2P with a view to identifying its status – legal and political – prior to events in Libya so as to facilitate comparative analysis. In the final section I discuss the structure of the book.

The Arab Spring and Libya

During the 1980s, Colonel Gaddafi's support for various international terrorist organizations, his direct involvement in murderous attacks against the US, the UK, France and Germany, and his ill-fated attempts to unite the Arab world in a coalition hostile to Western interests, led him to become arguably the most reviled international figure in the West (see Chapter 4). All this changed, however, in the wake of the 2003 invasion of Iraq; evidently fearing a similar fate, Gaddafi disbanded his chemical weapons programme and began a rapid process of reintegrating with the West and the international community more generally (Vandewalle 2006, p. 177). The new strategy produced immediate results and Gaddafi's 'rehabilitation' was regularly cited by proponents of the 'war on terror' as evidence of the efficacy of 'the Bush Doctrine' (Frum and Pearle 2004: 260). In late 2009 *The Guardian* published a review of Colonel Gaddafi's 40-year reign, which concluded:

> . . . many things are going his way; Western oil companies and investors are flocking to Tripoli, domestic repression has eased somewhat, and even tourism is developing . . . Gaddafi stills turns heads everywhere he goes, even sharing a photo call with Barack Obama at the G8 Summit in Italy. Shortly after the 40th anniversary celebrations he will address the United Nations in New York as Chair of the African Union. The handsome young Colonel has come a long way. (Black 2009)

At the time the idea that two years later Gaddafi would be deposed, and brutally murdered, during a NATO-led military intervention would have seemed absurd. Indeed, the idea of a region-wide eruption of popular resistance was arguably inconceivable until it actually began. Certain observers were aware of the existence of societal discontent in the Arab World but the scale, duration and consequences of the Arab Spring was not predicted, even by Middle East specialists (Gause 2011).

Prior to the Arab Spring, civil society in the Arab World had often been depicted as undeveloped and incapable of generating momentum for democratic change (Yom 2005; Stephan and Robertson 2003). The 'Orientalist' notion that Arabs were pre-disposed to authoritarianism certainly facilitated this conception (Santini 2011). As is now clear, however, underneath the facade of order, tensions were mounting. In Libya, Gaddafi's failure to create a strong sense of national citizenship amongst the population, coupled with his oppressive policies and remoteness, had created a dangerous disjuncture between the people and the regime. Indeed, with almost unique foresight, in 2006 Dirk Vandewalle warned that, while Gaddafi's aberrant rule had demonstrated remarkable continuity, his system '. . . will face considerable challenges in the future' (2006: 1). While Libya displayed few overt signs of looming rebellion, people in the Eastern province of Cyrenaica had traditionally been hostile to Gaddafi's rule and were becoming more publicly vocal; from 2007 protests had been regularly taking place in Benghazi over the massacre at the Abu Salim prison in 1996, albeit without generating much international attention (Becker 2011).

In pursuing the 'war on terror' the West supported a number of undemocratic regimes, overlooking their repressive domestic policies to secure their support against al-Qaeda and Islamic fundamentalism more generally (Hollis 2012: 93). Libya served as a site for 'extraordinary rendition'; thus Gaddafi's new international utility facilitated his domestic repression (Amnesty International 2012; Cobain 2012). His international rehabilitation had diminished his perceived threat to international security, while his new role as international statesman cemented his self-image as the archetypal 'strongman' crucial to the maintenance of domestic order. According to a 2010 report by Amnesty International,

> Libya's reintegration into the international community has not been accompanied by significant reforms or long-lasting improvements in the domestic human rights situation . . . members of the EU and the USA . . . are turning a blind eye to the human rights situation in order to further national interests. (2010: 9)

The combination of Gaddafi's hostile intransigence and the lack of external support led the disaffected within Libya to conclude that they would have to act unilaterally to initiate democratic reform (Hollis 2012: 85–6). As a result, by the end of 2010 Libya was, according to the International Crisis Group, 'a large pressure cooker ready to explode' (2011: 2). The uprisings in Tunisia and Egypt, driven by the cries *Ash-sha'b yurīd isqāṭ an-niẓām* (the people want to bring down the regime), served as the direct catalyst and on 15 February mass demonstrations held in Benghazi soon spread throughout the rest of the country.

From the perspective of international observers the sudden eruption of unrest in Libya was certainly a surprise; as Bellamy notes,

> None of the world's various risk-assessment frameworks viewed the country as posing any sort of threat of mass atrocities. Neither was a conflict widely anticipated. For example, CrisisWatch, the early-warning arm of the International Crisis Group, did not even mention Libya in its report of February 2011, and did not issue a 'conflict risk alert' until after the conflict had actually erupted. (2011: 4)

A report by UNICEF in 2010 noted that Libya had experienced a 'buoyant' growth rate, high per capita income, high literacy rates and high life expectancy and ranked the country 55th out of 182 states (International Crisis Group 2011: 2). The Minorities at Risk Coalition's list of 68 states 'at risk' did not include Libya (Bellamy and Williams 2011: 838). Internationally Libya was elected uncontested to the UN Human Rights Council in May 2010 and in October the EU and Libya agreed a deal on migration cooperation, to the dismay of many human rights organizations (Human Rights Watch 2011: 567).

Libya's decent into violence provoked an unusually rapid and robust response from both regional organizations and the UN. On 22 February the Organisation of Islamic Conference criticized Gaddafi's tactics as having caused, 'a humanitarian disaster incompatible with Islamic and human values' (2011) while, more significantly, the Arab League suspended Libya. The following day the African Union's Peace and Security Council declared it '. . . strongly condemns the indiscriminate and excessive use of force and lethal weapons against peaceful protestors'. Condemnatory statements were issued by the UN High Commissioner for Human Rights, the UN Special Adviser on the Prevention of Genocide and the Special Adviser on the Responsibility to Protect (Bellamy 2011: 2). On 25 February the UN Human Rights Council convened a special session during which they condemned the violence and called for Libya to be suspended. The formal suspension, the first of its kind, was unanimously endorsed by the General Assembly on 1 March.

On 26 February the Security Council invoked its Chapter VII powers and passed Resolution 1970. The Resolution referred the situation to the ICC and imposed an arms embargo, travel ban and asset freeze against the Libyan authorities. Given that significant protests had begun only eleven days earlier, and China and Russia's historically conservative approach to external involvement in intra-state conflicts, Resolution 1970 was in itself an unusually unified and rapid response (Weiss 2011). Despite this pressure, and appeals from regional organizations, the violence continued. On 17 March the Security Council passed Resolution 1973 which sanctioned the imposition of a no-fly zone over Libya. The Resolution condemned 'the gross and systematic violation of human rights . . . committed by the Libyan authorities' and warned that these acts may 'amount to crimes against humanity'. The Security Council sanctioned 'a ban on all flights in the airspace of the Libyan Arab Jamahiriya' and, most significantly, authorized states to 'take all necessary measures . . . to protect civilians and civilian populated areas under threat of attack'. The Resolution was passed with ten states voting affirmatively while China, Russia, Germany, Brazil and India abstained.

Military action began on 19 March and was initially led by the US, France and the UK. Despite the concerns of prominent members such as Germany and Poland, NATO agreed to lead the operation on 24 March and on 4 April the US withdrew its forces from direct combat though it continued to play a central role in coordinating the mission (Barry 2011: 5; Daalder and Stavridis 2012). A number of non-NATO members – Sweden, Jordan, Qatar, Morocco and the UAE – also took part in the operation.

NATO had three official aims; police the arms embargo, patrol the no-fly zone and protect civilians (Daalder and Stavridis 2012). The third aim proved by far the most difficult to achieve and it was this which ultimately led to the major controversy surrounding NATO's prosecution of the campaign. The rebels proved to be unable to defend many of their positions and without NATO support there is little doubt that they would have been overrun (Barry 2011: 9). To prevent this, and the slaughter of civilians that would allegedly follow, NATO's strategy changed from the initial focus on debilitating the regime's military bases and heavy weapons to a more expansive set of targets, including, most controversially, regime change (International Crisis Group 2011: i). China, Russia and South Africa publicly criticized what they saw as NATO's illegitimate interpretation of Resolution 1973 (Barry 2011: 6).

By the end of May, the mission was faltering as the rebel-held cities Misrata and Jebel Nafusa seemed about to fall, prompting France to unilaterally (and illegally) air-drop weapons to the rebels (Barry 2011: 7).

On 26 April the African Union called for an end to NATO's campaign and rejected calls for Gaddafi to step down warning, '. . . it should be left to Libyans to choose their leaders and international actors should refrain from taking positions or making pronouncements that can only complicate the search for a solution' (African Union 2011: 12). To ensure success, NATO stretched the terms of Resolution 1973 beyond breaking point and by August this, combined with defections from Gaddafi's regime, arms illegally smuggled to rebels from the UAE, Qatar and France, and military support from Sudan (see Chapters 4 and 9) turned the tide (Smith 2011: 75). Operation Unified Protector officially ended on 31 October, 222 days after it had started; Colonel Gaddafi was dead and a National Transitional Council was in power.

The responsibility to protect (R2P)

As detailed in many of the subsequent chapters, Resolution 1973, the intervention itself and the outcome, were greeted with jubilation by many of R2P's more vocal proponents and championed as evidence of a new disposition amongst the Security Council and the international community more generally. Prior to the intervention R2P had a mixed record, characterized by the widespread recognition of the term but modest actual impact. The concept had undoubtedly made rapid progress in terms of achieving global publicity and a place in the international political lexicon. Two paragraphs of the 2005 World Summit *Outcome Document* referred directly to R2P constituting significant official, if not quite legal, recognition (Stahn 2007). In 2009 the General Assembly held a special three-day debate on R2P and the overwhelming majority of states spoke in favour of the basic principles at the core of R2P (Hehir 2011). The new office of the Special Adviser on the Responsibility to Protect was established in 2008 and by the end of the decade R2P was officially referred to in a number of Security Council and General Assembly resolutions. Additionally, a number of NGOs, think tanks and research centres were established to specifically focus on promoting R2P, while within academia the concept was the subject of myriad books and articles – including a journal established in 2009 to focus solely on R2P – on a remarkably diverse range of subjects from climate change to women's rights.

Yet, despite these achievements, the real-world impact of R2P was modest. Various crises within R2P's purview raged unabated; where, many asked, was R2P during the conflagrations in Sri Lanka, the Democratic Republic of the Congo (DRC) and, most notably, Darfur? If

R2P was championed by its many proponents as 'revolutionary', how could it be that in the first ten months of 2008 alone some 290,000 people were displaced from Darfur while four million required humanitarian assistance (Coalition of NGOs on Darfur 2008: 7–8). At the time the UN Special Rapporteur on Sudan stated that 'violence and sexual abuse of women and children . . . continue almost unabated throughout Darfur' (UN General Assembly 2008: 12). Kofi Annan, indeed, stated that the reaction to Darfur showed, '. . . we had learnt nothing from Rwanda' (Fisher 2007: 103).

Yet in his report to the General Assembly prior to the 2009 debate on R2P, UN Secretary-General Ban Ki-Moon defended R2P's record. While accepting that the international response to the crises in Darfur, the DRC and elsewhere were lamentable, he claimed: 'Nonetheless, when confronted with crimes or violations relating to the responsibility to protect or their incitement, today the world is less likely to look the other way than in the last century' (Ban Ki-Moon 2009: 24). The evidence he advanced in defence of this appraisal was the role of Juan Méndez, then Special Adviser on the Prevention of Genocide, in defusing the crisis in the Ivory Coast in November 2004 when he (successfully) warned the Ivorian government to cease the proliferation of hate speech. His second example was the international response to the crisis in Kenya following the presidential election in December 2007. Following 1,000 fatalities and over 250,000 displaced persons, Francis Deng, the new Special Adviser on the Prevention of Genocide, invoked R2P in calling for an end to the violence, a call which was ultimately heeded.

Of course, while no-one can deny that in both crises R2P was employed as a rhetorical tool by external actors appealing for calm, whether this was a causal factor in the eventual cessation of the violence in an altogether different matter. It is certainly *not* the case that prior to the advent of R2P external actors lacked the means to condemn violence or that successful external mediation is a post-R2P phenomenon (Hehir 2012: 132). Additionally, despite the near ubiquity of the term, questions began to be raised as to its actual meaning and, crucially, whether states shared an understanding of its remit. While the 2009 General Assembly debate had demonstrated almost universal support for R2P, the precise nature of the R2P recognized varied considerably; one of the more effusive endorsements came from the government of Sudan which obviously held a markedly different interpretation of host-state responsibility to that of Western states (Hehir 2011: 7). The absence of thresholds determining precisely when an issue moved from the host state's jurisdiction to the international community's concern was an additional and obviously troubling ambiguity (Focarelli 2008; Reinold 2010). The proliferation of literature on R2P and its association with a wide variety of only tangentially related issues meant that its very meaning had been – paradoxically – irrevocably diluted by virtue of its ubiquity. As a result there was a growing consensus that R2P was little more than a political slogan destined to suffer the same sorry fate as 'make poverty history' and 'sustainable development'.

This ambiguity related also to R2P's legal status; while the 2005 World Summit *Outcome Document* certainly provided the concept with a more definite legal character than the original report by the ICISS, paragraphs 138 and 139, which recognized R2P, simply reiterated existing international law (Hakimi 2010: 343; Hehir 2010; Peters 2009: 538). As Simon Chesterman wrote, the *Outcome Document* '. . . essentially provided that the Security Council could authorize, on a case-by-case basis, things that it had been authorizing for more than a decade' (2011: 2). The International Commission on Intervention and State Sovereignty (ICISS) had been set up to establish 'clearer rules, procedures and criteria for determining whether, when and how to intervene' (2001: 11) and thus the fact that R2P has evolved to the point where it merely reconfirmed the existing discretionary powers of the Security Council naturally led many to wonder how it could possibly be effective given the system was exactly the same (Meyer 2009: 45; Berman 2007: 157).

Thus, by the end of 2010 R2P faced three key criticisms; first, that evidence of its efficacy was lacking; second, that states held widely divergent understandings of its remit and this ambiguity diminished its putative status as a norm; and third, that it had catalyzed no actual legal reform and thus the very system it was established to change remained intact.

Resolution 1973 and the subsequent intervention in Libya provided R2P's supporters with a much-needed boost; this was, Gareth Evans declared, '. . . a textbook case of the R2P norm working exactly as it was supposed to' (Evans 2011) and Ban Ki-Moon (2011) declared triumphantly: 'By now it should be clear to all that the Responsibility to Protect has arrived.' This book seeks to assess the validity of these claims; though not all chapters focus specifically on R2P the analysis in each should help us to formulate a more accurate understanding of the unique constellation of factors which aligned to facilitate the decision to intervene. The book is not an attempt to uncover nefarious agendas or determine the 'real' reasons for the intervention; the analyses here individually and collectively highlight those particular aspects of the intervention which challenge the sweeping, and often grandiose, claims made in its wake which, in our view, overlooked many troubling nuances in favour of unsubstantiated generalizations. The book is heavily orientated towards R2P but the analyses can also, of course, be situated within the more traditional – and ostensibly old-fashioned – 'humanitarian intervention' debate and the Libyan intervention must surely be seen as a modern example of this debate/trend which predates R2P.

The structure of this book

In Chapter 2, Robert Murray deals with the contestation surrounding the impetus for the intervention in Libya. He summarizes the humanitarian argument – that the intervention was impelled by concerns for the suffering demonstrators and thus 'R2P in action' – and the strategic-necessity argument, namely that the intervention was motivated by a desire to prevent further destabilization in this geo-strategically important region. Linking his analysis to historical patterns, Murray argues that the intervention is best explained as primarily driven by the logic of the latter; this has obvious implications for assessments of the intervention in Libya but, more broadly, suggests the strategic calculations states make remain largely unaltered by the rise of 'human security' and its most prominent manifestation, R2P.

In Chapter 3 I seek to explain the logic underpinning the strategy adopted by R2P's proponents and in particular the emphasis on 'mobilizing political will' through the proliferation of 'moral norms' over legal reform. This strategy, I argue, derives from the teleology inherent in the liberal 'end of history' thesis which considers progress – in the form of the spread of capitalism and liberal democracy – inevitable and irresistible. Concurrent with this vision of the future is the conviction that democracies are responsive to popular advocacy, hence the preference for normative pressure rather than legal reform. This is a strategy, I argue, which is at variance with the record of normative advocacy in the post-Cold War era and one which ultimately overlooks the implications of the looming structural change represented by the rise of China and Russia.

In Chapter 4 Alex de Waal provides a detailed overview of both Gaddafi's relationship with the African Union (AU) and the League of Arab States prior to the 2011 uprisings, and insights into the diplomatic machinations which took place after the rebellion began. This sheds light both on the divisions within the AU and the potentially viable diplomatic options rejected by the Transitional National Council (TNC) and ultimately 'killed by France, Britain and the United States' (p. 78). The manner in which Gaddafi's regime – odious as it was – fell has had, de Waal notes, serious negative implications for the future stability of Libya and the region. Of arguably greatest interest and indeed concern is de Waal's revelations regarding the role played by Sudan in supporting the overthrow of Gaddafi. Given the Sudanese government's record in Darfur, the fact that NATO worked closely with the Sudanese military – to the extent that the Sudanese at times directed NATO air strikes – obviously calls into question the ethical claims made about the intervention in Libya.

In Chapter 5 Theresa Reinold interrogates the notion of an 'African' security culture. While the AU has often been presented as adhering to the logic of R2P – in particular by virtue of article 4(h) of its constitutive act – the intervention in Libya highlighted the disjuncture between rhetoric and reality and the fissures within the AU. Reinold argues that the AU's often tepid and ambivalent attitude towards the crisis in Libya can be explained by factors from different levels of analysis – the societal, national, (sub-)regional and global. R2P's absorption into the AU has, naturally she suggests, been influenced and altered by these various levels throughout the member states, to the point that the concept is very obviously contested and thus its efficacy tempered.

Richard Nossal argues in Chapter 6 that the debate within Canada regarding the justifications for the intervention in Libya provides a qualitative insight into a general disposition amongst the Western states during the intervention, namely 'don't mention R2P'. Nossal provides a detailed analysis of the Canadian government's rhetorical creativity and contrasts this with others more eager to champion the intervention as 'R2P in action'. While, Nossal argues, the determination within Canada – and indeed the US, France and the UK – to refrain from mentioning R2P was intended as a rhetorical ploy, ultimately the intervention – and the mission creep which characterized it – has nonetheless been identified as indicative of the inevitable outcome of R2P-type action by states such as Russia and China, not least because of the celebratory rhetoric employed by R2P's more vocal champions. The fact that these states, cautious about R2P prior to the intervention in Libya, are now openly hostile to the idea, Nossal argues, greatly diminishes the prospect that Libya will herald a new precipitous era for R2P as many of its supporters claim.

In Chapter 7 Eric Heinze and Brent Steele argue that the intervention in Libya, though certainly unexpected, can be explained through the use of a generational analysis. Specifically, they argue that the post-2005 World Summit manifestation of R2P is a reflection of the 'lessons learned' by contemporary politicians whose formative experiences were the events of the 1990s. There remains since the 1990s, they suggest, a permissive normative environment for humanitarian intervention but actual intervention remains contingent on a confluence of circumstances which rarely occurs. Thus, rather than Libya constituting a 'new' type of intervention, it is consistent with the selective interventionism that characterized the 1990s and thus is an aberration rather than a harbinger.

Tom Keating, in Chapter 8, begins by providing an overview of the UN Security Council's approach to the use of force in the post-Cold War era. This has been, he notes, obviously characterized by a new willingness to creatively interpret Chapter VII of the UN Charter to facilitate 'humanitarian intervention'. Keating cautions, however, that this has been driven essentially exclusively by Western states who have not always applied a consistent approach to humanitarian crises, nor indeed to the need for Security Council authorization. He then analyses the debate at the Security Council on Libya and in particular the positions of those five states which abstained. While the passing of Resolution 1973 was widely heralded as a demonstration of a new resolve, Keating argues that the five abstentions must be recognized as being important barometers of the global disposition towards R2P given the status of the five states. The manner in which the provisions of the Resolution were stretched, Keating warns, has diminished the prospects of future unanimity around R2P.

While several of the preceding chapters challenge the manner in which the intervention was conducted, the nature of the support it was afforded and its broader implications, in Chapter 9 Alan Kuperman questions the veracity of the rationale advanced by the intervening coalition and its supporters and the efficacy of the action itself. Kuperman's analysis of the situation on the ground prior to the NATO intervention contradicts the conventional narrative, particularly with respect to the 'genocide' ostensibly looming in Benghazi. Kuperman advances a counter-factual analysis to argue that non-intervention would have resulted in fewer deaths and ultimately less disorder in Libya and the surrounding region. In terms of the 'lessons' of Libya, Kuperman warns in particular against calling for regime change, foreclosing as it does potentially viable diplomatic options.

References

African Union (2011) 'Report of the Chairperson of the Commission on the Activities of the AU High Level Ad Hoc Committee on the Situation in Libya',

PSC/PR/2(CCLXXV), 26 April. Available online at: www.peaceau.org/uploads/275reportonlibyaeng.pdf [Accessed 12 September 2012].

Amnesty International (2010) *'Libya of Tomorrow': What Hope for Human Rights?* (London: Amnesty International Publications).

Amnesty International (2012) 'Libyan Rendition Case Shows It's Time for UK to Come Clean', 18 April. Available online at: www.amnesty.org/en/news/libyan-rendition-case-shows-it-s-time-uk-come-clean-2012-04-18 [Accessed 2 May 2012].

Ban Ki-Moon (2009) 'Implementing the Responsibility to Protect: Report of the Secretary-General', A/63/677, 12 January. Available online at: http://globalr2p.org/pdf/SGR2PEng.pdf [Accessed 13 September 2012].

Ban Ki-Moon (2011) 'Remarks at Breakfast Roundtable with Foreign Ministers on "The Responsibility to Protect: Responding to Imminent Threats of Mass Atrocities"', UN News Centre, 23 September. Available online at: www.un.org/apps/news/infocus/sgspeeches/search_full.asp?statID=1325 [Accessed 28 November 2011].

Barry, B. (2011) 'Libya's Lessons', *Survival*, vol. 53, no. 5, pp. 5–14.

Becker, J. (2011) 'Events of Two Years Ago Sparked Current Uprisings in Libya', *Global Post*, 11 March. Available online at: www.hrw.org/news/2011/03/11/events-2-years-ago-sparked-current-uprising-libya [Accessed 1 August 2012].

Bellamy, A. (2011) 'Libya and the Responsibility to Protect: The Exception and the Norm', *Ethics and International Affairs*, vol. 25, no. 3. Available online at: www.carnegiecouncil.org/resources/journal/index.html [Accessed September 2011].

Bellamy, A. and P. Williams (2011) 'The New Politics of Protection? Côte d'Ivoire, Libya and the Responsibility to Protect', *International Affairs*, vol. 82, no. 7, pp. 825–50.

Berman, F. (2007) 'Moral Versus Legal Legitimacy', in C. Reed and D. Ryall (eds), *The Price of Peace* (Cambridge: Cambridge University Press).

Black, I. (2009) 'Libya under Muammar Gaddafi', *The Guardian*, 31 August. Available online at: www.guardian.co.uk/world/audioslideshow/2009/aug/31/libya-gaddafi [Accessed 3 August 2012].

Chesterman, S. (2011) '"Leading from Behind": The Responsibility to Protect, the Obama Doctrine, and Humanitarian Intervention after Libya', *Ethics and International Affairs*, vol. 25, no. 3, pp. 1–7. Available online at: www.carnegiecouncil.org/resources/journal/index.html [Accessed September 2011].

Coalition of NGOs on Darfur (2008) 'Rhetoric vs. Reality: The Situation in Darfur'. Available online at: www.hrw.org/sites/default/files/related_material/darfur1208.pdf [Accessed 2 May 2009].

Cobain, I. (2012) 'Special Report Rendition Ordeal that Raises New Questions about Secret Trials', *The Guardian*, 8 April.

Daalder, I. and J. Stavridis (2012) 'NATO's Victory in Libya', *Foreign Affairs*, vol. 91, no. 2, pp. 2–7.

Evans, G. (2011) 'The RtoP Balance Sheet after Libya', 2 September. Available online at: www.gevans.org/speeches/speech448%20interview%20RtoP.html [Accessed 28 November 2011].

Fisher, D. (2007) 'Humanitarian Intervention', in C. Reed and D. Ryall (eds), *The Price of Peace* (Cambridge: Cambridge University Press).

Focarelli, C. (2008) 'The Responsibility to Protect Doctrine and Humanitarian Intervention: Too Many Ambiguities for a Working Doctrine', *Journal of Conflict and Security Law*, vol. 13, no. 2, pp. 191–213.

Frum, D. and R. Perle (2004) *An End to Evil* (New York: Random House).

Gause, G. (2011) 'Why Middle East Studies Missed the Arab Spring', *Foreign Affairs*, vol. 90, no. 4, pp. 81–90.

Hakimi, M. (2010) 'State Bystander Responsibility', *The European Journal of International Law*, vol. 21, no. 2, pp. 341–85.

Hehir, A. (2010) 'The Responsibility to Protect: Sound and Fury Signifying Nothing?', *International Relations*, vol. 24, no. 2, pp. 218–39.

Hehir, A. (2011) 'The Responsibility to Protect in International Political Discourse: Encouraging Statement of Intent or Illusory Platitudes?', *International Journal of Human Rights*, vol. 15, no. 8, pp. 1329–46.

Hehir, A. (2012) *The Responsibility to Protect: Rhetoric, Reality and the Future of Humanitarian Intervention* (Basingstoke: Palgrave Macmillan).

Hollis, R. (2012) 'No Friend of Democratization: Europe's Role in the "Arab Spring"', *International Affairs*, vol. 88, no. 1, pp. 81–94.

Human Rights Watch (2011) *World Report 2011*. Available online at: www.hrw.org/sites/default/files/reports/wr2011.pdf [Accessed August 4 2012].

International Commission on Intervention and State Sovereignty (2001) *The Responsibility to Protect* (Ottawa: International Development Research Centre).

International Crisis Group (2011) 'Popular Protests in the Middle East and North Africa: Making Sense of Libya', Middle East/North Africa Report 107, 6 June.

Meyer, S. (2009) 'In Our Interest: The Responsibility to Protect', in R. H. Cooper and J. V. Kohler (eds), *Responsibility to Protect: The Global Moral Compact for the 21st Century* (Basingstoke and New York: Palgrave Macmillan).

Organisation of Islamic Conference (2011) 'OIC in the News', 22 February. Available online at: www.oic-oci.org/data/inthenews/en/OIC_Site3(10).pdf [Accessed 2 September 2012].

Peters, A. (2009) 'Humanity as the A and Ω of Sovereignty', *The European Journal of International Law*, vol. 20, no. 3, pp. 513–44.

Reinold, T. (2010) 'The Responsibility to Protect: Much Ado about Nothing?', *Review of International Studies*, vol. 36, supplement S1, pp. 55–78.

Santini, R. (2011) 'The Transatlantic Relationship after the Arab Uprisings: Stronger in North Africa, Shakier in the Middle East?', Brookings Institution, 9 June. Available online at: www.brookings.edu/research/papers/2011/06/09-arab-uprisings-santini [Accessed 30 December 2012].

Smith, B. (2011) 'The Arab Uprisings', House of Commons Library, Research Paper 11/73, 11 November.

Stahn, C. (2007) 'Responsibility to Protect: Political Rhetoric or Emerging Legal Norm?', *American Journal of International Law*, vol. 101, no. 1, pp. 99–120.

Stephan, A. and G. Robertson (2003) 'An "Arab" More than a "Muslim" Democracy Gap', *Journal of Democracy*, vol. 14, no. 3, pp. 30–44.

UN General Assembly (2008) 'Human Rights Situations that Require the Council's Attention: Report of the Special Rapporteur on the Situation of Human Rights in the Sudan, Sima Samar', A/HRC/9/13, 2 September. Available online at: www.reliefweb.int/rw/RWFiles2008.nsf/FilesByRWDocUnidFilename/EGUA-7JJNR2-full_report.pdf/$File/full_report.pdf [Accessed 24 September 2008].

Vandewalle, D. (2006) *A History of Modern Libya* (Cambridge: Cambridge University Press).

Weiss, T. (2011) 'R2P Alive and Well after Libya', *Ethics and International Affairs*, vol. 25, no. 3, pp. 1–6. Available online at: www.carnegiecouncil.org/resources/journal/index.html [Accessed September 2011].

Yom, S. (2005) 'Civil Society and Democratization in the Arab World', *Middle East Review of International Affairs*, vol. 9, no. 4, pp. 14–33.

2

Humanitarianism, Responsibility or Rationality? Evaluating Intervention as State Strategy

Robert W. Murray

Introduction

When Resolution 1973 was passed by the United Nations Security Council a strange contradiction quickly emerged regarding the justifications for this approval. On one side of the debate were pro-interventionists, who argued the mission was absolutely essential for humanitarian reasons, and that this mission could be a quasi-experiment of the Responsibility to Protect (R2P) doctrine. On the other side were those who didn't see the reasoning of the Security Council through human security eyes, but instead saw the mission as a necessary means to steady a region that, throughout 2011, had been extremely unstable. In the wake of the Libyan intervention by the UN, and then by NATO, observers are left to wonder exactly why international forces chose to intervene in Libya, and what the future of interventionism will be as a result of the multistate mission.

On the surface, humanitarianism is the most attractive explanation for why Libya was a target for intervention. Throughout what is now commonly referred to as the 'Arab Spring' there were calls for international, especially Western, support in the revolutions that erupted in Egypt, Tunisia, Bahrain and eventually Libya. National governments were waging war against their own people, and civilian casualties became increasingly prevalent. No distinction was made in most cases between a combatant and a civilian, as ordinary people rose up in opposition to oppression, authoritarianism and government-sponsored violence. It seemed as if the entire Arab world was enthralled by the bravery of these citizens, and thus the demand to help bring democracy to areas historically not known for democratic leanings, became louder and louder.

When Colonel Gaddafi turned Libya's national military resources against his own people, the pro-intervention lobby urged European Union and NATO states to draw the proverbial line in the sand, and to take action. Unlike various other instances of revolution in 2011, the Security Council and NATO decided to bring an end to humanitarian atrocity underway in Libya through the framework of Resolution 1973. Due to the success of the mission, the eventual ousting of Gaddafi, and the supposed ongoing transition to democracy, pro-interventionists have claimed victory, and there was even a sentiment that the Libyan mission could set a precedent for future missions of its kind.

At the core of this debate, and the debate about all instances of humanitarian intervention, which would include the theoretical precepts of R2P, is whether states have altered their strategic preferences in order to begin acting as moral agents. In order for states in the modern era to fullfil the obligations as humanitarian enforcers, they must shift many aspects of historical behaviour, and enter into a new era of selfless protectionism. It is in this context that scholars and policymakers are left with more questions than answers, as it is extremely difficult to determine if, and when, a marked change in state attitudes towards human security may have occurred.

Historically, states have acted out of rationality, not responsibility. States are motivated by their security, power and self-interest in an anarchic system, not by a desire to promote and protect domestic populations of all states across the globe. Though some may hope for such a world, it has never existed in the history of the inter-state system. As such, this chapter seeks to explain if and when states in the contemporary international system are actually shifting their strategic preferences towards protecting human populations. In doing so, attention must be given to the environment in which states are making strategy, the options available to them in pursuing national interests, and evaluating the strength of arguments surrounding the perceived responsibility of states to safeguard individuals in a global sense. It is the argument of this chapter that states are no more responsible now than they ever were for protecting humanity and that rational calculations premised on self-interest continue to dictate the foreign and defence strategies of states in the modern international system.

States as rational actors

At the heart of debates about whether states are capable of acting as moral agents is the question of how states evaluate their decisions in an anarchic international system. Realism, especially the structural variant, has spent considerable effort highlighting the rational calculations of self-interest states throughout the entire history of the state system, and certainly in instances of humanitarian inaction. In order to better comprehend the realist thesis that states are inherently rational, an analysis of how rational choice theory is applicable to the study of international politics might be helpful.

Rational choice postulates are not at all new to the study of international security, and remain an essential component of both scholarly and policy analyses. The driving assumption of rational choice theorists in IR is that the anarchic nature of the international system is a constant security dilemma, most commonly associated with Cold War explanatory models. Security dilemmas are not a new concept by any means, but the bipolar conflict between two superpowers in the international system allowed for rational choice models of theorizing to provide useful insight into interstate decision-making processes. In his 1950 article discussing anarchy and its effects on international politics, John Herz defines the security dilemma succinctly:

> Wherever such anarchic society has existed – and it has existed in most periods of known history on some level – there has arisen what may be called the security dilemma of men, or groups, or their leaders. Groups or individuals living in such a constellation must be, and usually are, concerned about their security from being attacked, subjected, dominated, or annihilated by other groups and individuals. Striving to attain security from such attack, they are driven to acquire more and more power in order to escape the impact of the power of others. This, in turn, renders the others more insecure and compels them to prepare for the worst. Since none can ever feel entirely secure in a world of competing units, power competition ensues, and the vicious circle of security and power accumulation is on. (Herz 1950: 157)

The specific dilemma which existed throughout the Cold War was focused chiefly on the tense and unfriendly relationship between the US and the USSR. Following the end of the Second World War, these two superpowers began a fifty-year standoff, primarily motivated by ideological and strategic differences. Of course, these factors paled in comparison to the main aspect which created the real dilemma, namely the vertical proliferation of nuclear weapons between the two largest powers in the world. From the time President Harry Truman dropped the atomic bombs on Japan to end the Second World War, the Soviet Union and the US were striving to win an arms race and supersede the military capabilities of each other. In essence, the objective for both sides was not to simply obtain more weapons, but to maximize their national security by winning the arms race; to fall behind the opposing side in relative military gains was to lose the race, thus providing the other power with the opportunity to strike first. Ironically, while both powers were dedicated to winning the race, both had little or no intention of using their enormous arsenals based on the knowledge that each side could totally annihilate the other. This is how the idea of Mutual Assured Destruction and deterrence theory kept the Cold War cold, and created the balance of power which is so central to structural realist theory (Waltz 1979: 102–28). With the fall of the USSR, however, traditional rational choice models of IR theory could not account for the events to follow.

Systems theorists in IR, like Waltz and Morton Kaplan, have described the relations between the superpowers in a bipolar international system as a *game*, and defined it by referring to economic or mathematical game theory. Game theory has been a part of social sciences research since the 1950s based on its applicability in situations where actors are forced to make strategic decisions. Its history can be traced to the 1920s, but game theory did not hit mainstream research studies until mathematician John von Neumann and economist Oskar Morgenstern published their seminal work, *Theory of Games and Economic Behaviour*, in 1944. This type of theory is based on assumptions regarding rationality and logic, and seeks to explain the motivations and outcomes of two or more actors when they are confronted with decision-making situations involving a number of other actors who must also decide which strategy to play. Frank Zagare explains:

> Underlying the structure of game theory is the key assumption that players in a game are *rational* (or *utility maximizers*). As game theorists use this term, rationality simply means that a player in an interactive situation will act to bring about the most preferred of the possible outcomes, given the constraint that other players are also acting in the same way. (Zagare 1984: 7)

Political science as a general field of study has employed various types of game theoretic models in its different subfields to explore the rationale behind decisions made in political outcomes like election behaviour, vote-trading behaviour, coalition formation and, more importantly for the purposes of this study, international decision-making.[1]

It is important to note here that within IR discussions, a number of game theoretic models have been presented and it is difficult to use one model to encompass every international consideration. These models include two-person zero-sum games, two-person non-zero-sum games, chicken, and the game which has endured throughout the recent history of IR is the model of mixed-motives games commonly known as the prisoner's dilemma.

The reason for the enduring nature of the prisoner's dilemma, which is a two person non-zero sum game (2 × 2), is its application to theories of the state in the structural realist school of IR theory. According to Steven Brams, 'political philosophers at least since Hobbes have used the anarchy of a stateless society to justify the need for an enforceable social contract and the creation of government, by coercion, if necessary' (Brams 1975: 33). The condition of anarchy described by virtually all realists tells a story of non-cooperation and constant distrust, building on Hobbes' state of nature. The prisoner's dilemma is used by international game theorists to explain the security dilemma faced by states in the structural realist conception of the international system because of the constant desire for states to pursue security, power and self-interest. Thus, cooperation is typically not seen by structural realists as the primary motivation for state interaction. The prisoner's dilemma is typically represented in the following manner:

Table 2.1 Traditional prisoner's dilemma matrix

		Suspect 2	
		Do not confess	**Confess**
Suspect 1	**Do not confess**	(−1, −1)	(−10, 0)
	Confess	(0, −10)	(−5, −5)

The dilemma presented here is explained by Zagare:

> Two suspects are taken into custody. The district attorney is convinced that they are guilty of a certain crime but does not have enough evidence to convince a jury. Consequently, he separates the suspects and tells each one that he has two choices: to either confess or not confess to the crime. The suspects are told that if both confess, neither will receive special consideration and will therefore receive a jail sentence of five years. If neither confesses, both will probably be convicted of some minor charge and have to spend one year in jail. But if one confesses and the other does not, the suspect who confesses will be set free for cooperating with the state while the

> suspect that does not will have the book thrown at him and receive a ten-year sentence. (Zagare 1984: 51)

The similarity to international politics is based on two major factors; first, questions are raised both in this game and internationally about whether actions are rationally calculated based on individual or collective interest, with structural realists preferring the individual, or state, self-interest argument; and second, this example does not depict a one-time game in the international sphere, but rather, each time a situation arises between states, this game replays itself and the world is doomed to witness the self-interested and distrustful nature of states always choosing the irrational outcome of noncooperation, though cooperation is clearly the optimal strategy for both players because it would provide a far more favourable outcome.

Commenting on why the prisoner's dilemma became so important for realists during the Cold War, Robert Jervis emphasizes three of its strengths:

> First, it builds upon central characteristics of international politics – anarchy, the security dilemma, and the combination of common and conflicting interests. Second, the approach is parsimonious and lends itself to deductive theorizing. Third, it seeks to bring together the study of conflict and the study of cooperation, and tries to explain a wide range of phenomena encompassing both security and political economy. (Jervis 1988: 319)

These seemingly attractive qualities of the prisoner's dilemma made for a number of analyses aimed at explaining the relations between nations throughout the tense climate of the Cold War and arms races.

The prisoner's dilemma model was used most often to describe the distrustful, arms-racing, though rational, behaviours of both the USSR and US throughout the Cold War. Case studies tend to centre on situations where the two superpowers were heavily focused on the continual arms buildup, and the ongoing negotiations to limit those arms as the Cold War progressed. According to Scott Plous,

> Typically, the United States and the Soviet Union are cast in a 2 × 2 game with one of four outcomes possible on each trial: mutual arms reductions, US armament and Soviet reductions, Soviet armament and US reductions, or a build up of nuclear weapons on both sides . . . According to a prisoner's dilemma, both sides ideally prefer to arm while the other disarms. (Plous 1993: 163)

Plous's description of the typical prisoner's dilemma described by international security theorists throughout the Cold War is represented in the following matrix:

Table 2.2 Cold War prisoner's dilemma matrix

		USSR	
		Disarm	*Arm*
US	*Disarm*	(3, 3)	(1, 4)
	Arm	(4, 1)	(2, 2)

While the prisoner's dilemma was such a sacred explanation for interstate behaviour throughout the Cold War, its continued relevance in the contemporary climate of international politics is questionable. The world is no longer bipolar. A variety of nations are beginning to make strides in power development, international institutions are playing vital roles in the daily outcomes of international politics and non-state actors are altering the security perceptions of states. As Stephen Walt notes,

> Formal rational choice theorists have been largely absent from the major international security debates of the last decade (such as the nature of the post-Cold War world; the character, causes, and strength of the democratic peace; the potential contribution of security institutions; the causes of ethnic conflict; the future role of nuclear weapons; or the impact of ideas and culture on strategy and conflict). These debates have been launched and driven primarily by scholars using nonformal methods, and formal theorists have joined in only after the central parameters were established by others. (Walt 2000: 43)

Walt does not completely discount the value of formal methods in international relations, but does argue that much of rational choice's explanatory power has been lost since the fall of the Soviet Union between 1989 and 1991.

As the Cold War was coming to an end, it is easy to see why structural realist theorists such as John Mearsheimer argued so vehemently in favour of a bipolar international system. This fear is perhaps best described as he claims: 'I argue that the prospects for major crises and war in Europe are likely to increase markedly if the Cold War ends' (Mearsheimer 1990: 6). Structural realist security arguments rest on the relative stability of the balance of power which is best arranged in a bipolar system, hence the preference for a 2 × 2 game like the prisoner's dilemma. The end of the Cold War would, according to structural realist theory, disrupt the balance of power, create conditions of multipolarity, and remove the deterrent effect of superpower nuclear arsenals. Ironically, none of these predictions came to fruition and structural realist theory lost much of its explanatory strength and respect.

The loss of explanatory power for structural realism has also led to broader, meta-theoretical concerns regarding the use of rational choice and game theory to examine inter-state behaviour. An area of criticism has been the strong case made by rational choice theorists regarding the use of formal methods. Rational choice approaches are accused of both not producing novel empirical facts and seeking to explain existing facts through their preferred framework. According to Donald Green and Ian Shapiro:

> What explains the gap between rational choice theory's formidable analytic advances and its lackluster empirical applications? Our view is that empirical progress has been retarded by what may be termed method-driven, as opposed to problem-driven, research . . . The method-driven proclivities of rational choice scholars may, in turn, be accounted for by their universalistic aspirations: to construct a unified, deductively based theory from which propositions about politics – or, indeed, all human behavior – may be derived. One of our central objections to the way in which rational choice is applied in political science concerns its proponents' drive to show that *some* variant of rational choice theory can accommodate every fact, an impulse that is not accompanied by an equally strong drive to test the proposed account against new phenomena. The rational choice approach inspires great commitment among its adherents, and too often this leads to scientific practices seemingly designed to insulate rational choice theories from untoward encounters with evidence. (Green and Shapiro 1995: 238)

Green and Shapiro's concerns regarding the use of formal methods in IR and the limitations of rational choice theory more generally are relevant based on traditional game theory's lack of explanatory power in the wake of the Cold War.

Also included in questions regarding the usefulness of rational choice theory in modern international relations is the assumption that actors are rational. Cox argues:

> neorealist theory has extended itself into such areas as game theory, in which the notion of substance at the level of human nature is presented as a rationality assumed to be common to the competing

> actors who appraise the stakes at issue, the alternative strategies, and the respective payoffs in a similar manner. This idea of a common rationality reinforces the nonhistorical mode of thinking. Other modes of thought are to be castigated as inapt; and there is no attempt to understand them in their own terms. (Cox 1996: 92)

To reinforce this criticism, Cox points out that structural realism's use of rational choice postulates prevent it from commenting on modern issues, like Islamic integralism. Taking this argument a step further in security discourse, rational choice models would be virtually incapable of discussing Islamic terrorism as well.

Common rationality among actors is difficult to defend when irrational behaviour occurs on a regular basis in global affairs. States will defect and sometimes embark upon foreign policy initiatives with little or no rational foresight. The American intervention in Vietnam speaks to this (Waltz 1969). This being so, two essential facts must be considered before dismissing the assumptions of rationality given to actors. First, individuals play virtually no role in affecting outcomes in the international system as it is presented by structural realists (Waltz 1979: 93–7). Asking structural realism to describe Islamic integralism, for instance, is asking more than the parameters of structural realist theory are capable of giving. Second, rational choice does not speak to the cognitive process but, rather, focuses on the presentation of choices facing rational actors. Christopher Achen and Duncan Snidal argue, 'the axioms and conclusions of utility theory refer only to choices. Mental calculations are never mentioned: the theory makes no reference to them' (Achen and Snidal 1989: 164). Therefore, while actors may not always act rationally, rational choice theory does not contend the decisions of states, or their cognitive processes, are entirely rational. Zagare claims:

> . . . there is almost unanimous agreement among its practitioners that rational choice theory seeks to explain and predict a specific form of human behavior: the choices of real-world decisionmakers. This is one important reason why it is called choice theory. Game theory and other theories based on the rationality assumption are not generally viewed as theories of the cognitive process. (Zagare 2000: 97)

Rational choice theory, while narrow and limiting, is able to outline the choices facing rational actors in a given framework. That framework, as it is currently applied, remains the anarchic international system, but rationality assumptions are now considered in a unipolar, and emerging multipolar, systemic structure. As such, while the Cold War bipolarity has gone, states have demonstrated themselves to still be rational actors, but their decisions are now calculated in a unipolar structure, making calculations far more clear with only one superpower to contend with.

International politics since 1991 have changed in the sense that liberal and critical theoretical agendas have grown exponentially. One stark example of this growth has been the discourse surrounding human rights and human security. Much of this comes as a result of the perceived failure of realism to predict the end of the Cold War, but more importantly, due to the various instances of humanitarian crisis that arose once the Soviet Union collapsed. In essence, observers now pay far more attention to humanitarian issues, though states are still bound by their inherent rationality. As such, it is difficult to believe any fundamental alteration to state behaviour has taken, or will take, place in the name of a common humanity.

States as morally responsible agents

In direct opposition to the realist thesis of states behaving rationally is the more recent emergence of responsibility discourse. Much of this discussion began in the early 1990s when scholars and UN policymakers attempted to take advantage of the end of the Cold War by compelling states to view themselves and each other as moral agents as well as political actors. Humanitarian failures, like those in Somalia, Rwanda and Sudan, certainly begged the question about whether states were truly willing to change their historical foreign policy decision-making processes, but as the human security agenda grew in prominence, so did the questioning of state responsibility.

Human security is predicated on the notion that people have a moral responsibility to one another, thus making states the political agents through which morality would be protected. Perhaps not intentionally, this line of argument leads to a questioning of the fundamental character and nature of states, and exactly what leads states and state-based institutions to behave as they do on the international stage. In order to better comprehend what a responsibility would be, one must engage the epistemological foundations of human security and what is expected of both people and states in this school of thought.

The issue of human security has become one of the most discussed and important issues on the global agenda in recent years. With the end of the Cold War came new ideas about the changing nature of conceptualizing the protection and enforcement of human rights on a world stage. These evolving notions began to discuss the security of humanity in a context that was not exclusively centered on the state, and included a variety of actors in the international arena (Hutchings 1999: 154–5). In the 1992 *An Agenda for Peace* report, the changing context of peacekeeping was highlighted as the debate shifted from traditional peacekeeping to what is now commonly referred to as peacebuilding and preventative diplomacy (Doyle and Sambanis 2007: 324). According to Section 15 of *An Agenda for Peace,* world organization must undertake the following steps to adapt to the changing nature of security:

- To seek to identify at the earliest possible stage situations that could produce conflict, and to try through diplomacy to remove the sources of danger before violence results;
- Where conflict erupts, to engage in peacemaking aimed at resolving the issues that have led to conflict;
- Through peace-keeping, to work to preserve peace, however fragile, where fighting has been halted and to assist in implementing agreements achieved by the peacemakers;
- To stand ready to assist in peace-building in its differing contexts: rebuilding the institutions and infrastructures of nations torn by civil war and strife; and building bonds of peaceful mutual benefit among nations formerly at war;
- And in the largest sense, to address the deepest causes of conflict: economic despair, social injustice and political oppression. It is possible to discern an increasingly common moral perception that spans the world's nations and peoples, and which is finding expression in international laws, many owing their genesis to the work of this Organization. (Boutros-Ghali 1992)

While the idealism and perceived need for change was met by many UN members in a positive manner, *An Agenda for Peace* ultimately failed with the outbreak of conflict in areas such as Somalia and Rwanda (Wheeler 2000: 219–30).

Building on the 1992 document, the UN and other agencies began to articulate a need to move beyond inter-state concerns about security and rights promotion toward an individual-focused program that could meet the needs of the global population. The *Agenda for Peace* saw its demise with the 1994 genocide in Rwanda (Barnett and Finnemore 2004: 135–55). In its wake came what can be described as a radical proposal for humanitarian security, found in the 1995 report of the Commission on Global Governance. Consisting of 28 prominent individuals and funded largely by the UN, this commission made a number of far-reaching suggestions to the UN General Assembly that would alter the landscape of international institutions and their role in upholding international peace and security. For instance, the final report of the commission calls for global taxation, a standing UN military force, the end of the veto power for the P5 Security Council members, a criminal court of justice and a larger role for the UN Secretary General (Commission on Global Governance 1995). Other than the suggestion for a criminal court, which was achieved in 2002 with the creation of the International Criminal Court and the signing of the Rome Statute, the other provisions of the report were largely ignored.

One area that the report focused heavily on was the perceived change to the nature of international security. Many, if not all, of the proposed changes to the UN system included in the document were aimed at giving the UN enough power to protect populations from human rights abuses on a regular and consistent basis. According to the report,

> To confine the concept of security exclusively to the protection of states is to ignore the interests of people who form the citizens of a state and in whose name sovereignty is exercised. It can produce situations in which regimes in power feel they have the unfettered freedom to abuse the right to security of their people . . . All people, no less than all states, have a right to a secure existence, and all states have an obligation to protect those rights. (Commission on Global Governance 1995: 81–4)

Clearly the 1995 report made little difference to those in the hierarchy of international society based on the continuation of humanitarian disaster and atrocity. As the 1990s drew to a close, there arose yet another discussion as to the necessity for a global initiative that focused on the individual and the emerging normative discourse surrounding the security of humanity. As Bellamy notes, by the end of the 1990s, 'The question was now not whether sovereigns had responsibilities but what those responsibilities were, how they were best realized and what role international society should play' (2009: 32). It is in this light that the International Commission on Intervention and State Sovereignty (ICISS) published its findings in the 2001 R2P document. Heavily sponsored by the Government of Canada, the report highlights the need for human security as a central driving force behind international policy formulation.

Among its findings, the ICISS called for major changes to the UN system as well as the basic motivations of state action. Security, according to the report, was no longer limited to states and a perceived outdated Cold War mentality. Rather, international security was to centre on the rights and interests of the global populus:

> Many new international institutions have been created to meet these changed circumstances. In key respects, however, the mandates and capacity of international institutions have not kept pace with international needs or modern expectations. Above all, the issue of international intervention for human protection purposes is a clear and compelling example of concerted action urgently being needed to bring international norms and institutions in line with international needs and expectations. (ICISS 2001: 3)

Under the findings of the ICISS, the realm of global security would look far different from that of traditional international security. States, under the legal direction of the UN, had an obligation to enforce three major provisions for the safety of humanity: the responsibility to prevent the outbreak of humanitarian disaster, the responsibility to intervene and protect populations if rights were being abused, and the responsibility to rebuild in the wake of humanitarian crisis (ICISS 2001: xi). While the international community took widespread notice of the initial 2001 report, the proposed changes to issues including state sovereignty, the role of the UN in natural disaster relief, and in post-conflict rebuilding, were all questioned by nations, especially the great powers who would likely incur the bulk of the costs in R2P-sanctioned missions.

By 2005, R2P had reached the UN agenda and was open for debate. Canadian Prime Minister Paul Martin was among those pushing very hard for the UN to adopt R2P and offer hope to those in areas experiencing human rights problems, specifically in Darfur. What became evident in 2005 to the entire membership of international society was that the society of states was not entirely prepared to sacrifice its independence and sovereignty for a Western ideal of natural rights. As a result, the 2005 World Summit Outcome Document, which ratifies parts of the R2P in principle only, outlines four key areas when interventionism may be a legitimate option: genocide, war crimes, ethnic cleansing and crimes against humanity (UN General Assembly 2005). The 2005 version of R2P adopted by the UN does not call for legal changes to the meaning of sovereignty nor does it affirm the responsibility of international society to intervene in every case where human rights are being abused. Bellamy lamented that the *Outcome Document* 'has done little to increase the likelihood of preventing future Rwandas and Kosovos'. So as to achieve consensus, he claimed, 'the concept's advocates have abandoned many of its central tenets, significantly reducing the likelihood of progress in the near future' (Bellamy 2006: 145–6).

Since the issuing of the 2005 version of R2P, nations have yet to operationalize and implement the provisions of the doctrine. One must wonder why this is the case, particularly when in the summer of 2009, the members of the UN General Assembly reaffirmed their support for R2P. Clearly the changes made between 2001 and 2005, and the lack of enforcement of human security since that time, reflect unwillingness on the part of states, especially the great powers, to introduce radical changes to interventionist strategy. There may be a variety of moral and normative arguments for why R2P *should* be implemented but, at this juncture of international history, it may be that the perceived costs of human security enforcement far outweigh any practical benefits to a group of self-interested states in international society.

Libya and state strategy

When describing both why and how states behave, it is very difficult to rely on a singular explanatory model, as states never act perfectly as either rational actors or moral agents. History has shown that, at times, states can be among the most irrational actors in the international system, which has led to some of the major foreign and defence policy blunders since the state system was created in 1648. That said, when states choose to use moral justification for their actions, rarely is a move made purely for any sense of common good. Rather, it appears far more appropriate to argue that, while states may be rationally self-interested actors, morality can coincide with security-maximizing actions. In recent history, Libya would seem to exemplify this claim.

The intervention in Libya throughout 2011 was by no means a strictly morally responsible mission on the part of either the UN or NATO. In fact, in order for the Chinese and Russians to allow the vote for intervention to pass the Security Council, all language related to R2P was forcibly removed because neither Russia nor China, along with their fellow BRIC members (Brazil and India), had any interest in actually allowing the doctrine to gain traction at the UN level. Though no formal invocation of R2P was used in the language of Resolution 1973, R2P advocates argued at the time that this was a clear victory for the doctrine, and that it was likely to set a new precedent in debates surrounding humanitarian crisis. According to the International Coalition for the Responsibility to Protect:

> The Security Council (UNSC) decision to mandate 'all necessary measures' to protect civilians in Libya came in response to the actions of Libyan leader Muammar Gaddafi, his security forces, and his hired hands . . . The initial decision under Resolution 1973 was a landmark for the norm, as it was the first time the UN Security Council had acted under the third pillar of the RtoP framework to mandate coercive measures to protect civilians at risk from imminent atrocities. (ICRtoP 2011)

Many other R2P advocates, including the American UN Ambassador Susan Rice, have been very quick to claim victory for R2P in the lead-up to and execution of the Libyan mission that eventually led to regime change in Libya. A closer look at Resolution 1973 enables us to assess the merit of these claims, though they certainly cannot be read in isolation.

According to the provisions of the Resolution, the UN Security Council has authorization under its Chapter VII mandate to act due to the ongoing civilian atrocities that were being committed by the Libyan regime under Gaddafi. The Resolution itself would certainly seem to fit the framework of R2P in many respects – the language of *responsibility* is used throughout the initial paragraphs of the Resolution and focuses almost exclusively on the civilian abuses taking place. However, when the Resolution arrives at the section that authorizes action by the Security Council, any mention of *responsibility* curiously disappears:

> Acting under Chapter VII of the Charter of the United Nations,
>
> 1. Demands the immediate establishment of a cease-fire and a complete end to violence and all attacks against, and abuses of, civilians;
> 2. Stresses the need to intensify efforts to find a solution to the crisis which responds to the legitimate demands of the Libyan people and notes the decisions of the Secretary-General to send his Special Envoy to Libya and of the Peace and Security Council of the African Union to send its ad hoc High Level Committee to Libya with the aim of facilitating dialogue to lead to the political reforms necessary to find a peaceful and sustainable solution;
> 3. Demands that the Libyan authorities comply with their obligations under international law, including international humanitarian law, human rights and refugee law and take all measures to

> protect civilians and meet their basic needs, and to ensure the rapid and unimpeded passage of humanitarian assistance.

If there was an R2P checklist to determine whether a Resolution adhered to the framework of the doctrine, Resolution 1973 would likely pass. Had the preventative measures designed to halt Gaddafi been tried and failed? Check. Had all other measures been exhausted before discussions of military intervention (that is, political and economic intervention) were employed? Check. Was the justification for the mission grounded in one of the four parameters outlined by the 2005 World Summit *Outcome Document*, being war crimes, crimes against humanity, genocide, and/or ethnic cleansing? Check. In principle then, it is difficult to argue against those that might claim a sense of victory for R2P, as the reasoning behind the mission was contingent upon humanitarian crises and not inter-state peace and security.

This does not, however, equate to states acting as moral agents, and this is where R2P advocates would prefer the discussion to stop. According to the provisions for action in Resolution 1973, a resounding civilian-focused intervention was not what the Security Council endorsed. The Resolution allowed for the following actions in seeking to protect the Libyan people from the egregious rights abuses being committed by their own government: the establishment of a no-fly zone; the enforcement of an arms embargo; a ban on flights; and an asset freeze. A noticeable addition to the Resolution was made under the section discussing protecting civilians:

> 4. Authorizes Member States that have notified the Secretary-General, acting nationally or through regional organizations or arrangements, and acting in cooperation with the Secretary-General, to take all necessary measures, notwithstanding paragraph 9 of resolution 1970 (2011), to protect civilians and civilian populated areas under threat of attack in the Libyan Arab Jamahiriya, including Benghazi, while excluding a foreign occupation force of any form on any part of Libyan territory, and requests the Member States concerned to inform the Secretary-General immediately of the measures they take pursuant to the authorization conferred by this paragraph which shall be immediately reported to the Security Council;

Why would an R2P mission overtly ban the ability of Security Council or NATO states from using boots-on-the-ground intervention if the humanitarian crisis was bad enough to earn intervention in the first place? The answer is both sad and simple – Libya was an example of R2P, but the term came to represent something different – *Rationality to Protect.*

In the wake of a decade-long NATO and UN mission in Afghanistan, the illegal and irrational mission of the US and UK in Iraq, and in the midst of a global economic recession, states could not afford a full-scale humanitarian intervention under the prototypical R2P auspices in political, economic or military terms. Instead, Security Council and NATO states showed themselves for what they truly are; rational survivalists. They looked at Libya and asked themselves the most important question of all – how can we benefit the most from a mission with it costing the least? Human security from 35,000 feet is as rational a strategy as possible when faced with regional spillover and the prospect of oil and gold reserves for those involved in the intervention.

Conclusion

States can be morally responsible, but only if acting in the name of humanity is a rationally beneficial calculation. The 2011 mission in Libya proves this argument beyond any shadow of a doubt. Yes, those intervening states acted in the name of civilian protection, but did so in a way that effectively minimized the costs of acting, and so that action would not disrupt their relative power capabilities in the international system. What seems to have emerged from the Libya mission is the more pragmatic and far less clandestine doctrine of *Rationality to Protect,* which allows states to carefully calculate where an intervention would take place, under what conditions, and just how beneficial such a mission might be to their own interests. Without this important rationality calculation involved, states are highly unlikely to ever operationalize a doctrine solely on the basis of human security or rights.

Of course, such a conclusion has major consequences for future cases of humanitarian crisis, and whether states or state-based institutions will be willing to intervene. The current case in Syria truly highlights much of this argument, as both the political and economic measures of interventionism have already taken place, yet no military option has been presented. Guy Taylor believes that inaction in Syria is almost entirely due to the precedent set in the Libyan case, and that both China and Russia are likely to veto any proposed intervention measures to erase the Western interventionist precedent set in 2011 (Taylor 2012). Libya may have been an example of human security in action, but it is a far cry from any sort of triumph for norms over self-interest.

In a recent critique of those questioning why R2P would apply in Libya and not Syria, Bellamy and Dunne refer to R2P as 'the art of the possible – working out what is needed to protect civilians in particular situations and persuading the powers-that-be to ensure their protection' (2012). In this case, Bellamy and Dunne are quite correct, but the persuasion of great powers to employ R2P, or doctrines like it, must, as they have always been, be based on rational calculations of states and not a utopian quest to save and protect everyone. Libya proved humanitarianism could work in a rational way. Unfortunately, in the year since, it also proved R2P critics right.

Note

1. For an excellent range of rational choice uses in political science, see the special edition of *Critical Review*, vol. 9, nos 1 & 2 (1995).

References

Achen, C. and D. Snidal (1989) 'Rational Deterrence Theory and Comparative Case Studies', *World Politics,* vol. 41, no. 2, pp. 143–69.

Barnett, M. and M. Finnemore (2004) *Rules for the World: International Organizations in Global Politics* (Ithaca: Cornell University Press).

Bellamy, A. (2009) *Responsibility to Protect* (Cambridge: Polity).

Bellamy, A. (2006) 'Whither the Responsibility to Protect? Humanitarian Intervention and the 2005 World Summit', *Ethics and International Affairs,* vol. 20, no. 2, pp. 143–69.

Bellamy, A. and T. Dunne (2012) 'Responsibility to Protect on Trail – or Assad?'. Available online at: www.ethicsandinternationalaffairs.org/2012/responsibility-to-protect-on-trial-or-assad-3/ [Accessed June 2012].

Brams, S. (1975) *Game Theory and Politics* (New York: The Free Press).

Boutros-Ghali, B. (1992) *An Agenda for Peace*. Available online at: www.integranet.un.org/Docs/SG/agpeace.html [Accessed May 2012].

Commission on Global Governance (1995) *Our Global Neighbourhood: The Report of the Commission on Global Governance* (Oxford: Oxford University Press).

Cox, R. (1996) 'Social Forces, States and World Orders: Beyond International Relations Theory', in R. Cox and T. Sinclair (eds), *Approaches to World Order* (Cambridge: Cambridge University Press).

Doyle, M. and N. Sambanis (2007) 'Peacekeeping Operations', in T. Weiss and S. Daws (eds), *The Oxford Handbook on the United Nations* (Oxford: Oxford University Press).

Green, D. and I. Shapiro (1995) 'Pathologies Revisited: Reflections on Our Critics', *Critical Review,* vol. 9, nos 1&2, pp. 235–76.

Herz, J. (1950) 'Idealist Internationalism and the Security Dilemma', *World Politics,* vol. 2, no. 2, pp. 157–80.

Hutchings, K. (1999) *International Political Theory* (London: Sage).

International Coalition for the Responsibility to Protect (ICRtoP) (2011) 'Libya, Syria, and the Responsibility to Protect (RtoP)'. Available online at: http://icrtopblog.org/2011/08/09/libya-syria-and-the-responsibility-to-protect-rtop/ [Accessed 25 June 2012].

International Commission on Intervention and State Sovereignty (ICISS) (2001) *The Responsibility to Protect* (Ottawa: International Development Research Centre).

Jervis, R. (1988) 'Realism, Game Theory, and Cooperation', *World Politics,* vol. 40, no. 3, pp. 317–49.

Mearsheimer, J. (1990) 'Back to the Future: Instability in Europe after the Cold War', *International Security,* vol. 15, no. 4, pp. 5–56.

Plous, S. (1993) 'The Nuclear Arms Race: Prisoner's Dilemma or Perceptual Dilemma?', *Journal of Peace Research,* vol. 30, no. 2, pp. 163–79.

Taylor, G. (2012) 'Libya Precedent Makes UN Unlikely to Back US Shift on Syria'. Available online at: www.worldpoliticsreview.com/trend-lines/9486/libya-precedent-makes-u-n-unlikely-to-back-u-s-shift-on-syria [Accessed June 2012].

Walt, S. (2000) 'Rigor or Rigor Mortis? Rational Choice and Security Studies', in M. Brown et al. (eds) *Rational Choice and Security Studies: Stephen Walt and His Critics* (Cambridge, MA: MIT Press).

Waltz, K. (1969) 'International Structure, National Force, and the Balance of World Power', in J. Rosenau (ed.), *International Politics and Foreign Policy* (New York: The Free Press).

Waltz, K. (1979) *Theory of International Politics* (New York: McGraw-Hill).

Wheeler, N. (2000) *Saving Strangers: Humanitarian Intervention in International Society* (Oxford: Oxford University Press).

Zagare, F. (1984) *Game Theory: Concepts and Applications* (Beverly Hills: Sage Publications).

Zagare, F. (2000) 'All Mortis, No Rigor', in M. Brown et al. (eds) *Rational Choice and Security Studies: Stephen Walt and His Critics* (Cambridge: The MIT Press).

3
The Responsibility to Protect as the Apotheosis of Liberal Teleology

Aidan Hehir

Introduction

Since it was recognized at the 2005 World Summit, states have routinely expressed their support for the Responsibility to Protect (R2P). The fact that it merely restates existing law, however, means that the utility of R2P is essentially predicated on its capacity to precipitate, either though socialization, inducement or mild coercion – such as rhetorical entrapment and/or a determination to avoid pariah status – a profound attitudinal change amongst states. As a result, R2P's advocates – academics, NGOs and political figures – have focused on stressing its alleged normative power; its ostensible capacity to 'shame' otherwise recalcitrant states by portraying non-compliance as anachronistic and reactionary.

This faith in R2P's normative power is sustained by an often unstated, though invariably discernible, belief in the progressive trajectory of international norms. 'Progress' in the post-Cold War era remains a liberal article of faith impelled and sustained by the teleological 'End of History' thesis and reflected in the positive predictions regarding the irresistible spread of democracy, free markets and human rights. These beliefs are informed by a more general conviction that the proliferation of liberal norms through public and political discourse catalyses a socialization process whereby compliance is achieved, even among the recalcitrant, without the need for actual structural reform.

The link between this evolutionary trajectory and the prevailing systemic configuration has been largely overlooked, however, as have the implications of this symbiosis. As the ascendancy of R2P is part of a broader normative shift derived from the post-Cold War structural changes, it stands to reason that imminent structural change from a unipolar to multipolar era necessarily has implications for the trajectory of normative evolution, and thus R2P. Shifts in the global distribution of power, therefore, disturb the prevailing norms and, given the disposition of the emerging powers – particularly China and Russia – this shift has potentially negative consequences for R2P given it is fundamentally predicated on its capacity to feed on the broader, and ostensibly ever-expanding, propitious framework generated by the irresistible rise of liberal norms. This chapter will argue that, even accepting the intervention in Libya, R2P's efficacy is fragile in the context of an unfolding structural realignment.

R2P and the law on humanitarian intervention

The International Commission on Intervention and State Sovereignty (ICISS) declared that its first objective was, '[to] establish clearer rules, procedures and criteria for determining whether, when and how to intervene' (2001: 11). Given this explicit aim, it is noteworthy that R2P has not impelled the drafting or codification of any new laws. Of arguably more significance, this determination to reform existing 'rules, procedures and criteria' has been all but dropped from the agenda of contemporary R2P advocates. Before discussing this turn away from legal reform, it is necessary to first identify the nature of the system and the rules the ICISS sought to change.

Chapter VII and the 1990s

While the UN Charter does not refer to a right of humanitarian intervention for either individual states or the UN Security Council, in the 1990s the Security Council expanded its interpretation of its Chapter VII powers to include intra-state humanitarian crises; this began with the landmark Resolution 688 in 1991 on the repression of Kurds in Iraq. While this new interpretation of Chapter VII provoked some controversy, an intervention authorized by the Security Council has a very strong legal case and such interventions have not, historically, been sources of great legal contestation (Peters 2009: 538). Of greater concern, however, was the inconsistent use of Chapter VII in the post-Cold War era and the related fact that the permanent five members of the Security Council (P5) had not advanced any coherent framework outlining how their new understanding of Chapter VII would be consistently and impartially applied (Chesterman, 2002: 5).

By the end of the 1990s, therefore, it was clear that the P5 understood Chapter VII as enabling it to authorize a military intervention for humanitarian purposes. Action taken without Security Council authorization proved a far more controversial issue, however, as evidenced by NATO's intervention in Kosovo in 1999. The ICISS, a self-described response to the legal deficiencies exposed by NATO's intervention, noted, '. . . the issue of international intervention for human protection is a clear and compelling example of concerted action urgently being needed to bring international norms and institutions in line with international needs and expectations' (2001: 3).

What's new?

The present contours of R2P originate with the ICISS report but find their most coherent, and legally relevant, expression in the 2005 World Summit *Outcome Document*. While the inclusion of two paragraphs on R2P in the *Outcome Document* was heralded by many as 'revolutionary', whether this constitutes a significant evolution or a meaningful commitment likely to have real impact is debatable. As Simon Chesterman reflects, '. . . by the time RtoP was endorsed by the World Summit in 2005, its normative content had been emasculated to the point where it essentially provided that the Security Council could authorize, on a case-by-case basis, things that it had been authorizing for more than a decade' (2011a: 4). Beyond this empirical observation, since at least the inception of the UN states have accepted the principle that they have certain responsibilities to their citizens that find legal expression in international human rights law and there has certainly not been a shortage of legal proscriptions (Bellamy 2010: 42; Stahn 2007: 112; Landman 2005: 14). It is not the case, therefore, that thirty years ago states accused of orchestrating and/or committing egregious internal crimes against humanity could have legitimately claimed the right to do *whatever* they wanted internally. There is nothing new in the fact that states have agreed that the international community has the right to become involved in the domestic affairs of states (Hakimi 2010: 343–4; Peters 2009: 525). In the first decade of the post-Cold War era the legality of external involvement was not an especially contentious issue – in principle – and not one of the key sources of controversy which compelled the ICISS to issue its report. Indeed, the ICISS found in its consultations, '. . . even in states where there was the strongest opposition to infringements on sovereignty, there was a general acceptance that there must be limited exceptions to the non-intervention rule for certain kinds of emergencies' (2001: 31). This acceptance of *a* role for the international community was reiterated time and time again during the negotiations at the World Summit in 2005 and the major General Assembly debate on R2P in 2009 (Hehir 2011). Yet, this is not significant in itself; the Security Council's use of Chapter VII in the 1990s had amply demonstrated that internal events, including humanitarian catastrophes, could be deemed of international concern and importance, and potentially, grounds for external intervention. In his 2009 report, 'Implementing the Responsibility to Protect', the UN Secretary-General acknowledged that R2P, 'rests on long-standing obligations under international law' while Francis Deng – credited by many as the inventor of the term the 'responsibility to protect' – admitted with respect to R2P 'perhaps there's nothing new here' (Ki-Moon 2009: 10; Deng 2010: 85–6).

The problem historically has been enforcement rather than enunciation; the proliferation of expressions of concern for, and commitment to, human rights have not been accompanied by an attendant alteration in the Charter's provisions for dealing with violations of human rights and compliance with international laws on human rights has been erratic. The result is a large body of both treaty and customary law which lacks a clear means by which these laws can be enforced in the event that a state willfully violates the law. States are subject to scrutiny by a variety of UN bodies but compliance with even just the supervisory role of these organizations is poor and their enforcement capacity is minimal (Henkin 1990: 250; Fitzmaurice 2006). As R2P has not changed either the legal architecture or the laws themselves, this unsatisfactory situation remains.

Following cases of non-intervention, such as the Rwandan genocide, many asked how the international response could be made more consistent and automatic. Indeed, the ICISS noted that one of its aims was 'crafting responses that are consistent' (2001: 5). Nothing has been achieved, however, which in any way alters the legal process governing the response to intra-state crises to ensure consistency and automaticity. During the 2009 General Assembly debate on R2P the P5 actually distanced themselves from any automaticity; indicatively, the UK ambassador warned, 'Every situation is different' and hence a political decision has to be agreed (UK 2009: 2). The Chinese ambassador stated unambiguously:

> . . . the Security Council has a role to play but it must make judgments and decisions tailored to specific circumstances and must act prudently. Here it must be pointed out that the responsibility entrusted to the Council by the Charter is the maintenance of international peace and security. (China 2009: 2)

This emphasis on maintaining 'international peace and security' is an obvious, and indeed legally accurate, reference to the limits of the

Security Council's raison d'être; while increased pressure has been put on the P5 to 'do something' in response to a number of intra-state crises since the end of the Cold War, humanitarian action was not, and is not, an explicit aspect of its mandate as detailed in Chapter V of the UN Charter.

Rather than suggest an alternative to the Security Council's monopoly on the authorization of intervention the better option, according to the ICISS, was to continue to respect the authority of the Security Council. 'The task,' the ICISS emphasized, 'is not to find alternatives to the Security Council as a source of authority but to make the Security Council work much better than it has' (2001: 49).

Libya and R2P's 'normative power'

The emergence of R2P, therefore, has not altered international law or the institutions which enforce and regulate it. Indeed, many of its key advocates dismiss, or certainly ignore, the utility of law in favour of normative pressure (Evans 2008: 7). Indicatively, when asked whether she felt R2P required legal codification, Sapna Chhatpar Considine, Project Manager for the International Coalition for the Responsibility to Protect, replied, 'No, personally I don't feel that way . . . I don't look at it as something that needs to actually become a treaty or international law . . . my personal belief is that it doesn't have to become international law for it to work'. Rather, she argued, the better strategy was to work towards 'strengthening normative consensus' (Considine and Sonner 2009). Existing organizations do not need to be reformed so much as taught to 'work better', as the Global Centre for RtoP states regarding the UN (2009: 3); likewise the ICISS emphasized that the aim 'is not to find alternatives to the Security Council as a source of authority but to make the Security Council *work much better* than it has' (2001: 49).

R2P is, therefore, predicated on an assumption that normative pressure will compel states to alter their foreign policies. This pressure stems from the agitation of advocacy groups and concerned individuals, and the declaratory acts of states which leaves them ostensibly 'rhetorically entrapped' (Glanville 2011: 471). Thus, R2P's efficacy is ultimately dependent on political will, the centrality of which, and the need to generate a new 'moral' disposition, has been acknowledged by many who have spoken in support of R2P (Evans 2008: 223). The ICISS report, for example, talked of the need to 'produce arguments appealing to morality' while Bellamy suggests the international response is dependent on 'the strength of individual leader's moral commitments'

(ICISS 2001: 72; Bellamy 2009: 3). Given the acknowledged centrality of political will, supporters of R2P have argued that the primary focus should be to 'mobilize' political will through NGO and popular advocacy (Power 2009: x; Global Centre for RtoP 2009). NGOs have been specifically established to 'apply targeted pressure on key actors within governments . . . about why R2P is important, why they should care and how it matters' (Considine and Sonner 2009). David Scheffer, indicatively, suggests that the message of R2P should be, '[championed by] school children and their parents . . . stamped on bumper stickers and broadcast through enlightened corporate sponsors [so that] policymakers ultimately comprehend this siren call of their peoples' (2009: 95).

Post-2005, however, R2P's capacity to mobilize political will seemed to be manifestly lacking with respect to a number of crises including Sri Lanka, the Congo and most notably Darfur; far from R2P having catalyzed a change in the way intra-state crises are dealt with, the international response to the crisis in Darfur suggested that, as UN Secretary-General Kofi Annan claimed, 'we had learnt nothing from Rwanda' (Fisher 2007: 103). The intervention in Libya, however, reinvigorated the optimists who declared it '. . . a textbook case of the R2P norm working exactly as it was supposed to' (Evans 2011). Paul Williams wrote, 'it is difficult to imagine how [Resolution 1973] could have been authorized without the preceding decade of pro-R2P advocacy' (2011: 259). Alex Bellamy and Paul Williams declared that the Security Council were now motivated by 'a new politics of protection' (2011: 826) while The International Coalition for the Responsibility to Protect (ICRtoP) declared that the intervention 'reflects a historic embrace of the RtoP principles' (2011). More emphatically, Simon Adams, Executive Director of the Global Centre for R2P, wrote that the intervention was 'unprecedented . . . because of its unanimous endorsement . . . of "the responsibility to protect" as its motivation for doing so' (2011). The intervention was similarly loudly praised by many other prominent proponents of R2P; Evans described it as a 'spectacular step forward' (2011); Ramesh Thakur characterized it as 'a triumph . . . for R2P' (2011); Lloyd Axworthy claimed the intervention heralded the dawn of 'a more humane world' (2011); former Canadian Ambassador to the UN Paul Heinbecker declared the intervention constituted 'a vindication for the international community, for the UN, for NATO, for the International Criminal Court and for American foreign policy' and was illustrative of the fact that 'human progress is possible' (2011). Ban Ki-Moon summed up the mood by announcing, 'By now it should be clear to all that the Responsibility to Protect has arrived' (2011). Such optimism, and the view of the world which underlies R2P's emphasis on 'norms' and 'people power', can be, and have been, dismissed as naïve utopianism, particularly in the light of the profoundly different international responses to the situations in Bahrain and Syria. These views can be understood, at least, when situated within framework of post-Cold War liberal teleology.

Liberal teleology

Defining 'liberal' is notoriously difficult and in the context of the discourse on human rights and R2P the difference between a 'liberal' and a 'cosmopolitan' is rarely obvious. Michael Barnett advances one definition which, I believe, captures the spirit of liberalism:

> [Liberals are] . . . intellectuals who believe in progress; the capacity of individuals to learn from the past; the construction of new political institutions to increase freedom and reduce the likelihood of physical violence; and thus the ability to improve the moral charter and material welfare of humankind. (2010: 26)

The end of the Cold War famously ostensibly constituted

> The triumph of the West, of the Western *idea* . . . the total exhaustion of viable systematic alternatives to Western liberalism . . . the end point of mankind's ideological evolution and the universalization of Western liberal democracy as the final form of human government. (Fukuyama 1989: 3)

Much of the post-Cold War human rights advocacy has been informed by this underlying belief in the 'end of history' and thus strategies have been designed with this in mind.

R2P and the ascent of liberalism

R2P's underlying rationale – this insistence on the efficacy of moral advocacy – is, I contend, a function of this broader post-Cold War consensus on 'progress' presented as the irresistible spread of liberalism. The new systemic configuration – unipolarity rather than bipolarity – allowed for doctrines like R2P to become popularized as part of a broader trend favouring norms over law. This is not to suggest that the US, or 'the West', has been a consistent supporter of the concepts of human security, humanitarian intervention or R2P, but rather that the new systemic configuration and the ascendency of liberalism catalyzed a vocal movement – championing the protection of human rights – inspired by a belief in the capacity of domestic and global civil society to alter the behaviour of the newly dominant liberal democracies. By virtue of their domestic political systems these states were (and are) deemed to be receptive to the blandishments of humanitarian NGOs and thus their foreign policy is ostensibly malleable and susceptible to moral pressure (Hehir 2008: 33–52). The end of bipolarity, therefore, facilitated the emergence of a discourse and movement – of which R2P is a part – seeking change through advocacy rather than institutional or legal (re)design.

R2P was born from the widely held perception that bipolarity was to blame for Security Council inaction. Indicatively, in 1991 the then UN Secretary-General Perez de Cuellar stated:

> The extinction of the bipolarity associated with the cold war has no doubt removed the factor that virtually immobilized international relations over four decades. It has cured the Security Council's paralysis. (1991: 2)

As Barnett notes, the end of the Cold War witnessed a proliferation of reports and commissions which 'wax eloquent about the transformational possibilities for global politics and about the role of the UN as the prospective global deliverer' (2010: 21). There was a general sense that this was a new era for the UN and the dawn of a world more concerned with human rights, and responsive in cases of dereliction. Regarding these perspectives Barnett observed:

> . . . their narratives are informed by a belief in progress; that modernization and interdependence are transforming the character of global politics; that institutions can be established to help manage these changes; that democracy is a principled issue and can enhance peace and security; and that the UN has an obligation to protect individuals, promote universal values, and create institutions that can encourage political and economic freedom. (ibid.: 30)

Advocates thus hailed 'the age of enforcement' (Robertson 2002: xvi) and the 'remarkable opportunity to replace the politics of military defence and deterrence with a politics of security based on international cooperation and addressing global inequalities' (Shaw 1994: 155). This belief in the imminence of a new era for the UN, described by Mats Berdal as 'the great illusion' (2003: 9), was widely held and predicated on an assumption that the recent systemic change would be more amenable to human rights enforcement and, crucially, a long-term reality rather than a temporal phase (Chesterman 2011b: 2).

The new era facilitated the emergence of a preference for norms over law for two key reasons; first, the newly dominant states were liberal democracies and hence naturally responsive to popular advocacy; second, altering international law would require the consent of powerful 'old-fashioned' states such as China and Russia which still retained seats (with vetoes) on the Security Council, and also a majority amongst the developing world which was also wedded to anachronistic notions of sovereign inviolability and national interest.

Receptive hegemony and 'liberal anti-pluralism'

The US's incontrovertible status as world leader, combined with its democratic credentials, facilitated both this prevailing sense of optimism and the focus on generating 'norms' rather than laws governing issues such as humanitarian intervention. The preference for norms stems from the democratic character (and unrivalled power) of the US and its Western allies; a character that ostensibly facilitates the efficacy of moral advocacy (Frost 2011: 42; Wheeler 2003: 207).

The spread of democracy thus became increasingly portrayed as a prerequisite for the realization of human rights and the broader normative agenda, a '. . . necessary condition for political emancipation' (Kaldor 2003: 12). Democratic states thus, unsurprisingly, were portrayed as more legitimate actors than non-democracies and inherently more receptive to global civil society's humanitarian advocacy (Weiss 2007: 100; Buchanan and Keohane 2004). Global civil society was variously described as, 'the guarantors of civil behavior both by official institutions (states and international institutions) and in the wider world at large' (Kaldor 2001: 210), '. . . a source of constant pressures on the state system' (Shaw 1994: 24) and '. . . a pervasive, significant, positive influence on the policies of the states and the other actors in the international system' (Hensel 2004: ix). Thus, the efficacy of global civil society, and by extension R2P, is a function of the rise of democratic states which are, so we are told, receptive to normative pressure; the project naturally collapses if states refuse to engage with, or cannot be swayed by, normative pressure.

This advocacy appeared to bear fruit in 1999 with the NATO intervention in Kosovo and the Australian-led peacekeeping mission in East Timor. Indeed, Human Rights Watch described 1999 as indicative of 'a new era for the human rights movement' in which humanitarians can 'count on governments to use their police powers to enforce human rights law'. 'Victims of atrocities', they claimed, will receive 'effective assistance *wherever* they cry out for help' (Orford 2003: 8). The intervention in Kosovo, of course, was controversial because NATO acted without the Security Council's authorization. This added further momentum to the campaign to reject international law in favour of a looser regulatory system based on moral norms, avowed by global civil society and defended by Western states. Unsurprisingly, therefore, it was argued that Western states should be afforded unique rights of intervention so that interventions such as Operation Allied Force could be facilitated but reserved for the few 'enlightened states' (Glennon 1999: 7).

This very obviously constituted an attempt to challenge sovereign equality in favour of 'the formal rehierarchisation of international society, whereby democratic states would gain special governance rights – particularly with regard to the legitimate use of force' (Reus-Smit 2005: 72). Such rehierarchisation is indicative of what Gerry Simpson describes as the '. . . second image of what it means to be a liberal. This is liberalism (sometimes characterized as neo-liberalism) endowed with a sort of moralistic fervor, a conviction and, at times, an intolerance of the illiberal' (2004: 78). This 'liberal anti-pluralism' is driving a change which 'undermines the system of equal sovereigns' and 'has been drawn to the idea of separating the globe into zones – the democratic-liberal or decent society of states operating in a sphere of cosmopolitan law and the failed state/outlaw state subsisting in the state of nature' (ibid.: 83). Indeed, Ann-Marie Slaughter, a proponent of this idea, admits, '[Liberal theory] permits, indeed mandates, a distinction among different types of states based on their domestic political structure and ideology' (1995: 509) while self-described liberal Geoffrey Robertson claimed, 'The reality is that states are not equal' (2002: 372). This rejection of law and existing legal institutions was of course, rationalized in terms of humanitarian need and justified as necessary for the progress of humanity.

It is, therefore, in the context of a rise of liberal democracies, a re-imagining of the state system as hierarchical, and the discrediting of international law and the institutions which regulate it, that moral norms and popular advocacy emerge as vital, and ostensibly effective, regulatory mechanisms. Hence the emergence of R2P with its emphasis on speech-acts and normative pressure, a strategy sustained by an underlying belief in both the moral rectitude of liberal states and progressive teleology. The following sections critically analyse these assumptions and the record of the strategy employed.

Flaws in the strategy

The strategy of normative advocacy and the 'mobilization' of political will was said to have demonstrated its efficacy with respects to the intervention in Libya in 2011. In this section, however, I argue that this intervention was consistent with the Security Council's inconsistent record of responding to intra-state crises since 1991. There remains scant evidence that the West has embraced a new understanding of its foreign policy priorities, let alone the P5, while the rise of China and Russia almost by definition diminishes the prospects that normative advocacy will influence the Security Council's response to intra-state crises.

Western interests

In the aftermath of the Rwandan genocide further iterations of 'Never Again!' peppered memorial speeches for years yet, in the face of the next major atrocity to come near to the scale of the murder in Rwanda – the crisis in Darfur – the international reaction was sadly all too similar (Slim 2004). Indeed, according to the UK Select Committee on Foreign Affairs, 'the international community's response to the events in Darfur has been slow and inadequate . . . lives have been lost unnecessarily as a result' (Berdal 2008: 184). According to Romeo Dallaire, 'Western governments are still approaching it with the same lack of priority [as they did in 1994]. In the end, it receives the same intuitive reaction: "What's in it for us? Is it in our 'national' interest?"' (2004). This desultory response to Darfur is all the more troubling because unlike in the cases of Sri Lanka and the DRC, global civil society mobilized a huge campaign in favour of action on Darfur which generated enormous international media attention. These pleas were, however, ignored. Likewise the enormous global campaign against the invasion of Iraq failed to convince the leaders of democratic states to choose a different course (Hehir 2012: 119–46).

Beyond just the obvious willingness on the part of the West to ignore pleas from their citizens, there is evidence that human rights protection is not a *sine qua non* for Western support. While NATO's intervention in Libya was heralded as evidence of the West's relatively advanced ethical foreign policy, the response to Bahrain points to a more mendacious Realpolitik. As the monarchy, from Bahrain's Sunni minority, struggled to contain the deteriorating situation the Gulf Cooperation Council (GCC) sent troops, largely from Saudi Arabia and the UAE, into Bahrain on 14 March 2011 to enable the enforcement of a state of emergency.

What followed was described by the International Crisis Group (ICG) as a 'campaign of retribution':

> Before the crackdown [on 14 March] Bahraini security forces were accused of using excessive force, beating, torturing and in some cases killing peaceful demonstrators. Following the GCC troops' arrival, these security forces came down on protestors and opposition groups even harder. (ICG 2011: 4)

Despite this, the ICG note that the US criticized the violence 'relatively mildly' and 'threw its weight behind the Crown-Prince's efforts to jump-start a substantive reform effort'. This was a consequence, they note, of the US's key desire to appease the Saudi royal family (ibid.: 21).

The West's response to the Arab Spring has been, therefore, markedly inconsistent (Crocker 2011). There has been a persistent suspicion that Europe's primary interests in the Arab world are twofold; to stem the flow of migrants (Hollis 2012: 84) and to secure access to the region's vast oilfields (Rutledge 2005: 21–37) and that these interests, more so than a concern for human rights, have always dictated policy towards the region. The US and Europe have supplied oppressive regimes in the Middle East with arms for decades, even during the Arab Spring; in February 2011 UK Prime Minister David Cameron travelled to Egypt, Qatar and Kuwait with representatives from eight defence and aerospace companies seeking new clients (Smith 2011: 84). A report by Amnesty International in 2011 condemned arms sales to the Middle East, highlighting trade between NATO states and regimes in Bahrain, Egypt, Libya, Syria and Yemen. The report noted that Belgium, France, Germany, Italy, Spain and the UK had supplied arms to Colonel Gaddafi since 2005 (Amnesty International 2011). Russia and China have also continued to supply arms to certain oppressive regimes, including Libya and Syria, while violence was being perpetrated (Barnard 2011; Branigan 2011; Amnesty International 2011).

A new norm or (same old) discretionary entitlement?

International history is replete with lofty declarations that have had little practical impact due to the fact that they were predicated on political will. Issues from climate change to poverty reduction have served as principles which world leaders have willingly endorsed but subsequently ignored safe in the knowledge that by virtue of the nature of international law both compliance and enforcement were a matter of discretion. The fate of the 1948 Genocide Convention is most illustrative of this trend; while the provisions of the Convention were lauded at the time, in 2001 UN Secretary-General Kofi Annan stated, '[the convention] has, for all practical purposes, remained a dead letter' (2001). This was, of course, evident during the Rwandan genocide when states with the capacity to halt the massacres did little to help (Shawcross 2001: 119). Wheeler's analysis of the response to the genocide found that the idea that international law on sovereign inviolability somehow prevented states from intervening is simply untrue (2006: 36). The inaction was overwhelmingly a function of the absence of political will amongst the P5, particularly the US.

There is no doubt that the decision to intervene in Libya was notable for both the speed of the decision-making and the degree of collective unity displayed (Weiss 2012). The decision to act had followed weeks of NGO activism and even the Russian and Chinese abstentions appeared to be in keeping with the ICISS's 'code of conduct'. Yet, to invoke the classic cliché, correlation does not imply causation; the intervention can arguably be situated in a broader pattern of Security Council responses to intra-state crises which pre-dates R2P, a pattern that is obviously erratic; the reason is that the Security Council may choose to take action, but it is under no obligation to do so. It thus has merely a 'discretionary entitlement' to act (Berman 2007: 161).

During the course of the debate on Resolution 794 on Somalia in 1992 a number of states on the Security Council argued that the Security Council had a responsibility and even in certain cases an 'obligation' to save lives. Hungary cited the existence of an obligation while, more importantly, Russia declared that the action was being taken because of the existence of 'obligations to put an end to the human tragedy in that country' (UNSC 1992, pars 49 and 27). At the time, of course, Russia's avowal of an obligation to protect human rights was, as Wheeler notes, 'groundbreaking'. In 1992 – nineteen years before the intervention in Libya – the debate on Somalia was shaped by '. . . the view expressed by several members that the Security Council had a moral responsibility to save the victims of famine and civil strife' (2002: 185). The fact that Russia suggested it had an 'obligation' of this nature today appears somewhat incredible, not least because we see this declaration in light of the subsequent response to Srebrenica, Rwanda, Darfur and others. This consensus in 1992, therefore, on a 'moral responsibility' appears to have quickly dissipated thereby diminishing its normative potentiality. In 1999, two years before the publication of the ICISS report, the Security Council passed Resolution 1265 which advanced an expansive summation of the Council's understanding of the responsibilities of states to adhere to international humanitarian law and the Council's remit to act in cases where states fail to meet this responsibility. The resolution noted the Council's '. . . willingness to respond to situations of armed conflict where civilians are being targeted . . . including through the consideration of appropriate measures at the Council's disposal'. One could say, in essence, that the responsibility to protect existed before R2P. Indeed, as Chesterman notes, formulations of the phrase 'responsibility to protect' were used even prior to the recognition by the UN of R2P at the 2005 World Summit; he recalls that in the context of the situation in Georgia, the Abkhazi were said by the Security Council in Resolution 1393 in 2002 to have 'a particular responsibility to protect' returnees (Chesterman 2011a: 2). States, including the P5, have, therefore talked about 'moral responsibilities' and even obligations prior to the emergence of R2P. This in itself does not preclude R2P from constituting a norm but given that R2P emerged as a putative solution to the international community's lamentable record of responding to intra-state crises, it is significant that the record of intervention post-R2P remains inconsistent, even accepting Resolution 1973. As discussed further later, the double veto twice cast by China and Russia against resolutions on Syria after the intervention in Libya surely confirms this.

The term 'norm' has been used loosely with respects to R2P; it is often used as though the near ubiquity of the term 'R2P' in international political discourse is sufficient evidence of its status as a 'norm'. We must distinguish, however, between genuine 'norms' and 'political catchwords' that are used when the will to act is occasionally mustered such as the occasional flashes of resolve discussed above (Stahn 2007: 120). There is a large body of academic literature which interrogates the meaning of 'norms' and the process by which a norm is established; true norms are certainly more than just popular terms (Finnemore and Sikkink 1998: 890).

The first issue with R2P's putative status as a norm is the lack of conceptual clarity surrounding key aspects of R2P, in particular the threshold criteria for intervention. This, by definition, impacts on the extent to which it can be deemed to constitute a 'norm'. Theresa Reinold's analysis of this confusion and contestation concludes that as a 'norm' constitutes 'an intersubjectively shared standard of appropriate behavior', the ambiguity surrounding R2P means 'norm internalisation cannot occur' (2010: 74). While the Security Council have used the term in resolutions and statements, they have demonstrated an unwillingness to explicitly cite R2P as the basis for action due, Jennifer Welsh suggests, to a general acceptance that the term does not have a shared meaning (2011: 4).

Beyond this issue of R2P's contested meaning, the relationship between a putative norm and legitimacy is, though often overlooked, of great importance. By definition a norm, whether legal or moral in nature, confers legitimacy on a practice; expressing adherence to a norm constitutes a means of legitimization (Clark 2007: 206–27). The real importance of norms, therefore, derives from their capacity to bestow legitimacy. According to Ian Hurd, legitimacy '. . . refers to an actor's normative belief that a rule or institution ought to be obeyed'. 'The operative process in legitimization,' Hurd argues, 'is the internalization by the actor of an external standard' (2007: 7, 31). Thus norms, commonly recognized as legitimate modes of behaviour, are incorporated into the decision-making calculus of states and manifest in the policies these states pursue. Hurd suggests there are three indicators that show this internalization has occurred:

> . . . that states treat the rule in question as a necessary part of the strategic landscape for decision making; that they cease making cost-benefit calculations about the effects of breaking the rule as they consider future behaviors; and that they use as resources the symbols that derive from the rule or institution. (ibid.: 79)

It could plausibly be argued that there is some evidence that the first of these three is evident in contemporary international politics with respects to R2P; states, even the P5, are today unwilling to publicly reject R2P and do appear eager to ensure their action is justified in a way which does not clash with the basic ethos of R2P, however minimally they interpret this (Hehir 2011). This does not, however, mean that R2P compels timely and effective action; policies are framed so as to at least appear to cohere with R2P, as was arguably the case with respects to the UK's and US's use of R2P to, ironically, justify *non-intervention* in Darfur (Bellamy 2006: 33). Evidence of the second and third indicators, however, is more obviously lacking. Statements by the P5 on Libya, including the three NATO states that supported Resolution 1973, clearly highlight that they will continue to treat each case put before the Security Council on a case-by-case basis and judge how to act on the basis of an evaluation of their respective interests and the cost of action. The response of China and Russia to the violence in Syria certainly suggests that they have not stopped making 'cost-benefit calculations'. The fact that there were so few official public avowals of R2P certainly suggests, with respects to Hurd's third indicator, that R2P is not yet seen to constitute an essential positive symbol of legitimization

(Welsh 2011: 1). The source of legitimacy routinely cited by supporters of Resolution 1973 was Chapter VII of the Charter.

Multi-polarity and R2P

Beyond the receptiveness of the West to moral advocacy and the question of R2P's status as a 'norm', there remains a further problem with the strategy adopted by its supporters which have ominous implications for the efficacy of R2P. The belief in the irresistible spread of liberal democracy is increasingly untenable as rivals to Western power – particularly China and Russia – rapidly emerge.

R2P can only work if the theory on the efficacy of normative advocacy is true. This is dependent on the capacity of global civil society to influence the behaviour of states. This capacity is itself contingent on the nature of the political system within states; democratic states are, ostensibly, more susceptible to the blandishments of global civil society than other states. As the current systemic configuration is one dominated by democratic powers then there is at least some logic to the notion that the contemporary hegemonic powers can be prevailed upon to respond to humanitarian crisis. However, as the previous section argues, even this propitious systemic configuration has not ensured much more that the occasional intervention (Weiss 2011). In a new era where non-democratic states are as influential as democracies the likelihood of moral advocacy influencing key decision-making is naturally reduced.

R2P's focus on moral norms has – by virtue of being a function of liberal teleology – essentially overlooked the capacity of the system to change and thus to foresee that the rise of new powers will alter the prevailing norms (Hehir and Murray 2012). The fact that R2P has not advanced a coherent proposal to reform the laws governing the use of force or the powers of the institutions charged with enforcing these norms means that as systemic change lessens the normative impact of R2P (which was modest at best) the Security Council remains as powerful as ever; it is in essence a organ which has survived the shifting distribution of power and fluctuations in prevailing norms.

This matters because if R2P fails to even constitute a norm its claims to influence the behaviour of states is greatly undermined. It is worth reiterating that as the P5 retain the monopoly on the authorization of the use of force the efficacy of R2P is dependent on its capacity to influence China and Russia. While their decision not to veto Resolution 1973 on Libya was historic, there is no evidence that it was a function of normative pressure or humanitarian intent. Some have argued that their decision to abstain was wholly cynical; Michael Walzer (2011) suggested they welcomed another ill-conceived, costly and potentially divisive Western intervention in the region. This aside, China's statement to the Security Council following its abstention offers the clearest explanation for its decision; their ambassador acknowledged they '. . . attach great importance to the position of African countries and the AU. In view of this . . . China abstained' (UNSC 2011: 11). The fact that the three African states on the Security Council – Nigeria, Gabon and the influential South Africa – supported the Resolution, as did the Arab League, understandably influenced China given its growing economic and political ties with Africa and the Middle East. Russia also referred to regional opinion in its statement, citing in particular the position taken by the Arab League in its 12 March statement calling for a no-fly zone (ibid.: 8). This is an explanation, indeed, accepted by some proponents of R2P. Referring to the position taken by the Arab League, Gareth Evans wrote: 'its political support was absolutely crucial in ensuring that there was both a majority on the Council and no exercise of the veto by Russia or China' (2011). According to Bellamy, without the support of key regional organizations such as the LAS and AU, 'China and Russia would have certainly vetoed Resolution 1973' (2011: 4). Thus, the explanation for these abstentions is relatively clear and not related to R2P. This alone – to say nothing about China and Russia's subsequent liberal use of the veto over Syria – must temper the claims made about the intervention in Libya.

The perennial problem remains: the Security Council

The UN system, of course, was designed by the victorious Allies, particularly the US, the UK and the Soviet Union, who reserved significant competencies for themselves, most notably the veto powers of the P5; a form of 'legalised hegemony' (Simpson 2004: 68). The new organization could only function, it was suggested by the Great Powers in 1945, if it reflected, rather than sought to limit, the post-Second World War political hierarchy (Briggs 1945: 670). The power of the Security Council at the zenith of the new system and the constitutional competencies at its disposal were particularly evident with respects to two features of the P5's power; their entitlement to sanction action under Chapter VII and the veto (White 2004: 666). The structure of the new organization and the lack of judicial review of Security Council decision-making meant that the provisions of Chapter VII were, in effect, a matter for the P5 to conceptualize and utilize as they saw fit (Mertus 2009: 98).

The veto served as a means by which the P5 acquired 'the legal and constitutional weapon with which they could defend their interests and position' (Bourantonis 2007: 7).

The Security Council does, of course, exercise its power within the Charter's stipulated framework. The Security Council's powers, therefore, technically 'cannot be unlimited' (White 2004: 646) a point reiterated by the International Court of Justice (ICJ) in 1948 (Gowlland-Debbas 2000: 304) and the ruling in the 1995 Tadic case at the Appeals Chamber of the International Criminal Tribunal for the former Yugoslavia. Nonetheless, despite these formal legal constraints, in reality the Security Council has acted as the principal interpreter of the Charter's rules and hence its own powers (Franck 2005: 206). Bourantonis notes that as the clamour for reform of the Security Council grew in the post-Cold War era the P5 'reached a tacit agreement and adopted a common stance on the reform issue: to resist claims for reform and to do their utmost to prevent discussion on the subject in the UN' (2007: 35).

The fact that the powers vested in the Security Council are as extensive today as they were in 1991 is surely problematic; more so in the context of the increasing power of China and Russia and their evident willingness to resist Western-backed draft resolutions, as evidenced twice in the case of Syria. The key issue with respect to the Security Council is that the P5 has always acted, and likely will always act, in accordance with its members' respective national interests. There is little evidence that moral pressure can be, or has been, effective with respect to the P5's outlook; 'self-abnegation' on the part of the P5, Alan Buchanan and Robet Keohane note, 'is highly unlikely' (2011: 51). This means the response to intra-state crises will remain a function of a coincidence between national interest and humanitarian need, as it always has.

The only conceivable way in which the primacy of the Security Council could have been maintained and *not* constitute a barrier to the consistent enforcement and protection of human rights was if there had been a profound reassessment of the P5's respective national interests. R2P clearly sought to achieve this and thus this project coheres with Reinhold Niebuhr's critique of the 'children of light'. Niebuhr defined the children of light as 'those who seek to bring self-interest . . . in harmony with a more universal good' (1986: 166). Niebuhr criticized 'The social and historical optimism' prevalent among this group as 'the typical illusion of an advancing class which mistook its own progress for the progress of the world' (ibid.: 162). The children of light seek to advance humanity without recognizing the existence of the 'children of darkness' who take advantage of the normative idealism of the children of light. While the children of light construct democratic systems, nationally and internationally, and accept promises at face value, the children of darkness exploit the regulatory weakness of these systems to pursue their own self-interest (ibid.: 166).

'The children of light,' Niebuhr argued, 'have not been as wise as the children of darkness.' The fatal mistake they made, he warned, is that they 'underestimated the power of self-interest' (ibid.: 166). Self-interest therefore exists, and will likely always exist, but this need not induce fatalism as law can act as a means by which individual avarice is tamed; anarchy would reign in every country across the world if this were not the case (Koskenniemi 2006: 57). Currently the international legal system actually facilitates the influence of self-interest through the powers vested in the Security Council. For this reason, it is obvious that legal reform is required; it is thus curious that R2P's advocates have abandoned this original goal; as Bellamy admits, the project has 'sidestepped the question of Security Council reform almost entirely' (2009: 63). A popular definition of insanity is doing the same thing over and over again while expecting different results; given the system is the same today as it was in 1945 can we be surprised that inconsistency remains the norm?

Conclusion

Despite the ICISS report, the 2005 World Summit *Outcome Document* and the 2009 General Assembly debate on R2P, the manner in which an intra-state humanitarian crises will be, and legally can be, dealt with today is exactly the same as was the case in 1990. This was evident in the manner in which the Security Council responded to the situation in Syria in 2012; the response of the 'international community' was ultimately predicated on the disposition of the P5, and particularly in this case, the view from Beijing and Moscow. There is very little concrete evidence that R2P in any way influenced the Chinese and Russians with respect to Libya and even less so in the case of Syria, as they have twice vetoed resolutions against the Assad regime. This may well be indicative of the growing power of these two states and their new willingness to throw their weight around at the Security Council. This can only have ominous implications for R2P.

The optimism which abounded in the wake of the intervention in Libya, therefore, is misplaced. While this intervention was potentially laudable in itself, it is not indicative of a broader trend or the dawning of a new era. A more holistic perspective on the Arab Spring demonstrates that twin problems of parochial interests and the power of the P5 remains a barrier to the consistent enforcement of human rights law. R2P is predicated on idealistic understanding of the disposition of Western states and a mistaken belief in the permanence of liberal hegemony.

References

Adams, S. (2011) 'R2P and the Libya Mission', *Los Angeles Times*, 28 September.

Amnesty International (2011) 'Arms Trade to Middle East and North Africa Shows Failure of Export Controls', 19 October. Available at: www.amnesty.org/en/news-and-updates/report/arms-trade-middle-east-and-north-africa-shows-failure-export-controls-2011-1 [Accessed 4 February 2013].

Annan, K. (2001) 'Message Honoring Raphael Lemkin', Press Release SG/SM/7842, 13 June.

Axworthy, L. (2011) 'In Libya, We Move Toward a More Humane World', *Globe and Mail*, 23 August.

Barnard, A. (2011) 'China Sought to Sell Arms to Qaddafi, Documents Suggest', *The New York Times*, 4 September.

Barnett, M. (2010) *The International Humanitarian Order* (London: Routledge).

Bellamy, A. (2006) 'Whither the Responsibility to Protect? Humanitarian Intervention and the 2005 World Summit', *Ethics and International Affairs*, vol. 20, no. 2, pp. 143–69.

Bellamy, A. (2009) *Responsibility to Protect: The Global Effort to End Mass Atrocities* (London: Polity).

Bellamy, A. (2010) 'Kosovo and the Advent of Sovereignty as Responsibility', in A. Hehir (ed.), *Kosovo, Intervention and Statebuilding* (London: Routledge).

Bellamy, A. (2011) 'Libya and the Responsibility to Protect: The Exception and the Norm', *Ethics and International Affairs*, vol. 25, no. 3. Available at: www.carnegiecouncil.org/resources/journal/index.html [Accessed September 2011].

Bellamy, A. and P. Williams (2011) 'The New Politics of Protection? Côte d'Ivoire, Libya and the Responsibility to Protect', *International Affairs*, vol. 82, no. 7, pp. 825–50.

Berdal, M. (2003) 'The UN Security Council: Ineffective but Indispensable', *Survival*, vol. 45, no. 2, pp. 7–30.

Berdal, M. (2008) 'The UN, Multilateralism, and International Order', in G. Andreani and P. Hassner (eds), *Justifying War?: From Humanitarianism to Counterterrorism* (Basingstoke: Palgrave Macmillan).

Berman, F. (2007) 'Moral Versus Legal Legitimacy', in C. Reed and D. Ryall (eds), *The Price of Peace* (Cambridge: Cambridge University Press).

Bourantonis, D. (2007) *The History and Politics of Security Council Reform* (London: Routledge).

Branigan, T. (2011) 'Chinese Arms Companies "Offered to Sell Weapons to Gaddafi Regime"', *The Guardian*, 5 September.

Briggs, H. (1945) 'Power Politics and International Organization', *American Journal of International Law*, vol. 39, no. 4, pp. 664–79.

Buchanan, A. and R. O. Keohane (2004) 'The Preventive Use of Force: A Cosmopolitan Institutional Proposal', *Ethics and International Affairs*, vol. 18, no. 1, pp. 1–22.

Buchanan, A. and R. Keohane (2011) 'Precommitment Regimes for Intervention: Supplementing the Security Council', *Ethics and International Affairs*, vol. 25, no. 1, pp. 41–63.

Chesterman, S. (2002) *Just War or Just Peace?* (Oxford: Oxford University Press).

Chesterman, S. (2011a) '"Leading from Behind": The Responsibility to Protect, the Obama Doctrine, and Humanitarian Intervention after Libya', *Ethics and International Affairs*, vol. 25, no. 3, pp. 1–7. Available online at: www.carnegiecouncil.org/resources/journal/index.html [Accessed September 2011].

Chesterman, S. (2011b) 'The Outlook for UN Reform', New York University School of Law, Public Law & Legal Theory Research Paper Series, Working Paper No. 11–55, August. Available online at: http://ssrn.com/abstract=1885229 [Accessed September 2011].

China (2009) 'Statement by the Permanent Representative of China to the UN', 23 July. Available online at: http://responsibilitytoprotect.org/Statement%20by%20Ambassador%20Liu%20Zhenmin.pdf [Accessed June 2012].

Clark, I. (2007) *Legitimacy in International Society* (Oxford: Oxford University Press).

Considine, S. C. and H. Sonner (2009) 'Interview between Author and Sapna Chatpar Considine, Project Manager, International Coalition for the Responsibility to Protect, and Heather Sonner, International Secretariat of the Institute for Global Policy', Tuesday, 18 August, New York.

Crocker, C. (2011) 'The Arab Spring', United States Institute for Peace, 25 April. Available online at: www.usip.org/publications/the-arab-spring [Accessed August 2012].

Dallaire, R. (2004) 'Looking at Darfur, Seeing Rwanda', *New York Times*, 4 October.

de Cuellar, J. P. (1991) 'Report of the Secretary-General on the Work of the Organization', UN Document A/46/1, 13 September.

Deng, F. (2010) 'JISB Interview: The Responsibility to Protect', *Journal of Intervention and Statebuilding*, vol. 4, no. 1, pp. 83–9.

Evans, G. (2008) *The Responsibility to Protect: Ending Mass Atrocity Crimes Once and For All* (Washington, DC: Brookings Institution Press).

Evans, G. (2011) 'The RtoP Balance Sheet After Libya', 2 September. Available online at: www.gevans.org/speeches/speech448%20interview%20RtoP.html [accessed November 2011].

Finnemore, M. and K. Sikkink (1998) 'International Norm Dynamics and Political Change', *International Organization*, vol. 52, no. 4, pp. 887–917.

Fitzmaurice, M. (2006) 'The Practical Working of the Law of Treaties', in M. Evans (ed.), *International Law* (Oxford: Oxford University Press).

Fisher, D. (2007) 'Humanitarian Intervention', in C. Reed and D. Ryall (eds), *The Price of Peace* (Cambridge: Cambridge University Press).

Franck, T. (2005) 'Interpretation and Change in the Law of Humanitarian Intervention', in J. L. Holzgrefe and Robert O. Keohane (eds), *Humanitarian Intervention: Ethical, Legal and Political Dilemmas* (Cambridge: Cambridge University Press).

Fukuyama, F. (1989) 'The End of History and the Last Man', *The National Interest*, Summer.

Frost, M. (2001) 'The Ethics of Humanitarian Intervention', in K. E. Smith and M. Light (eds), *Ethics and Foreign Policy* (Cambridge: Cambridge University Press).

Glanville, L. (2011) 'Darfur and the Responsibilities of Sovereignty', *International Journal of Human Rights*, vol. 15, no. 3, pp. 462–80.

Glennon, M. (1999) 'The New Interventionism', *Foreign Affairs*, vol. 78, no. 3, pp. 2–7.

Global Centre for R2P (2009) 'Frequently Made Assertions', 16 June. Available online at: http://globalr2p.org/media/pdf/Frequently_made_assertions_16_June_Final.pdf [Accessed June 2011].

Gowlland-Debbas, V. (2000) 'Functions of the United Nations Security Council in the International Legal System', in M. Byers (ed.), *The Role of International Law in International Politics* (Oxford: Oxford University Press).

Hakimi, M. (2010) 'State Bystander Responsibility', *The European Journal of International Law*, vol. 21, no. 2, pp. 341–85.

Hehir, A. (2008) *Humanitarian Intervention after Kosovo: Iraq, Darfur and the Record of Global Civil Society* (Basingstoke: Palgrave Macmillan).

Hehir, A. (2011) 'The Responsibility to Protect in International Political Discourse: Encouraging Statement of Intent or Illusory Platitudes?', *International Journal of Human Rights*, vol. 15, no. 8, pp. 1329–46.

Hehir, A. (2012) *The Responsibility to Protect: Rhetoric, Reality and the Future of Humanitarian Intervention* (Basingstoke: Palgrave Macmillan).

Hehir, A. and R. W. Murray (2012) 'Intervention in the Emerging Multipolar System: Why R2P will Miss the Unipolar Moment', *Journal of Intervention and Statebuilding*, vol. 6, no. 4, pp. 387–406.

Heinbecker, P. (2011) 'Plenty of Credit to Go Around in Gadhafi's Fall', *Montreal Gazette*, 23 August.

Henkin, L. (1990) 'Compliance with International Law in an Inter-state System', *Academie de droit international, Recueil des cours 1989* (Dordrecht: Martinus Nijhoff).

Hensel, H. (2004) 'Introduction', in H. Hensel (ed.), *Sovereignty and the Global Community* (Aldershot: Ashgate).

Hollis, R. (2012) 'No Friend of Democratization: Europe's Role in the "Arab Spring"', *International Affairs*, vol. 88, no. 1, pp. 81–94.

Hurd, I. (2007) *After Anarchy: Legitimacy and Power in the United Nations Security Council* (Princeton: Princeton University Press).

The International Coalition for the Responsibility to Protect (2011) 'FAQs on Impact of Action in Libya on the Responsibility to Protect', 6 May. Available online at: www.responsibilitytoprotect.org/index.php/component/content/article/35-r2pcs-topics/3436-icrtop-2-page-faq-on-the-impact-of-action-in-libya-on-rtop [Accessed November 2011].

International Commission on Intervention and State Sovereignty (ICISS) (2001) *The Responsibility to Protect* (Ottawa: International Development Research Centre).

International Crisis Group (2011) 'Popular Protests in the Middle East and North Africa: Bahrain's Rocky Road to Reform', Middle East/North Africa Report 111, 28 July.

Kaldor, M. (2001) 'Transnational Civil Society', in T. Dunne and N. Wheeler (eds), *Human Rights in Global Politics* (Cambridge: Cambridge University Press).

Kaldor, M. (2003) *Global Civil Society: An Answer to War* (London: Polity).

Ki-Moon, B. (2009) 'Implementing the Responsibility to Protect: Report of the Secretary-General', A/63/677, 12 January. Available online at: http://globalr2p.org/pdf/SGR2PEng.pdf [Accessed June 2012].

Ki-Moon, B. (2011) 'Remarks at Breakfast Roundtable with Foreign Ministers on "The Responsibility to Protect: Responding to Imminent Threats of Mass Atrocities"', UN News Centre, 23 September. Available online at: www.un.org/apps/news/infocus/sgspeeches/search_full.asp?statID=1325 [Accessed November 2011].

Koskenniemi, M. (2006) 'What is International Law For?', in M. Evans (ed.), *International Law* (Oxford: Oxford University Press).

Landman, T. (2005) *Studying Human Rights* (London: Routledge).

Mertus, J. (2009) *The United Nations and Human Rights* (London: Routledge).

Niebuhr, R. (1986) 'The Children of Light and the Children of Darkness', in R. McAfee Brown (ed.), *The Essential Reinhold Niebuhr* (New Haven: Yale University Press).

Orford, A. (2003) *Reading Humanitarian Intervention* (Cambridge: Cambridge University Press).

Peters, A. (2009) 'Humanity as the A and Ω of Sovereignty', *The European Journal of International Law*, vol. 20, no. 3, pp. 513–44.

Power, S. (2009) 'Foreword', in R. H. Cooper and J. V. Kohler (eds), *Responsibility to Protect: The Global Moral Compact for the 21st Century* (Basingstoke and New York: Palgrave Macmillan).

Reinold, T. (2010) 'The Responsibility to Protect: Much Ado About Nothing?', *Review of International Studies*, vol. 36, Supplement S1, pp. 55–78.

Reus-Smit, C. (2005) 'Liberal Hierarchy and the License to Use Force', in D. Armstrong, T. Farrell and B. Maiguashca (eds), *Force and Legitimacy in World Politics* (Cambridge: Cambridge University Press).

Robertson, G. (2002) *Crimes against Humanity* (London: Penguin).

Rutledge, I. (2005) *Addicted to Oil* (London: I. B. Taurus).

Scheffer, D. (2009) 'Atrocity Crimes: Framing the Responsibility to Protect', in R. H. Cooper and J. V. Kohler (eds), *Responsibility to Protect: The Global Moral Compact for the 21st Century* (Basingstoke and New York: Palgrave Macmillan).

Shaw, M. (1994) *Global Civil Society and International Relations* (London: Polity).

Shawcross, W. (2001) *Deliver Us from Evil* (London: Bloomsbury).

Simpson, G. (2004) *Great Powers and Outlaw States* (Cambridge: Cambridge University Press).

Slaughter, A-M. (1995) 'International Law in a World of Liberal States', *European Journal of International Law*, vol. 6, no. 1, pp. 503–38.

Slim, H. (2004) 'Dithering over Darfur?', *International Affairs*, vol. 80, no. 5, pp. 811–28.

Smith, B. (2011) 'The Arab Uprisings', House of Commons Library, Research Paper 11/73, 11 November.

Stahn, C. (2007) 'Responsibility to Protect: Political Rhetoric or Emerging Legal Norm?', *American Journal of International Law*, vol. 101, no. 1, pp. 99–120.

Thakur, R. (2011) 'Has R2P Worked in Libya?', *Canberra Times*, 19 September.

UK (2009) 'Statement by the Permanent Representative of the United Kingdom to the UN', 23 July. Available online at: www.responsibilitytoprotect.org/UK_ENG(1).pdf [Accessed June 2010].

UNSC (United Nations Security Council) (1992) 'S/PV.3145', 3 December. Available online at: http://daccess-dds-ny.un.org/doc/UNDOC/PRO/N92/621/12/PDF/N9262112.pdf?OpenElement [Accessed November 2011].

UNSC (United Nations Security Council) (2011) 'Security Council 6498th Meeting', S/PV.6498, 17 March.

Walzer, M. (2011) 'The Case against Our Attack on Libya', *The New Republic*, 20 March. Available online at: www.tnr.com/article/world/85509/the-case-against-our-attack-libya [Accessed November 2011].

Weiss, T. (2007) *Humanitarian Intervention* (Cambridge: Polity).

Weiss, T. (2011) 'R2P Alive and Well After Libya', *Ethics and International Affairs*, vol. 25, no. 3, pp. 1–6. Available online at: www.carnegiecouncil.org/resources/journal/index.html [Accessed September 2011].

Welsh, J. (2011) 'Civilian Protection in Libya: Putting Coercion and Controversy Back into RtoP', *Ethics and International Affairs*, vol. 25, no. 3, pp. 1–8. Available online at: www.carnegiecouncil.org/resources/journal/index.html [Accessed September 2011].

White, N. (2004) 'The Will and Authority of the Security Council After Iraq', *Leiden Journal of International Law*, vol. 17, no. 4, pp. 645–72.

Wheeler, N. (2002) *Saving Strangers: Humanitarian Intervention in International Society* (Oxford: Oxford University Press).

Wheeler, N. (2003) 'Humanitarian Intervention after September 11, 2001', in A. Lang (ed.), *Just Intervention* (Washington, DC: Georgetown University Press).

Wheeler, N. (2006) 'The Humanitarian Responsibilities of Sovereignty', in J. Welsh (ed.), *Humanitarian Intervention and International Relations* (Oxford: Oxford University Press).

4

'My Fears, Alas, Were Not Unfounded': Africa's Responses to the Libya Conflict

Alex de Waal

Introduction

Like the 'Brother Leader' Colonel Muammar Gaddafi, Chadian President Idriss Déby Itno was born into a Bedouin lineage in the central Sahara. Over three decades as a soldier and politician, Déby came to know his Libyan enemy, rival and colleague as well as anyone. Déby was a senior officer in the Chadian army, which spent over a decade fighting the Libyan army, and, as President of Chad from 1991, he had two further decades' worth of experience in managing the impacts of the mercenarized tribalism with which his neighbour ruled the Libyan Sahara. As soon as the Libyan uprising developed into a civil war, Déby warned of impending instability and the spread of terrorist groups across the Sahara and Sahel (Déby Itno 2011a). He was no friend of Gaddafi, but predicted a potential blowback – or perhaps 'blow-around' – following an uncontrolled dismantling of the Brother Leader's patronage of miscellaneous armed groups and an opening of his vast arsenals to all comers. Speaking to *Jeune Afrique* six weeks after Gaddafi's death, Déby recalled his warnings and said, 'I think history will prove me right . . . my fear, alas, were not unfounded' (2011b). A further six weeks later, about 3,000 armed men, a combination of Tuaregs who had formerly served under Gaddafi and radical Islamists who had been drawn to the Libyan insurrection and its promise of unlimited weaponry, invaded Mali. Their insurrection triggered a train of events that resulted rapidly in a military coup that destroyed a fragile but precious democracy and a unilateral declaration of independence by Tuareg insurgents to assert the desert state of Azawad.

While the Arab world, Europe and the United States tended to view the 2011 Libyan uprising as a turbulent version of Tunisia's democratic uprising, sub-Saharan African leaders saw the contest between Gaddafi and his rivals as a variant of the Chadian wars, threatening a lawless mercenarism that could easily spill across borders. African leaders found Gaddafi erratic, egotistical and frequently offensive, but many were leery of forcible regime change, fearing that what followed could be worse. The warnings expressed by Déby concerning regional destabilization were repeated in four statements by the African Union Peace and Security Council from March 2011 onwards. The African Union (AU) consistently spoke of an 'inclusive transition' to democracy in Libya, meaning a process in which Gaddafi would step aside peaceably.

The efforts by the AU's 'Ad Hoc High Level Committee' of five heads of state to mediate a ceasefire and a negotiated political settlement in Libya were spurned by western leaders and the Transitional National Council (TNC) and did not prevail. Moreover, Africa's caution about the regime change project led by the TNC and NATO was dismissed and derided by most international commentators. For example, when the AU leaders arrived in Libya with ceasefire proposals on 10 April, the BBC's Will Ross wrote:

> The African Union does not have a good reputation when it comes to solving crises . . . any intervention which does not involve the removal from power of Col Gaddafi will be seen by some as the AU saving the Libyan leader. It has often been accused of standing up for the incumbents and is criticized as being a club which serves the interests of the continent's presidents more than the people. The situation is muddied by money. Col Gaddafi has bankrolled the AU for years and he has bought friends in Africa. South Africa and Uganda are on the AU panel. Col Gaddafi has previously supported both South Africa's ruling party, the ANC, and Uganda's President Yoweri Museveni before they came to power. Although neither country would admit this history influences their stance on Col Gaddafi, some may say it means they cannot be honest brokers in peace talks. (Ross 2011)

Barak Barfi of the New America Foundation made a similar charge, writing that Gaddafi had 'declared that he planned to "throw in his lot with Africa" and backed up his words by lavishing his country's oil wealth on the continent's impoverished nations . . . Today, Qaddafi's African largesse has paid off' (Barfi 2011).

These are misrepresentations and caricatures of the AU position. The AU's Libya initiative did not succeed, and left the organization at odds with the United States, Europe and the Arab League, and internally divided. However, with the passing of time, the wisdom of the African position is becoming more widely acknowledged.

The NATO intervention in Libya has been subject to many criticisms, including from those who advocated negotiations for a political transition (Roberts 2011). However, such critiques tend to contrapose the regime change option with a hypothetical political settlement, without attending to the specifics of what the AU actually proposed, and why. Additionally, the AU position was not unanimous, and several African states, notably Sudan, actively supported the TNC.

This chapter explores the sub-Saharan African dimension of the Libyan civil war and the diverse policies adopted by African governments and the AU towards Libya during 2011. It begins with a tour d'horizon of Libya's adventures in sub-Saharan Africa during the 42 years of Gaddafi's rule, outlines the hopes and fears of Africa's leaders when the uprising in Tripoli began, details the key elements of the AU response to the crisis, and concludes with some reflections on the aftermath.

Background

Colonel Gaddafi cut a unique figure in African politics – divisive, controversial and ambiguous. Although Gaddafi's African policies had many twists and turns, they were marked by a persistent anti-imperialism, and although many Africans found him tiresome, egotistical and mercurial, they also considered him no less hypocritical and dangerous than his adversaries, including the former imperial powers and the United States. During four decades in power Gaddafi was actively engaged in conflicts and political affairs in many Saharan and sub-Saharan African countries, including military adventurism, support to proxies, patronage of governments, and an active role in continental organizations, including sparking the creation of the AU.

From the outset, Gaddafi was as an active anti-colonialist and supported the southern African liberation movements and the African National Congress. In this regard, he was no different to Gamal Abdel Nasser in Egypt and Ahmed Ben Bella and Houari Boumédiènne in Algeria, except that he continued for much longer. Gaddafi extended similar solidarity to post-colonial liberation fronts, including the POLISARIO in Western Sahara, the Eritrean Liberation Front (up to the Ethiopian revolution), the National Resistance Movement (NRM) in Uganda, and (briefly) the Sudan People's Liberation Movement (SPLM).

Gaddafi could be relied upon to serve as a consistent and vocal pole of opposition to Africa's dependence on former colonial powers and the United States. Libya's role in creating the AU was consistent with this; having lost confidence in the anti-imperialism of the League of Arab States he became an enthusiast for African unity.

But, as AU Chairperson Jean Ping delicately put it, 'For too long, the political system in Libya has been at variance with the relevant instruments of our Union' (African Union 2011g: para. 17). Gaddafi's enthusiasm for any and all forms of avowedly anti-imperialist armed struggle long outlasted his fellow Africans'. In 1999, when Gaddafi made the bold proposal to replace the Organisation of African Unity (OAU) with a United States of Africa, setting in motion the rapid setting up of the AU, he found himself dealing with a different generation of African leaders. Among the principles enshrined in the AU's Constitutive Act are a prohibition on unconstitutional changes in government and a provision for intervention in the internal affairs of member states in cases of grave human rights abuses. The Libyan 'Brother Leader', of course, considered himself not to be bound by such rules and when he assumed the Presidency of the Union in 2009, it took considerable effort on the part of African leaders to persuade him that he was not President for life but needed to step down after a year, in accordance with the rules of the organization. Libya's presidency was shambolic, marked by repeated public arguments between Gaddafi and other African leaders. Recurrently at AU Summits, Gaddafi disrupted proceedings both with his unrealistic agenda items and his disregard for procedures. At the AU's inaugural summit in Durban in 2002, he was ruled out of order by South Africa's President Thabo Mbeki, who was in the chair, and stormed out after Nigerian President Olusegun Obasanjo cut him off when he was speaking out of turn. At Accra in 2007, Gaddafi's attempts to fast-track a united Africa earned him the opposition of longtime friends including President Robert Mugabe of Zimbabwe and Ugandan President Yoweri Museveni. At the Europe-Africa conference in Tripoli in 2010, Gaddafi tried to prevent a scheduled meeting of the PSC, but was overruled by President Jacob Zuma of South Africa.

Military adventurism was a feature of Libya's sub-Saharan policy, and its immediate neighbours Chad and Sudan bore the brunt of this (Burr and Collins 1999). In 1972, Libyan forces occupied the Aouzou Strip along the northern border of Chad. Libyan engagement increased during the decade 1978–87, during which time Libya launched a full-scale invasion and supported Chadian factions in the civil war. In response, France dispatched ground and air forces (Operation Épervier) and the CIA set up its biggest covert operation in Africa, providing assistance to anti-Libyan factions. The confrontation culminated in the battle of Ouadi Doum in 1987, when mobile Chadian forces loyal to President Hissène Habré defeated a far larger conventional Libyan army. Demoralized and unsure why they were fighting, the Libyan army retreated, leaving thousands of prisoners of war whom Gaddafi promptly disowned. Thereafter, Gaddafi retreated, licked his wounds, and accepted that the Aouzou Strip was part of Chad. He also retired many army officers and instead relied ever more heavily on mercenaries and personally loyal security services.

Having achieved their goals, the US and France distanced themselves from Habré, partly because of his appalling human rights record, and stood aside when his army commanders rebelled and one of them, Idriss Déby, overthrew him with Sudanese assistance in 1990. Déby achieved a *modus vivendi* with both Gaddafi and Sudan's President Omar al Bashir that lasted until the outbreak of the Darfur war in 2003.

Gaddafi's engagement with Sudan was as long and deep, marked by intimate enmity from the earliest days in which he and President Jaafar Nimeiri (also of the class of 1969 free officers) avowed Arab nationalism. Relations soon soured and Libya supported the sectarian and Islamist National Front that in 1976 invaded Sudan from Libya, its forces reaching as far as Omdurman before they were defeated. Gaddafi's hostility to Nimeiri did not dim, in particular because of Sudanese support for the Chadian contras. Relations thawed after Nimeiri was overthrown in 1985 and Sadiq al Mahdi, earlier one of the leaders of the National Front, was elected Prime Minister a year later. Al Mahdi allowed Gaddafi a free hand in Darfur, especially when, after the 1987 defeat at Ouadi Doum, Libya used Darfur as a route for resupplying its Chadian Arab proxies, helping to spark the first Darfur war (1987–89) and creating the Janjawiid (Flint and de Waal, 2008). In 1989, al Mahdi was overthrown by Omar al Bashir, who maintained an accommodation with Libya.

The Sudan-Chad-Libya triangle was destabilized when the Darfur war erupted in 2003, and at first the three countries were united in trying to resolve it. However, by December 2005, the prominent role of Zaghawa in the Darfur rebellion dragged their kinsman Déby into the war on the rebel side. For the next four years, Chad was in a state of undeclared war with Sudan. Gaddafi was simultaneously public peacemaker and patron of different warring factions at different moments. Notably, he became financier, arms supplier and protector of the Justice and Equality Movement (JEM) and its leader, Khalil Ibrahim. In May 2008,

JEM launched an attack right across the desert from Chad, reaching the Nile at Omdurman, using vehicles and supplies provided by Libya. This attack was partly retaliation for a Sudanese-sponsored Chadian rebel assault that had reached N'djamena three months earlier and had, for a day, looked as though it would overthrow Déby. Thereafter, al Bashir and Déby realized that they had better return to their earlier security pact, and that agreement was consummated with the signing of the Sudan-Chad Accord on 15 January 2010 (Tubiana 2011).

Déby pressed Khalil to negotiate with Khartoum, and drafted a Framework Agreement which Khalil duly signed the next month. Khalil refused to go further, hopeful that his strong political and family ties with the Chadian leadership would allow him to circumvent the Accord. But in May, he was refused entry at N'djamena airport and flew to Tripoli. Gaddafi received him: he had refused to be part of the re-normalization, and continued to host JEM and other Darfurian groups. One reason for this was that the Darfur peace talks were hosted and sponsored by Qatar, and he disliked Qatar's aspirations to Arab leadership. At the time when the Libyan uprising began, the JEM leadership was in Tripoli, planning its next military moves against Khartoum.

Among the forces that Gaddafi recruited for his Chadian adventures were Saharan nomads and sub-Saharan migrants, several thousand of whom were moulded into an 'Islamic Legion' and others who became fractions of the diverse Libyan military apparatus. Among these were, in particular, Tuareg from Mali, who nurtured wild ideas about restoring Saharan kingdoms that had been eclipsed during the European colonial conquest. According to a former Libyan military officer,[1] Gaddafi's preference for the Tuareg from Mali, which does not share a border with Libya, was because recruits from Niger or Chad would have been able to defect more easily and threaten him from the neighbouring countries. Much of the subsequent talk of 'African mercenaries' in Libya has its roots in the Saharan peoples – Libyan, non-Libyan and those with multiple territorial identities – who joined his military forces.

Gaddafi's reach extended much further across the continent. In the Horn of Africa, Gaddafi was an early supporter of the Eritrean nationalist fronts, but then switched to become part of an axis with revolutionary Ethiopia and South Yemen. He was engaged in various sides in the Somali conflicts. After the Ethio-Eritrean war of 1998, Libya was one of the few friends and financiers of Eritrea. In West Africa, Gaddafi backed a number of coups and insurgencies from the late 1980s. He considered Thomas Sankara, the charismatic leftist coup-maker in Burkina Faso, as his protégé, and like every other African leader, despised his successor Blaise Compaoré. Nonetheless, Gaddafi used Compaoré as his principal intermediary to support the rebellions of Charles Taylor in Liberia and Foday Sankoh in Sierra Leone; one of the many ironies of Europe's relationship with Libya is that Compaoré, who for fifteen years was the major agent of destabilization in West Africa and a client of Gaddafi, was subsequently rehabilitated as a French gendarme and lauded for peacemaking roles in Ivory Coast and Mali.

Libyan patronage also financed impecunious governments, including when they had an urgent need to pay their dues to the AU so that they could cast their votes at summit meetings. But Gaddafi's brashness and disdain for protocol offended in equal measure. He responded to brush-offs from Nigeria in 2010 by advocating dismembering the country, first into two and then into several states (BBC 2010). Consistent with his insistence that he was not a 'head of state' but rather the representative of the people, Gaddafi latterly began circumventing Africa's official leaders and aspiring to lead the continent through chiefs and monarchs, taking for himself the title 'King of Kings'.

By the 2000s, African governments had become adept at managing Gaddafi, doing the minimum necessary to avoid his meddling. The leaders of the biggest countries, such as Ethiopia, Nigeria and South Africa, dealt with Libya through gritted teeth. For others, the Libyan leader was an embarrassment, and they paid lip service to his usually unwanted attention, while finding ways of continuing to do their own thing. The AU pursued this minimalist strategy. For example, following the coup in Mauritania in August 2008, General Mohamed Ould Abdel Aziz overthrew the country's first democratic government, headed by President Sidi Mohamed Ould Cheikh Abdallahi. The AU imposed sanctions. Shortly after assuming the presidency of the AU, Gaddafi took the opposite position and argued that Mauritanians should accept military rule as a fait accompli. Aziz squared the circle by resigning from the army and running for president in elections, which he won.

Two years later, Gaddafi was outraged when Aziz refused to return the favour and was among the African leaders who called for democracy in Libya. Aziz's position reflected how Gaddafi had become at best out of step with, and at worst loathed by, other African leaders. He was neither respected not trusted, but barely tolerated. By 2010, only those who had nowhere else to turn, such as Eritrea's Issayas Afewerki, or those who continued to pocket Libyan money indiscriminately, such as Gambia's Yahya Jammeh, could be considered Libyan allies or reliable clients.

The African Union initiative

The first protests in Libya occurred immediately in the wake of the uprisings in Tunisia and Egypt, and the AU response should be seen partly in the context of those revolutions. The guiding principles for the AU were the Lomé Declaration on Unconstitutional Changes in Government (2000) and the Constitutive Act of the African Union (2002), which prohibited unconstitutional changes in government. The drafters had not foreseen the possibility of democratic uprisings, although these had occurred in Sudan (1964 and 1985) and non-violent demonstrations and civil society mobilization had hastened the democratization of many African countries after 1990.[2] But the AU did not use these principles to buttress the status quo, but rather to stress the democratic nature of the uprisings and the continuities with the democratization wave in sub-Saharan Africa of the late 1980s and early 1990s (African Union 2011d: paras 6–12). The AU Peace and Security Council (PSC) condemned the repression of demonstrations in Tunisia on 15 January and in Egypt on 16 February, in each case calling for democratic change. The AU Chairperson Jean Ping explained:

> . . . the AU exhibited the necessary flexibility, basing its response not on a dogmatic interpretation of the existing texts, but rather on the need to contribute to the attainment of the overall AU objective of consolidating democracy in the continent. Notably, the African leaders welcomed the developments in Tunisia and Egypt, stressing that they provided an opportunity for Member States to renew their commitment to the AU agenda for democracy and governance. (Ping 2011: 1)

The first AU discussion on the Libyan crisis was at the PSC meeting of 23 February, and focused on the Libyan authorities' repression of demonstrations and the threats that Gaddafi was making against the opposition. This was the brief 'Tripoli Spring' and the meeting reflected it. The Libyan ambassador in Addis Ababa spoke at length but did not sway the Council, whose communiqué condemned excessive use of force against demonstrators (African Union 2011a).[3] But over the next week it became clear that the uprising was turning into a civil war, and by the time of the next PSC meeting, two weeks later, the AU was thinking differently.

The 10 March PSC meeting, held at the level of heads of state, forged the African diplomatic response to the Libya crisis. The first agenda item of that meeting was the final report by the AU's High-Level Panel on Côte d'Ivoire, which demanded that Laurent Gbagbo vacate the presidency and insisted President-elect Alessane Ouattara be able to take his post. The Commission drew upon the lessons of the Ivorian crisis, and decided at once that, given the seriousness of the crisis in Libya, effective action required the involvement at the highest level of the Member States. Hence the PSC proposed a high-level ad hoc committee made up of heads of state, anticipating that this would have the required clout and influence to facilitate a negotiated solution in Libya and rally the international community behind the AU's efforts. The meeting was chaired by the Mauritanian President Mohamed Ould Abdel Aziz. He and other heads of state had quickly recognized that the Arab Spring meant that Gaddafi could not survive. The other key intervention was from Déby: 'beware of opening the Libyan Pandora's box.' The themes of the meeting included the need for a ceasefire, for humanitarian assistance (including the rescue of African migrant workers) and for an inclusive peace agreement combined with a democratic transition. The members also worried about the destabilization of Libya's southern neighbours and invoked the OAU Convention on the Elimination of Mercenarism in Africa (1977). Instead of applying its newly developed doctrine of supporting democratic uprisings, the AU interpreted the Libyan conflict through its more familiar lens of responding to a civil war.

The communiqué captured all these issues (African Union 2011b). It underscored the legitimacy of the aspirations of the Libyan people for democracy, political reform, justice, peace and security, and reiterated the AU's 'strong and unequivocal condemnation of the indiscriminate use of force and lethal weapons, whoever it comes from, resulting in the loss of life, both civilian and military, and the transformation of pacific demonstrations into an armed rebellion'. This was not objected to or watered down by the presidents participating in the meeting.

The most substantive element was paragraph 7, which became known as the 'roadmap':

> The current situation in Libya calls for an urgent African action for: (i) the immediate cessation of all hostilities, (ii) the cooperation of the competent Libyan authorities to facilitate the timely delivery of humanitarian assistance to the needy populations, (iii) the protection of foreign nationals, including the African migrants living in Libya, and (iv) the adoption and implementation of the political reforms necessary for the elimination of the causes of the current crisis.

Although Gaddafi leaving office was not explicitly mentioned, the roadmap was designed as a way for the Brother Leader to step down in a timeframe of months, handing over to an inclusive interim government that would pave the way for elections. The AU set up an Ad Hoc High Level Committee to pursue the roadmap, including the presidents of Mauritania (in the chair, representing the North African subregion[4]), Republic of Congo (Central Africa), Mali (West Africa[5]), South Africa and Uganda (East Africa). By dint of South Africa's presence on the UN Security Council, the AU would bring the UN onside. The first meeting of the Ad Hoc High Level Committee was scheduled for the Mauritanian capital Nouakchott on 19 March, after which the members would fly to Libya.

Meanwhile, the US, France and Britain were following a different track, and driving UN policy. A week later, the UN Security Council met to consider the escalating crisis and especially the threat to Benghazi. The three African countries on the Security Council (Gabon, Nigeria and South Africa) all voted for Resolution 1973. If just one had voted against, or two had abstained, the Resolution would not have passed. The Resolution refers to the AU efforts in its preambular section, including calling for a ceasefire and noting the decision of the AU 'to send its ad hoc High Level Committee to Libya with the aim of facilitating dialogue to lead to the political reforms necessary to find a peaceful and sustainable solution'. But the operative provisions of Resolution 1973 were different entirely.

President Sarkozy of France had no patience for the AU and its diplomatic approach. He invited Ping to Paris for the 19 March 'Summit for the Support of the Libyan People', even though it clashed with the AU's previously scheduled meeting in Nouakchott. Amr Moussa, Secretary-General of the Arab League, went to Paris, and Ping later commented that he was surely right not to go for a lunch and a photo opportunity, lending legitimacy to an agenda different from that of the AU.

The Ad Hoc Committee met in Nouakchott on 19 March, hosted by President Aziz. Present were Denis Sassou Nguesso of the Republic of Congo; Amadou Toumani Touré ('ATT') of Mali; and ministers representing Presidents Yoweri Museveni of Uganda and Jacob Zuma of South Africa. Mauritania provided a plane to fly to Tripoli the following day, but 19 March was the day on which the no-fly zone came into effect. The Panel members received a curt message from the US and the UN saying that, should they proceed with their visit, their security could not be guaranteed. The communiqué published at the end of the meeting reflected the disappointment and anger of the participants for not having been allowed to travel to an African country for a peace mission.

Neither did they, or the Chairperson of the AU, go to London for the 29 March meeting of Foreign Ministers and leaders from the UN, the Arab League, the Islamic Conference, the European Union and NATO. At that meeting, the Libya Contact Group was established, and the AU was conspicuously not included.[6] The Contact Group called for Gaddafi to relinquish power and expressed support for the TNC, with some of its members extending recognition to the TNC as the sovereign authority of Libya.

The Ad Hoc Committee met again in Nouakchott on 9 April. Four presidents were there: Aziz, Sassou Nguesso, ATT and Zuma, with Museveni represented by his foreign minister. This time the UN gave permission to fly to Tripoli and they met with Gaddafi the following day. In the meeting, Gaddafi insisted that his country was victim of an aggression and that Africa should stand on his side. He was unhappy with the 10 March PSC communiqué and rejected accusations that his army and security services had killed a countless number of civilians. Instead he levelled accusations against the demonstrators in the east of Libya, whom he described as drug addicts, criminals and Al Qaeda-linked terrorists. On this basis, Gaddafi adamantly opposed any visit to Benghazi by the High Level Ad Hoc Committee.

In response, the Heads of State insisted that the communiqué was fair and that attacks against civilians had to stop. Pointing out that Gaddafi had advised other African leaders that they had no option but to enter into dialogue with opposition groups, they said that the Libyan government similarly had no choice but to negotiate with the TNC, and that any solution had to be based on the aspirations of the Libyan people to democracy and respect for human rights. The members of the Ad Hoc Committee also argued that Libya lacked the means to stand up to the international coalition and its leader should therefore be realistic about its options. Finally, they told Gaddafi that the delegation would continue to Benghazi whether he liked it or not: they were not seeking his authorization.

Gaddafi accepted, in principle, the AU roadmap including the ceasefire and negotiations. The next day the AU leaders (with the significant absence of President Zuma) flew to Benghazi, where the TNC leadership rejected the plan. Mustafa Abdel Jalil announced that the roadmap was not acceptable because it did not include the immediate departure of Gaddafi. 'Gaddafi must leave immediately if he wants to survive,' he said. 'Any initiative that does not include the people's demand, the popular demand, essential demand, we cannot possibly recognize . . . We cannot negotiate with the blood of our martyrs' (McElroy 2011a).

The AU's principal diplomatic advantage was that only African leaders could make with any credibility the case to Gaddafi that he should both stop his assault on civilian populations and step down. A combination of African access to Gaddafi and NATO leverage over the TNC could have provided the basis for a negotiated settlement. However, this possibility was never pursued.

In addition to the TNC's rejection, the AU roadmap had several major problems. First, the nature of Gaddafi's departure was not specified. In particular, it was not clarified whether he should depart the country or go into internal exile. Following the adoption of the roadmap, the AU began discreet talks with leaders across Africa to find a country willing to receive Gaddafi. A number of hopeful openings were registered, and the AU passed on information about these efforts to its international partners. Another idea floated was that Gaddafi could retire to Sirte or Sebha, where the AU would provide a small military force to guard him.

Another problem was that while the AU had proposals for a ceasefire, including monitors (such as in Misrata) or an inter-positioning force (such as on the front line near Benghazi), member countries did not show enthusiasm in coming up with the military observers and troops needed. Not a single African country volunteered to send observers to Misrata when the AU proposed the idea at its Extraordinary Summit on 25 May, and none was ready to send the battalions needed to enforce a ceasefire. The AU regretted that the ceasefire plan was never tried, less because of its confidence that it would have worked, and more because had Gaddafi violated it, this would have helped to generate African consensus for tougher measures.

Third, Africa was divided. While most of the continent wanted Gaddafi gone with minimal disruption, a few leaders were still sympathetic to the 'Brother Leader', among them Museveni and Zimbabwe's President Robert Mugabe.[7] Mahmoud Jibril has reported travelling to South Africa to meet with President Zuma, who proposed that the TNC leaders 'present their demands through the proper constitutional channels', a suggestion that enraged them and caused them to lose confidence in him as a mediator. They were also unimpressed by his failure to visit Benghazi. Some other African leaders were so antipathetic to Gaddafi that they would have no truck with compromise. Sudan was heavily involved in supporting the TNC. The Ethiopian Prime Minister Meles Zenawi not only nurtured personal disgust towards Gaddafi, but was also furious over Libyan support to Eritrea, and insisted that Gaddafi should step down.[8] Nigerian leaders were also eager to see Gaddafi depart.

Lastly, not unrelated to the TNC position, the NATO countries were opposed. This hampered the AU financially as well as politically. The European Union funded a major part of the AU's conflict response budget, including a small but flexible fund for rapid response to political emergencies. The response to the AU's request for funding was delayed for weeks.

On 25 April the Ad Hoc Committee met with representatives of the Libyan government and the TNC in Addis Ababa. There was no breakthrough. The following day the PSC met to receive the report on the Committee's efforts to date (African Union 2011c). Among other questions, participants asked under what authority had the UN been able to prevent the AU from pursuing its peace mission, mentioned in the preamble of Resolution 1973, postponing it to a date at which its effectiveness had been seriously, probably fatally, compromised? Three other concerns arose again: mercenaries recruited to fight in Libya, migrant workers in Libya, and the concerns of Saharan and Sahelian countries concerning arms proliferation, terrorism and transnational crime (African Union 2011c: para. 12).

At an Extraordinary Summit meeting a month later, the AU called for an immediate pause in fighting, for ceasefire monitors, and for a Framework Agreement for Political Solution. The Chairperson's report stated:

> It is becoming increasingly clear that the pursuit of the military operations will not only undermine the very purpose for which resolutions 1970 and 1973 (2011) were adopted, i.e. the protection of civilians, but also compound any transition to democratic institutions, while adding to the threats facing the countries of the region in terms of security and terrorism and the socio-economic burden resulting from the repatriation of migrant workers. This is all the more urgent as the military campaign is significantly expanding beyond the objectives for which it was in the first place authorized, raising questions about the legality and legitimacy of some of the actions being carried out and the agenda being pursued. (African Union 2011d: para. 51)[9]

The AU's denunciation of the one-sided interpretation of Resolution 1973 sprang in part from its fear that if members of the Security

Council could interpret resolutions as they wanted, in order to pursue any specific agenda, then Africa would be at risk of other foreign interventions. As a politically weak continent, Africa's interest and protection lie in a strict compliance with international law.[10]

Five days later, President Zuma flew to Tripoli to present the proposals, focusing on a ceasefire to be monitored by the AU, UN and Arab League, leading to a transitional period culminating in elections. The key question was, would Gaddafi be ready to step down? The African leaders who had interacted with him in April were convinced that his commitment to the roadmap remained, including his promise not to be part of the transition. However, the meeting with Gaddafi was a disappointment: he restated his commitment to 'not being part of the negotiation process' (AU High Level Ad Hoc Committee on Libya 2011: para. 6(ii); Al Jazeera 2011) but also insisted he was not ready to leave the country (Spencer 2011). Gaddafi's family members and close supporters had reportedly vetoed the plan for transition. The next day in Benghazi, Mustafa Abdul Jalil again said that there was no possibility of talking to Gaddafi, who had irredeemably lost credibility and was just playing games. The clearest statement from the chair of the AU Ad Hoc Committee followed a week later, when President Abdel Aziz told AFP that Gaddafi 'can no longer lead Libya. His departure has become necessary . . . He must be made to leave without causing more damage' (AFP 2011a).

The AU pressed on, hoping that the way in which the war had apparently descended into stalemate would make both sides accept the need for a negotiated solution. The Ad Hoc Committee spelled out its plan for the transition at a meeting in Pretoria on 26 June (AU High Level Ad Hoc Committee on Libya 2011). At the six-monthly Summit in Malabo, Equatorial Guinea, in July, the African Heads of State endorsed the Ad Hoc Committee's Proposals on a Framework Agreement for a Political Solution to the crisis in Libya (African Union 2011f). However, international actions were heading in the opposite direction. On 27 June, just days before the summit, the Prosecutor of the International Criminal Court (ICC), requested arrest warrants for Colonel Gaddafi, his son Saif al Islam and Abdalla al Sanussi, head of military intelligence. The ICC had never before acted with such speed, assembling what was required to demand an arrest warrant in the four months since the Security Council referred Libya to the Court, at a time when the fighting made it difficult to gather evidence on the ground. The arrest warrants threatened to close the door on any solution that involved Gaddafi going quietly into exile. The Summit resolved that Africa would not cooperate with the ICC warrants, a decision that was derided by the international press as evidence for the AU's preference for siding with rich dictators (Meldrum 2011). This publicity overshadowed the fact that African leaders overwhelmingly preferred for Gaddafi to relinquish power, and indeed the 'Brother Leader' soon afterwards began intimating that he might indeed talk to France and the TNC on that basis (AFP 2011b).

The summit was followed by a meeting in Addis Ababa (a 'technical interaction') on 19 July to address the steps required for a ceasefire and a transition. The Libyan government came to Addis Ababa for the meeting but the TNC did not. The TNC received a delegation from the AU on 9 August and communicated a general but non-committal appreciation of the AU efforts a week later (African Union 2011g). On 21 August, TNC fighters entered Tripoli and the war swung decisively in their favour. Key African governments such as those of Nigeria and Ethiopia recognized the TNC in the following days, and called for the AU to do the same.

Thereafter, the AU's diplomatic efforts were at best remedial, reiterating its proposal for a national dialogue and an all-inclusive transitional government. For example, the Communiqué of the PSC on 26 August was a largely pro forma statement in which the PSC:

> 5. Strongly reaffirms that the AU stands with the people of Libya, and encourages all the stakeholders in Libya to come together and negotiate a peaceful process that will lead to democracy;
> 6. Encourages the Libyan stakeholders to accelerate the process leading to the formation of an all-inclusive transitional Government that would be welcome to occupy the seat of Libya at the AU. (African Union 2011g)

The TNC was irritated by the AU's reluctance to recognize it as the legitimate authority in Libya. Even after the President of the AU, President Teodoro Obiang Nguema of Equatorial Guinea, stated that the 'AU recognizes the TNC as the representatives of the Libyan people as they form an inclusive transitional government' at the UN General Assembly in New York in September it took a further month for the AU to decide that, 'taking into account the uniqueness of the situation in Libya and the exceptional circumstances surrounding it, and without prejudice to the relevant AU instruments, to authorize the current authorities in Libya to occupy the seat of Libya in the AU and its organs' (African Union 2011h).

Sudanese military support to the TNC

In parallel to the AU peace initiative for Libya, an African country – Sudan – was closely engaged in the TNC's military campaign against Gaddafi. When NATO began its air campaign in March, military planners were concerned that it would have limited impact without effective ground forces. Moreover, the TNC fighters were poorly trained and coordinated. Part of the gap was filled by special forces from Britain and France, and part by Jordanians and Qataris. However, the Jordanians had relatively little experience of combat operations and the Qataris had only what the TNC fighters called 'Qatari weapons' – dollars and riyals. The greatest contribution came from Sudan.

Sudan had a long-term concern with destabilization from Libya, and an immediate concern over the presence of the Darfurian rebel group JEM in Libya, and the possibility that it would acquire weapons, either as a reward for fighting on Gaddafi's side or because of the generalized opening of Libyan arsenals (Sudan Tribune 2011a). Supporting the TNC was therefore a chance to eliminate JEM and to ensure that the Libyan arsenals did not fall into the hands of rogue groups. Second, backing the TNC presented the opportunity for helping sympathetic Islamists to power. Lastly, it was a chance to consolidate alliances with Qatar and, very discreetly, with NATO.

Even before the uprising the Sudanese National Intelligence and Security Service (NISS) had agents in Libya, and Sudan was hosting the Libyan opposition and training some of the men who would soon become the leaders of the TNC. Among them was Abdel Hakim Belhaj, who was later the TNC's military commander for Tripoli. As soon as Gaddafi's authority began to crumble, Sudanese intelligence spoke to their counterparts in Egypt and Chad, seeking a joint alliance in favour of the opposition. Chad was leery of taking sides against Gaddafi, and Egypt was worried both about reprisals against Egyptian migrant workers in Libya and of arms falling into the hands of Islamists. So Sudan went it alone.

The first major Sudanese operation was to take control of the oasis of Kufra, the key point on the trans-Saharan road to Darfur. Press reports indicate that on 2 April, Kufra was under control of the Libyan opposition, that it was recaptured by loyalists on 28 April and was then under opposition control a week later. Sudanese sources say that most of the fighting was between JEM and an armoured battalion of the Sudanese army. On 1 July Sudanese military forces were publicly reported to be in full occupation of Kufra (McElroy 2011b). This enabled the TNC to control oilfields in the south-east of Libya and the pipelines to the sea. It also opened a road whereby foreign military assistance, including from Qatar, could be channelled to the TNC in advance of the TNC's strategic offensives that culminated in the assault on Tripoli. Supporting the TNC was a major logistical operation by the Sudanese army, especially at a time when it was mobilizing to confront threats from the Sudan People's Liberation Army at the time of South Sudan's independence.

The Sudanese analysis was that the war threatened to descend into a de facto partition of Libya between west and east, and that Gaddafi could be removed only by an assault from the west. The TNC needed to establish a military presence capable of moving onto the offensive from western Libya. To that end, the Qataris provided cash to bring around tribal leaders in that area and the Sudanese provided personnel and logistics to open the new front. They also helped plan and execute seaborne operations. Meanwhile, the Sudanese army withdrew most of its troops from Kufra and left a smaller unit, principally for training and coordination purposes. The Libyan opposition had no need for additional heavy weapons, but was sorely in need of specialized training in the use of tanks and artillery.

For the TNC, the most important Sudanese contribution was communications equipment and expertise in the tactical coordination of ground forces. 'The Sudanese gave us anything and everything,' said a former Libyan general who assisted the TNC with training.[11] The Sudanese NISS and Military Intelligence provided security officers to coordinate, both among the different TNC contingents and between them and their backers, including NATO. Sudanese trainers were present in Benghazi, Misrata, western Libya and around Tripoli. According to Sudanese sources, these officers were directly in communication with NATO special forces on the ground, helping to direct air strikes; the Sudanese called for NATO planes to attack loyalist forces that were regrouping in southern Libya, without success. Both NATO and the Sudanese intelligence have been tight-lipped about this operation, although both Sudanese President Omar al Bashir and TNC leaders have acknowledged that it took place. Speaking at a rally in the eastern Sudanese town of Kassala, Bashir said that 'Our weapons reached the revolutionaries in Misrata, Al-Jabal al-Gharbi and Zawiya . . . the forces that liberated Tripoli were armed 100 percent by Sudan' (Sudan Tribune 2011c). Allowing for Bashir's hyperbole, the essence of the claim was not untrue. Mustafa Abdel Jalil confirmed the support, welcoming President Bashir to Tripoli in January 2012.

Ironically for an intervention that began with enunciating the 'responsibility to protect', NATO's military operations were conducted in close coordination with Sudanese intelligence and its Islamist protégés. It may even be the case that, without Sudanese assistance, the NATO-TNC military campaign would have been unable to break the stalemate.

Blowback

The first regional fallout of the Libya conflict was felt in Sudan. When the uprising began, JEM appealed for foreign help to 'rescue' its leaders in Tripoli, and shortly afterwards the UN planned to evacuate Khalil to join the Darfur peace talks in Qatar, but Gaddafi reportedly blocked him from leaving (Tubiana 2011: 52). Sudan accused JEM of contributing mercenaries to Gaddafi's forces, a claim that JEM denies. During the middle months of 2011, Sudanese NISS agents tried to find, isolate and destroy the JEM leadership in Libya but did not succeed. 'We were in a race with the Sudanese intelligence who were seeking to catch us in Libya,' Khalil Ibrahim told the Sudanese press (Sudan Tribune 2011b). He re-entered Sudan in September, evading Sudanese, Chadian and French efforts to apprehend JEM forces as they crossed the desert.

Re-equipped from Gaddafi's arsenals, JEM fighters posed a major threat to the Sudanese government. They ranged across both Darfur and Kordofan and then crossed the savanna to newly independent South Sudan, which provided it with a safe haven. Also, JEM had established links with the Ugandan government and army. En route to South Sudan, Khalil Ibrahim was killed in an air strike on 25 December 2011. The Sudanese air force insists that during a routine patrol by a fighter-bomber, the pilot identified a group of six vehicles matching the description of JEM fighting units in a location known to be a JEM operational area, and opportunistically destroyed them. Only later, when JEM itself announced the death and burial of Khalil and several of his aides and bodyguards, did the pilot discover that he had killed the JEM leader.[12] This account is consistent with JEM reports of the incident.

More than one hundred 'technical' vehicles and several thousand JEM fighters did reach their destination in South Sudan. In February and March 2012, in close coordination with the SPLA, two groups of JEM vehicles re-crossed the border northwards, entering Southern Kordofan where they played an important role in the fighting between Sudan and South Sudan in the oil-producing area of Heglig. With their high mobility, desert fighting skills, and fighters drawn from both their core Zaghawa constituency and several Arab groups in Kordofan, JEM provided a strike force that complemented the SPLA's South Sudanese and Nuba infantry.

Mali was next in line. The Libyan armed forces had included two brigades drawn from the Malian Tuareg, and miscellaneous other Saharan groups descended on Libya during the conflict. President Déby of Chad warned as early as March 2011 that '[t]he Islamists of al-Qaeda took advantage of the pillaging of arsenals in the rebel zone to acquire arms, including surface-to-air missiles, which were then smuggled into their sanctuaries in Tenere' (Al Arabiya 2011) referring to the ungoverned desert area straddling Niger, Chad and Libya. Until this point, al-Qaeda in the Islamic Magreb (AQIM) had been a numerically tiny group, principally Algerian Islamists, who combined trans-Saharan smuggling operations with intermittent hostage-taking. As Déby predicted, AQIM acquired both weapons and soldiers in Libya. With some exaggeration, he said, 'AQIM is becoming a genuine army, the best equipped in the region'. Western security specialists were particularly concerned with the possibility of AQIM and other terrorist groups obtaining 'man-portable air defence systems' (MANPADS), which are shoulder-launched missiles capable of shooting down a warplane or a civilian airliner during takeoff or landing (Stewart 2011, 2012).

In January 2012, a coalition of up to 3,000 Tuareg separatists who had long sought an independent Azawad nation in the Sahara, along with AQIM fighters and a newly established Tuareg Islamist group, Ansar al-Dine, invaded Mali. This threat had been foreseen but, unlike his neighbours, President Touré did little to prepare. Indeed he had presided over a marked deterioration of governance in Mali, once an exemplar of democratization. The Malian army was wholly unequipped to deal with the threat and turned upon Touré. Captain Anadou Sanogo mounted a coup on 21–22 March. Although Captain Sanogo and his fellow officers agreed to African and international demands to return the country to civilian rule, Mali's crisis was unresolved.

The National Movement for the Liberation of Azawad (NMLA) continued its offensive, overrunning all the cities of northern Mali, and declared an independent Azawad state, covering the northern half of Mali, on 6 April. Alongside the NMLA forces were units of AQIM and Ansar al-Dine. The Nigerian extremist group Boko Haram also sent fighters to join the rebellion. As they no doubt anticipated, the presence of avowedly terrorist groups associated with al-Qaeda ruled out the possibility of negotiations.

In Niger, the danger of civil war, including Tuareg secessionism, was also very real. But, unlike its neighbour, it was prepared. Niger had suffered a series of rebellions in the north, the most recent of which (2007–09) was led by the Niger Movement for Justice (MNJ) and the Niger Patriotic Front (NPF). This conflict was ended by the joint mediation of Mali, Algeria, Libya, the UN and Canada (the latter because AQIM had taken a Canadian diplomat as a hostage). Following a peace agreement in May–June 2009, the Niger government was proactive in accommodating Tuareg leaders, including appointing one as Prime Minister in April 2011, while also pursuing disarmament and integration programmes for MNJ and NPF fighters. As the Libyan regime imploded, Niger took a tough line on security, making good use of the US Pan-Sahelian Counter Terrorism Initiative to patrol the skies, and its own army, backed by Western special forces, to disarm infiltrators, including former Tuareg rebels who had fought for Gaddafi (Hicks 2012). Nonetheless, Niger is fragile. Libyan fugitives, including Saadi al Gaddafi, fled to Niger with arms and money, and their presence there will prove destabilizing.

In Chad, President Déby was also prepared. During the Libyan war, the northernmost ethnic groups, including Tubu, Goraan and Zaghawa/Bideyat, acquired even greater stockpiles of weapons than those they possessed before. The Tubu, who inhabit the Tibesti massif in northern Chad and neighbouring parts of southern Libya, were beneficiaries of Gaddafi's policy of Africanizing his security forces. From the late 1990s, the Tubu were in rebellion against the N'djamena government, as a result of which Tibesti became cut off from its own capital, lost its income from the now-closed Libya–Chad trade routes, and was deprived of services such as health and education. When the uprising began, the Tubu quickly abandoned Gaddafi and associated themselves with the TNC. They assisted the Sudanese to take over Kufra. Now better armed than ever, the Tubu could again present a military threat to Chad.[13]

The AU itself has suffered in the aftermath. The Commission's decision to set up the Ad Hoc Committee of heads of state was, in part, an effort at reducing political risk to the Commission itself and especially to its Chairperson. The correct response from the Commission would have been to apply the AU principles, regardless of the size and power of the state in question, to condemn the repression of the demonstrations, condemn violence by all parties and call for a transition to democracy. The PSC statement of 23 February, while substantively correct, was no substitute. In failing to take a lead, the Commission appeared to put its Libya policy in the hands of states, many of which had, or appeared to have, specific political interests in the outcome. Although the Ad Hoc Committee made a sound proposal and its individual members generally took principled positions, its efforts were not as rapid, high-profile, and sustained as could have been the case if the Commission itself had decided to lead the initiative. And outsourcing the handling of Libya to the Ad Hoc Committee did not, in the event, protect the Commission and its head. Chairperson Ping's failure to provide leadership on the Libyan issue was a major reason why South Africa challenged his position at the helm of the AU in January 2012, a challenge that led to paralysis at the top of the organization.

Implications

The AU roadmap for a negotiated transition to a post-Gaddafi order in Libya had no guarantee of success. The internal political dynamics in Libya made it a difficult proposition, like the negotiated end to civil wars in many African countries. However, the approach of an inclusive negotiated settlement was not given a serious chance. It was killed by France, Britain and the United States.

As the months pass since the demise of Colonel Gaddafi and his unlamented regime, African concerns appear well founded and history may judge the AU more kindly. A more orderly negotiated settlement to the Libyan crisis stood a serious chance of avoiding the current political and military problems in Libya, where the TNC struggles to manage the proliferation of independent militias. The fallout for neighbouring countries has also been problematic, complicating domestic problems. Chad and Niger have thus far managed their security problems, while the issue of JEM would have arisen in Sudan regardless of the Libyan dimension. While the crisis in Mali is fundamentally internal, it was triggered by Tuareg returnees from Libya. The challenge of how to handle former mercenaries would have existed whatever political option were chosen, but could have been handled more effectively in the light of the warnings given.

The outcome has damaged Africa. The AU was not able to convince Libyans, Africans or the world that it was a credible interlocutor for peace in Libya. Africa did not present a united position, and did not provide the financial, military or diplomatic resources necessary for the AU initiative to prevail. Africa did not even provide a good account of its intent and strategy to the general public, as a result of which the AU position has been widely misunderstood, and the AU itself has suffered a crisis of leadership. Africa's weakness has benefited nobody. The Libyan people, the new government and NATO may regret that the African option was not pursued.

The African dimensions to the Libyan war shine a spotlight on any justifications for NATO's intervention in terms of R2P. The blocking of the AU diplomatic initiative indicates that the decision to escalate the military intervention beyond the defence of Benghazi to an agenda of regime change could not be justified as a last resort. There were options for a negotiated settlement that could have been pursued. Indeed, a partnership between the UN and the AU could have benefited Libya and both organizations. Meanwhile, the secret liaison between NATO and the Sudanese intelligence forces, which turned out to be a critical element in the overthrow of Gaddafi, illustrates the truism that a military intervention is a war, and that, in common with wars, its conduct may entail making alliances from military necessity. The Libyan campaign may indeed become an exemplar of the practice of R2P, but one that illustrates the problems of the doctrine, not its unalloyed success.

The last word on the Euro-American enthusiasm for regime change by force of arms may belong to President Déby, who described NATO's operation as 'a hasty decision that can have serious consequences for regional destabilization' (2011a). Fortunately, in foreseeing the problem, Déby was able better to manage it. At the end of the year the Chadian soldier-president, who had matched Gaddafi in combat and intrigue for three decades, added:

> In reality, no head of state of the continent was against the departure from power of Gaddafi, but the brutal way in which it has pushed him could only be generating unrest in a country without institutions or Constitution. But Africa needs a strong and organized new Libya. (Déby 2011b)

Notes

1. Interviewed 15 April 2012.
2. The AU response to the 2009 overthrow of the government in Madagascar reflected the ambiguous nature of that uprising: it applied its principle of opposition to unconstitutional changes in government rather than the democratic principle.
3. On 26 February, UN Security Council Resolution 1970, using its far greater authority, referred Libya to the ICC, and imposed an arms embargo, and a travel ban and asset freeze on senior members of the government.
4. Algeria would not have been a good candidate because of its longstanding tensions with Libya. Tunisia and Egypt were in turmoil. Morocco is not a member of the AU.
5. Nigeria was the obvious candidate, as the biggest state and also a member of the UN Security Council. But Nigerian elections were scheduled for April.

6. AU Chairperson Jean Ping attended the second Contact Group meeting in Rome on 5 May 2011 as a guest.
7. At the January 2012 AU Summit, Mugabe excoriated the AU leadership. 'We should have said no, no to NATO . . . We fought imperialism and colonialism and forced them out of Africa. Our founding fathers did not have the means but they stood up and said "no". But here we are absolutely silent' (New Zimbabwe 2012).
8. Visiting Addis Ababa in July 2011, the French Foreign Minister Alain Juppé said that Meles Zenawi supported the international consensus that the way out of the Libyan crisis was for Gaddafi to leave power (AFP 2011b).
9. This report was adopted and summarized in a later report, see African Union (2011e), esp. para 11.
10. Emperor Haile Selassie's speech to the League of Nations appealing for international solidarity in the face of Fascist aggression is the locus classicus of Africa's stand on consistency in applying international law.
11. Interviewed 15 April 2012.
12. Interview with Sudan Armed Forces officer, 30 January 2012.
13. Unpublished note by Jérôme Tubiana, April 2012.

References

AFP (2011a) 'Kadhafi Can No Longer Lead Libya: Mauritania President,' *AFP*, 7 June. Available online at: www.google.com/hostednews/afp/article/ALeqM5hrFBFXmDdrFY6HVYxgjHKPuAto8A?docId=CNG.0188ac6bd8569c2fcac4194065f4834d.2c1 [Accessed September 2012].

AFP (2011b) 'Possible Diplomatic Opening in Libyan Crisis,' *AFP*, 12 July. Available online at: http://m.rnw.nl/english/node/60918 [Accessed September 2012].

African Union (2011a) 'Communiqué of the 265th Meeting of the Peace and Security Council, PSC/PR/COM(CCLXI), 23 February.

African Union (2011b) 'Communiqué of the 265th Meeting of the Peace and Security Council', PSC/PR/COM.2(CCLXV), 10 March.

African Union (2011c) 'Report of the Chairperson of the Commission on the Activities of the Ad Hoc High Level Committee on the Situation in Libya', PSC/PR/2(CCLXXV), 26 April.

African Union (2011d) 'Report of the Chairperson of the Commission on Current Challenges to Peace and Security on the Continent and the AU's Efforts: Enhancing Africa's Leadership, Promoting African Solutions', Extraordinary Session of the Assembly of the Union on the State of Peace and Security in Africa, Addis Ababa, 25–26 May, Ext/Assembly/AU/2.

African Union (2011e) Report of the Chairperson to the Executive Council, Nineteenth Ordinary Session, Malabo, 23–28 June.

African Union (2011f) 'Proposals to the Libyan Parties for a Framework Agreement on a Political Solution to the Crisis in Libya', letter dated 22 July 2011 from the Secretary-General addressed to the President of the Security Council, Annex 2, S/2011/455. Available online at: www.securitycouncilreport.org/atf/cf/%7B65BFCF9B-6D27-4E9C-8CD3-CF6E4FF96FF9%7D/Libya%20S2011%20455.pdf [Accessed September 2012].

African Union (2011g) 'Report of the Chairperson of the Commission on the Situation in Libya and the Efforts of the African Union for a Political Solution to the Libyan Crisis', PSC/AHG/3(CCXCI), 26 August.

African Union (2011h) 'Communiqué of the 297th Meeting of the Peace and Security Council', PSC/PR/COMM/2.(CCXCVII) 20 October.

AU High Level Ad Hoc Committee on Libya (2011) 'Meeting of the AU High Level Ad Hoc Committee on Libya: Communiqué', Pretoria, South Africa, 26 June.

Al Arabiya (2011) 'Al-Qaeda snatched missiles in Libya: Chad President', *Al Arabiya News*, 25 March. Available online at: http://english.alarabiya.net/articles/2011/03/25/143013.html [Accessed September 2012].

Al Jazeera (2011) 'Gaddafi Vows to Stay Out of AU Peace Talks', *Al Jazeera*, 26 June. Available online at: http://english.aljazeera.net/news/africa/2011/06/20 1162615731797543.html [Accessed September 2012].

Barfi, B. (2011) 'Can Africa Really Help Libya Find Peace? Why the Rebels Rejected the AU Ceasefire', *The New Republic*, 13 April.

BBC (2010) 'Gaddafi Says Nigeria Should Split into Several States', BBC News, 29 March. Available online at: http://news.bbc.co.uk/2/hi/8593355.stm [Accessed September 2012].

Burr, M. and R. Collins (1999) *Africa's Thirty Years' War: Chad-Libya-the Sudan, 1963–1993* (Boulder: Westview Press).

Déby Itno, I. (2011a) 'Si la Libye implose, les conséquences seront incalculables pour la région', *Jeune Afrique*, 6 April.

Déby Itno, I. (2011b) 'En Libye, l'Histoire me donnera raison', *Jeune Afrique*, 26 December.

Flint, J. and A. de Waal (2008) *Darfur: A New History of a Long War* (London: Zed Books).

Hicks, C. (2012) 'Tuareg Rebels Make Troubled Return from Libya to Mali', BBC, 29 February. Available online at: www.bbc.co.uk/news/world-africa-17192212 [Accessed September 2012].

McElroy, D. (2011a) 'Libya: Opposition Rejects African Union Peace Plan', *Daily Telegraph*, 11 April. Available online at: www.telegraph.co.uk/news/worldnews/africaandindianocean/libya/8443982/Libya-opposition-rejects-African-Union-peace-plan.html [Accessed September 2012].

McElroy D. (2011b) 'Sudanese Army Seizes Southern Libyan Town', *Daily Telegraph*, 1 July. Available online at: www.telegraph.co.uk/news/worldnews/africaandindianocean/libya/8611199/Sudanese-army-seizes-southern-Libyan-town.html [Accessed September 2012].

Meldrum, A. (2011) 'African Union Refuses to Arrest Gaddafi', *Global Post*, 1 July. Available online at: www.globalpost.com/dispatches/globalpost-blogs/africa-emerges/african-union-refuses-arrest-gaddafi [Accessed September 2012].

New Zimbabwe (2012) 'Mugabe: AU a Toothless Bulldog', *New Zimbabwe*, 31 January. Available online at: www.newzimbabwe.com/news-7067-Mugabe+AU+a+toothless+bulldog/news.aspx [Accessed September 2012].

Ping, J. (2011) 'The African Union and the Libyan Crisis: Putting the Records Straight', African Union Commission, Letter from the Chairperson, November.

Roberts, H. (2011) 'Who Said Gaddafi Had to Go?', *London Review of Books*, vol. 33, no. 22, 17 November.

Ross, W. (2011) 'Analysis: Libya: Benghazi Rebels Reject African Union Truce Plan', BBC News Africa, 11 April, Available online at: www.bbc.co.uk/news/world-africa-13035501 [Accessed September 2012].

Spencer, R. (2011) 'Col. Gaddafi "Emphatic" He Will Not Leave Libya', *Daily Telegraph*, 31 May, Available online at: www.telegraph.co.uk/news/worldnews/africaandindianocean/libya/8548594/Col-Gaddafi-emphatic-he-will-not-leave-Libya.html [Accessed September 2012].

Stewart, S. (2011) 'Will Libya Again Become the Arsenal of Terrorism?', *Security Weekly*, 10 March. Available online at: www.stratfor.com/weekly/20110309-will-libya-again-become-arsenal-terrorism [Accessed September 2012].

Stewart, S. (2012) 'The Continuing Threat of Libyan Missiles', *Security Weekly*, 3 May. Available online at: www.stratfor.com/weekly/continuing-threat-libyan-missiles [Accessed September 2012].

Sudan Tribune (2011a) 'Sudan Concerned over Proliferation of Weapons from Libyan Crisis', *Sudan Tribune*, 19 March. Available online at: www.sudantribune.com/Sudan-concerned-over-proliferation,38319 [Accessed September 2012].

Sudan Tribune (2011b) 'Exclusive: JEM Leader Says He Has Arrived in Darfur', *Sudan Tribune*, 11 September. Available online at: www.sudantribune.com/EXCLUSIVE-JEM-Leader-says-he,40110 [Accessed September 2012].

Sudan Tribune (2011c) 'Bashir Says Sudan Armed Libya Rebels', *Sudan Tribune*, 27 October. Available online at: www.sudantribune.com/Bashir-says-Sudan-armed-Libyan,40547 [Accessed September 2012].

Tubiana, J. (2011) 'Renouncing the Rebels: Local and Regional Dimensions of the Sudan-Chad Rapprochement', Geneva, Small Arms Survey, HSBA Working Paper no. 25.

5

Africa's Emerging Regional Security Culture and the Intervention in Libya

Theresa Reinold

Introduction

Just as nation-states are imagined communities (Anderson 1983), so are regions. A hitherto under-researched dimension of imagining regions as communities is the construction of regional security cultures. These are dynamic artifacts of human practice that are constantly evolving as the local, national, regional and global normative contexts change. Consequently, with the concept of 'security' itself currently undergoing reinterpretation – with global discourses about the moral purpose of the state increasingly pointing to the protection of human security as the state's primary *raison d'être* – regional security cultures are expected to mirror this normative shift in their own constitutive norms and practices.

While the notion of human security has been embraced (rhetorically) by most governments around the world, its implications for the international community's responsibility to protect endangered civilians (R2P), militarily if necessary, continue to be highly controversial. R2P is a concept whose opaqueness has made it possible for regional actors to attach markedly different meanings to it and thus make it congruent with their respective political agendas. The lack of consensus over what R2P actually means, that is, what kind of (military) action it permits (or even dictates), was exposed by NATO's intervention in Libya, which sparked a heated controversy over the proportionality and necessity of military action as well as issues of right intention and just authority. Despite these controversies, what was remarkable about the international response to the carnage in Libya was the rhetorical momentum generated by the global discourse about the responsibility to protect. The crisis quickly rose to the top of the international agenda – not least thanks to the vocabulary provided by the proponents of R2P, which provided the advocates of forceful action against the Gaddafi regime with a powerful tool for rallying the international community around their cause.

Yet despite the international outrage at the atrocities committed by Colonel Gaddafi and his henchmen, the African Union (AU) – which should have been the primary addressee of calls for intervention – initially shirked its responsibility to protect Libyan civilians from the havoc wrought upon them by their own leader. The AU's lack of resolve during the crisis in Libya stands in stark contrast to the organization's rhetorical commitment to R2P, which is at the heart of the AU's security architecture; At least on paper, the AU has strongly embraced the notion of military intervention on behalf of endangered civilians – witness the inclusion of Article 4(h) into the organization's Constitutive Act. Yet words have not always been followed by deeds, and when the international community decided to intervene in Libya, the African Union's response was rather tepid. As a result, the organization was sidelined in international efforts to end the carnage. While the AU still called for a diplomatic solution to the crisis, NATO went ahead with its military campaign, interpreting its fallback responsibility to protect rather broadly to include the toppling of the murderous regime which had failed in its primary responsibility to protect its own citizens. Even though NATO obviously believed that sufficient legal cover for regime change existed, the AU objected to such a broad interpretation of R2P, fearing this would legitimize neocolonial interference in African affairs under the cloak of humanitarianism. The intervention in Libya has thus exposed the continuing contestation surrounding R2P and has also shown that many African leaders continue to privilege regime security over human security, especially when the target regime is one which has long played a central role as the prime financier and ideological mastermind of the AU.

This chapter draws on the concept of regional security culture to make sense of the AU's ambiguous role in the Libyan crisis. In line with the notion of norm localization (Acharya 2004) I shall argue that the culture of regional security is the result of a peculiar blend of factors from various levels of analysis; first, world political culture (reflected, for instance, in global discourses about human security, sovereign responsibilities and good governance); second, regional political dynamics, norms and bargaining processes; and third, variables from the state and sub-state levels, such as domestic regime type, leadership (or absence thereof) from individual political figures, societal pressures, and so on. The interplay of these variables has given rise to markedly diverse security cultures in different regions of the world, ranging from rather interventionist regimes, which have incorporated evolving global norms about responsible sovereignty into their regional security architecture, to more inert arrangements, which continue to adhere to the classical rules of the international game. According to the concept of norm localization, regional actors do not simply refute or accept new global norms, but more often than not adapt them to local circumstances by 'pruning' them, that is, modifying them to make them more responsive to the local context (ibid.: 251). The responsibility to protect is especially prone to pruning as it continues to be an essentially contested concept whose opaqueness has made it possible for regional actors to make it congruent with their respective political agendas. As the crisis in Libya has shown, the R2P discourse offers ample opportunity for contestation, re-interpretation, and modification – in short, for norm localization.

This chapter is roughly divided into two sections; in the first, I seek to grasp the concept of regional security culture theoretically, that is, I will suggest a set of variables which I believe contribute to the formation of regional security cultures. The second part of the chapter then applies these insights to the AU's response to the crisis in Libya, which was widely viewed as constituting an 'R2P situation', but which has triggered rather diverging reactions from different diplomatic players. In the concluding section I will wrap up my findings and suggest directions for future research.

The culture of regional security: disentangling the concept

Even a cursory look at the literature reveals that research on regional security cultures is still in a fledgling state, even though in recent years there has been a surge in publications on the subject (see, for example, Haacke 2003; Haacke and Williams 2008; Jaye 2008; Williams 2007). More than a decade ago, Peter Katzenstein published his seminal volume on *The Culture of National Security*, which argued – rather innovatively at the time – that the definition of states' security interests is not determined by material factors alone, but also cultural ones (Katzenstein 1996: 1). As regions are made up of nation-states, it would seem logical to export the concept of security culture to the regional context, even though the set of variables shaping the culture of regional security will likely differ from the factors influencing national security cultures. In the following, I shall attempt a first theoretical approximation to the concept of regional security culture by suggesting a set of variables which influence what kind of security culture a region will adopt in the first place, and which shape its response to subsequent threats and challenges.

Katzenstein posited that national security cultures do not emerge in a vacuum, but are products of the surrounding normative environment (Katzenstein 1996: 9). As states are embedded in a wider material and ideational structure, so are regions, which respond to stimuli from the sub-regional and global levels. (Regional) security cultures can thus be defined as discourses in which actors collectively develop durable security preferences regarding the role, legitimacy and efficacy of particular approaches to protecting values (Johnston 1995: 6). Now, what factors influence the formulation of these durable collective security preferences of regional actors? I argue that the development of regional security cultures is a complex process involving variables from different levels of analysis – global, regional, national (state-level) and local (societal level). To begin with, regions are embedded in what Katzenstein et al. have dubbed 'world political culture' (Katzenstein et al. 1996: 12), that is, the foundational pillars of the global normative order, such as notions of legitimate statehood, sovereign equality, the non-use of force, and so on. For centuries, the global normative structure was rather thin in that international law merely provided a parsimoniously formulated set of rules of the road regulating the peaceful co-existence of sovereign nation-states. In the course of the past decades, however, the scope of international law has expanded dramatically. It has permeated many issue-areas of international relations and has begun to make substantive claims upon the internal make-up of sovereign states. In constructing a particular ideal of good governance, international law has pushed for a homogenization of existing states according to a liberal-democratic blueprint offered by the West.

As all nation-states were socialized into an international system built on a set of (Western) notions of good governance, human rights, legitimate sovereignty, and so on we should expect a certain mimetic dynamic to operate at the regional level, that is, we should expect regional security cultures across the globe to reflect a similar set of norms. Yet empirically, we find substantial cross-regional variation. This is due to the coincidence of various factors; first, a global norm's status as hard or soft law influences how it will be received regionally. It seems intuitively plausible that norms that have crystallized into customary international law, treaty law or general principles of law are more likely to be integrated into regional security cultures than ideas and concepts to which we would refer as soft law – that is, political or moral values which have not (yet) attained the status of law.

Second, regional norms, preferences and political dynamics must be taken into account. Universal norms are usually not transferred across the board to the regional level but must travel through different regional contexts, where they are 'localized', that is, reconstructed, 'to ensure the norms fit with the agents' cognitive priors and identities' (Acharya 2004: 239). In these processes of norm localization, global norms that are compatible with indigenous traditions stand a better chance of being incorporated into the security culture of regional organizations than norms that lack congruence (ibid.: 244). If a global norm is at odds with regional norms and beliefs, it will either be rejected altogether or 'pruned', that is, made compatible with regional values. This process of pruning means that regional actors accept those elements of the norm in question that can be reconciled with regional values and interests, and jettison the rest (ibid.: 251). These values and interests obviously vary from region to region. In the developing world, for instance, the incentives for regionalization are probably not the same as in the developed world. While regionalization may serve a variety of purposes, a major rationale for pooling resources at the regional level is what has come to be known as 'soft balancing' in IR theory. Soft balancing aims at 'preventing the powerful from laying down the law to weaker states, from imposing their own worldviews and norms' (Hurrell 2006: 16). In this perspective, regionalization in the developing world is (among other things) a strategy to balance the power of the West. This we must take into account when trying to understand how global norms (which are usually of Western provenance) are received in the developing world. While regionalization is about balancing, it is also about creating social cohesion. Regional organizations constitute themselves as 'value communities' (*Wertegemeinschaften*), which are built on a set of shared norms and narratives. Hence, regional political dynamics as well as regional identities impact upon the extent to which global norms are integrated into a region's security culture. Another explanatory variable from the regional level of analysis is the type of threats faced by a region. Regions which are internally pacified and politically stable will most likely adopt a different type of security doctrine and allocate resources for different purposes than regions which face a multitude of internal challenges (such as state failure, or intra- or inter-state wars).

To sum up thus far, regional security cultures are shaped by universal norms, which are made compatible with regional identities, threat perceptions and political dynamics. In order to understand these regional political dynamics, we must of course look to the preferences of national governments, which in turn respond to societal pressures to varying degrees. Factors from the state level as well as the societal level thus exert a significant influence on the development of regional security cultures. We should expect to find substantial cross-regional variation depending on the type of polity prevalent in a region, that is, depending on whether a region is primarily made up of autocratic regimes and/or dysfunctional democracies, or whether mature democracies prevail in any given region. In the former case, variables from the sub-state level will probably be less salient than in the latter case, as dictators are much less responsive do societal pressures than democratic governments, whose publics exert a significant influence on the conduct of their foreign and security policies. For example, we should expect that the extent to which democracy has spread across a region determines whether the region's security culture privileges human security over regime security, or vice versa. If a regional security culture is premised on the primacy of human security, this is most likely partly due to the strength of civil society actors in the region, who are crucial norm entrepreneurs and as such contribute to the formation of the region's security culture. In regions with mostly authoritarian regimes, by contrast, the relevant norm entrepreneurs shaping the regional organization's security culture are likely to be state officials rather than civil society representatives. While civil society norm entrepreneurs are usually motivated by a firm belief in the intrinsic qualities of the norm in question, state officials may be guided by a more complex balancing of interests, which includes utilitarian calculations regarding the norm's potential for consolidating the official's power at home or enhancing his or her international prestige. Finally, apart from cost-benefit considerations, historical and cultural forces must also be taken into account. Historical experiences of subjugation, wars, colonization and the like play a vital role in determining the threat perceptions of political elites and their societies, their willingness to cooperate in regional security arrangements, as well as their reactions to outside interference.

In sum, regional security cultures are complex and malleable social constructs which, due to the multitude of factors shaping their content, are likely to respond rather differently to stimuli such as humanitarian crises. The following case study of the AU's role in the Libyan crisis will serve to illustrate this argument. While the case study provides a first plausibility probe intended to underline the merits of the theoretical approach sketched in this section, it is clearly nothing more than a hoop test, which underlines the need for further empirical corroboration, for instance through cross-regional comparisons (see Dembinski and Reinold 2011).

R2P – genesis of a concept

Although the International Commission on Intervention and State Sovereignty (ICISS) is usually credited with kicking off the debate over sovereignty as responsibility, it was in fact Sudanese national Francis Deng who introduced a broader audience to the notion of responsible sovereignty. In 1996 Deng et al. developed a framework to guide nation-states and the international community in meeting their respective responsibilities (Deng et al. 1996). Their concept is based on the idea of a dual social contract – between each government and its citizens, and between nation-states and the international community as a whole: 'The sovereign state's responsibility and accountability to both domestic and external constituencies must be affirmed as interconnected principles of the national and international order. Such a normative code is anchored in the assumption that in order to be legitimate, sovereignty must demonstrate responsibility' (ibid.: xvii). Hence, sovereignty should not merely be regarded as the right to be left alone, but as the responsibility to discharge governmental duties: 'Normatively, to claim otherwise would be to lose sight of its purpose in the original context of the social contract, taking the means for the end' (ibid.: xviii). The authors go on to argue that if a government manifestly fails to fulfil its part of the social contract, its claim to sovereign immunity becomes void. Consequently, discharging the responsibilities of sovereignty is in effect the best guarantee for sovereignty (ibid.: 1, 15).

This changed understanding of sovereignty is informed by a wider notion of security – one that takes not the state but the individual as its primary unit of analysis. Traditional concepts of security are concerned with the state's right to territorial integrity, that is, its ability to ward off external threats. The concept of human security, by contrast, places the individual and its protection needs at the core of policy. It highlights the challenges to individual human rights posed by the emergence of complex threats, including threats to human life emanating from the state itself, which sometimes fails to discharge its security obligations. Proponents of the concept of human security define as its prime purpose the protection of 'the vital core of all human lives in ways that enhance human freedoms and human fulfilment' (Commission on Human Security 2003: 4).

The norm entrepreneurship of Deng – coupled with the effects of state practice in the 1990s – bore fruit when in 2001 the ICISS published its widely cited report *The Responsibility to Protect*. The gist of the ICISS's argument is that 'state sovereignty implies responsibility, and the primary responsibility for the protection of its people lies with the state itself' (ICISS 2001: p. xi). However, if a state proves unwilling or unable to live up to its responsibilities, that is, if it violates basic human rights or does not prevent such violations, the international community has a residual responsibility to act. The principle of non-intervention thus yields to the international responsibility to protect (ibid.: xi). This argument is derived from the idea that both the prohibition of the use of force and respect for basic human rights form part of international *jus cogens*. If a state violates the latter, it cannot shield itself from intervention by invoking the former.

Borrowing from just war theory, the report listed a number of legitimacy criteria that should guide intervention on behalf of endangered civilians: just cause (gross violations of fundamental human rights); right intention (putting an end to these violations); last resort (military means as *ultima ratio*, after all non-military measures have been exhausted); proportional means (minimal duration and intensity of military strikes); and, lastly, reasonable prospects of success (ibid.: xii). In particular, the issue of right intention has proven to be a major bone of contention, as Western countries time and again were suspected of ulterior motives when intervening abroad to save strangers. Geopolitical developments post-9/11 have only served to reinforce developing countries' worries that R2P could be abused as a fig leaf for the reckless pursuit of the national interests of the powerful. At first glance, the ICISS report therefore seems to posit a narrow scope for the application of R2P, which shall be neither invoked to justify the redrawing of borders or to support the self-determination claims of any particular belligerent party (ibid.: 35). The sole rationale for intervention is the protection of civilians; hence any type of military action must be strictly confined to this goal, and should not be used as a pretext for pursuing regime change (ibid.). However, the drafters of the ICISS report also acknowledge that the protection of civilians will often require disabling the target regime's capacity for hurting its own people, 'and what is necessary to achieve that disabling will vary from case to case' (ibid.). Thus, despite its unequivocal commitment to a narrowly circumscribed mandate for civilian protection, the ICISS deliberately left some wiggle room for assessing the legitimacy of any military action in context-specific terms, thus avoiding an all too rigid application of the right intention criterion. This deliberate indeterminacy is also reflected in the statement that while occupation of a territory could never be an end in itself, it could be necessary for an interim period (ibid.). In order to operationalize the right intention criterion, the commissioners suggest the following indicators; any action that is multilateral in nature, that has the clear support of the target population, and that is endorsed by other countries in the region satisfies the right intention criterion; conversely, military action that flunks one or more of these tests is less legitimate (ibid.: 36).

Another yardstick for assessing the legitimacy of an intervention is the proportionality criterion. Here again, the ICISS used the same reasoning as in the case of the principle of right intention. While at the outset positing strict adherence to the principle of proportionality in order to avoid the impression that R2P could be used as a vehicle for advancing hidden imperialist agendas, it subsequently allows for some leeway in assessing the proportionality of any military action in context-specific terms:

> The scale, duration and intensity of the planned military intervention should be the minimum necessary to secure the humanitarian objective in question. The means have to be commensurate with the ends, and in line with the magnitude of the original provocation. The effect on the political system of the country targeted should be limited, again, to what is strictly necessary to accomplish the purpose of the intervention. While it may be a matter for argument in each case what are the precise practical implications of these strictures, the principles involved are clear enough. (ibid.: 37)

Both necessity and proportionality are elusive concepts which are collapsed into a single legitimacy criterion in the ICISS report, where the commissioners define proportionality as the minimum necessary force for realizing the goal of civilian protection. Even though the ICISS argues that 'the principles are clear enough', their application in practice might not be as straightforward, as we shall see later on in the section discussing NATO's intervention in Libya. As I have argued elsewhere with regard to the use of force in counter-terrorism operations (Reinold 2011: 267), the application of the criteria of necessity and proportionality requires an elusive calculation, which becomes even more complex when necessity is defined in teleological, or 'outcome-determinative' terms (Printer 2003: 343). NATO's campaign in Libya was justified on the basis of such a purposive reading of necessity, which however, met with fierce criticism from the AU, as we shall see below.

Finally, the ICISS also dealt with the issue of just authority. While emphasizing the Security Council's primary responsibility for the maintenance of international peace and security, it did not duck the problem of Security Council paralysis and tentatively suggested possibilities for action outside the Security Council. The commissioners made the following propositions: first, states must in all cases seek Security Council authorization prior to carrying out any military action; second, in cases of massive human rights violations, the Council's permanent members should agree not to use their veto power, unless vital national interests are at stake; and third, should the P5 exercise their veto nonetheless, recourse may be made to the General Assembly under the Uniting for Peace procedure and to regional arrangements, subject to seeking subsequent authorization from the Security Council (ibid.: xiiff). To its credit, the ICISS reminded the P5 that in the case of failure to discharge its primary responsibility for the maintenance of international peace and security, states might not rule out unilateral means to address 'conscience-shocking situations', which in turn would adversely affect the credibility of the Security Council (ibid.).

Subsequently, R2P was affirmed by the major UN bodies in a string of resolutions including the 2005 World Summit *Outcome Document.*[1] Nonetheless, more than anything, it continues to be a moral aspiration; it has certainly not hardened into a norm of customary international law, because what is currently lacking is an intersubjective consensus over what R2P actually *means*, that is, which obligations exactly it imposes on the international community, and which actors are the primary duty bearers. In the World Summit *Outcome Document*, paragraph 139, states insisted on treating each case on its own merits and hence rejected a generalized duty to intervene to protect endangered civilians. While international law has long recognized that nation-states have a duty to protect their own citizens, the novelty introduced by the concept of R2P is the notion that the international community not only has a *right*, but a *responsibility* to protect fundamental human rights, militarily if necessary. Yet it is exactly the scope of this responsibility borne by the international community at large which continues to be the subject of major controversy. Currently unresolved issues include: is there a qualitative difference between the responsibility of the host state and the fallback responsibility of the international community? Do states, acting through the Security Council, have an obligation to respond to mass atrocities in areas outside of their jurisdiction, possibly against the will of the host state? If the Security Council fails to act, can states or regional organizations enforce R2P in the absence of a Security Council mandate? Can Security Council authorization also be sought *post hoc*? (Reinold 2010, 2012).

These and related questions strongly suggest that R2P – at least as regards the military dimension – is an essentially contested concept, which has emerged as a popular soft law category and a discursive frame, but which has certainly not hardened into a norm of customary international law, because what is currently lacking is both *opinio juris* and state practice. As we shall see in the following, the lack of agreement over what R2P actually means has also affected the degree of its internalization into the regional security cultures of the African Union.

The AU and R2P – from non-intervention to non-indifference?

In March 2001 the Assembly of Heads of State and Government of the Organization of African Unity (OAU) at their meeting in Sirte, Libya, declared the establishment of the African Union, which marked a turning point in African perspectives on sovereignty and (non-)intervention. Unlike its predecessor organization, which exalted traditional sovereignty norms such as the principles of non-interference and *uti possidetis juris*, the AU Constitutive Act mandates the organization to deal with human rights issues in member states which are no longer regarded as matters essentially within the domestic jurisdiction of states. The AU's founding fathers equipped their organization with a significantly broader mandate and a more interventionist posture than its predecessor organization could have ever dreamed of. Yet the transition from a security culture characterized by the overarching principle of non-intervention to one founded upon the doctrine of 'non-indifference' (Mwanasali 2008; Williams 2007) remains incomplete. Even though the AU has increased its election monitoring and mediation activities, and launched a number of pro-democratic interventions as well as peacekeeping operations with civilian protection components, its commitment to implementing R2P in practice remains rather fickle. Before analysing the AU's practical application of R2P in more detail, however, let us have a look at the norms and institutions on which the AU's security policy rests.

The continental security architecture is built on two main pillars; the Common African Defense and Security Policy (CADSP), adopted in 2002, and the Peace and Security Council (PSC), which was launched in 2004 as a standing decision-making body for the prevention, management and resolution of conflicts on the African continent. Even though the AU Assembly is nominally the supreme organ of the AU, the PSC, which is composed of 15 representatives of member states, is arguably the most important continental body in the maintenance of peace and security. It is authorized, for instance, to recommend to the Assembly interventions in the internal affairs of member states. The other elements of the continental security architecture are the Continental Early Warning System (CEWS), the Panel of the Wise, the Military Staff Committee as well the African Standby Force (ASF). These newly minted institutions operate on the basis of a set of principles enshrined in the AU Constitutive Act, which can be said to reflect the core tenets of the AU's emerging security culture; the principles of sovereign equality (Art. 4a), non-intervention by member states (Art. 4g), *uti possidetis* (Art. 4b), non-use of force (Art. 4e, 4f, 4i), rejection of unconstitutional changes of government (Art. 4p), and the AU's right to intervene in the internal affairs of member states in the event of gross human rights abuses (Art. 4h). The most revolutionary feature of the AU's security culture is certainly Art. 4h, which indicates a rethinking of traditional concepts of sovereignty:

> The establishment of the African Union as a supranational legal entity with significant powers of intervention in domestic crisis situations challenges traditional notions of the Westphalian state system and in fact offers us an insight into how a post-Westphalian – or post-nation-state – system might be constituted. In fact, the constitution of the African Union offers an alternative framework for organizing a political community. (Murithi 2009: 103f)

After the adoption of the AU Constitutive Act, African governments reaffirmed their (rhetorical) commitment to R2P in a report known as the 'Ezulwini Consensus', which reiterated states' obligations to protect their own citizens, affirmed the UN Security Council's primary responsibility for the maintenance of international peace and security, but also noted that in certain cases regional organizations might intervene on behalf of human rights without prior Security Council approval (African Union 2005).

Art. 4h of the AU Act as well as the Ezulwini Consensus testify to Africa's rhetorical support for R2P, yet as previously noted, words have for the most part not been matched by deeds. Despite all the high-sounding rhetoric R2P has clearly not yet become internalized in the AU's security culture, as indicated by the AU's lackadasical response to the crisis in Darfur, for instance, where it failed to equip its peacekeepers with sufficient resources and an appropriate mandate for effectively protecting endangered civilians, or its decision not to cooperate with the International Criminal Court (ICC) in the arrest and surrender of Sudanese President Omar Al-Bashir. Old habits of non-intervention and impunity obviously die hard. When the ICC issued an arrest warrant for Bashir on charges of war crimes and crimes against humanity, the AU asked that the warrant be suspended, effectively privileging political haggling with the recalcitrant Sudanese regime over promoting the international rule of law. When the Security Council failed to act on the AU's request for deferral, the AU decided not to cooperate with the ICC in bringing Bashir to justice:

> The AU, in a political evasion of its own legal mandate, is seeking to ultimately avoid respecting the ICC's indictment because of its implications for the culture of impunity and non-interference which has dominated the approach of its member states to peace and security on the continent. (Murithi 2009: 104)

When the ICC issued an arrest warrant for another African leader manifestly failing to live up to his responsibility to protect his own people – namely Libya's Muammar Gaddafi – the world witnessed a replay of the Bashir episode, with the AU declaring its resolve not to cooperate with the ICC in the arrest of Gaddafi (CNN.com 2011). In the following section, I try to account for this gap between aspiration and reality by analysing the AU's security culture against the backdrop of the variables put forward in the first part of this chapter.

The global level, I argued earlier, has an impact upon regional security cultures through the diffusion of what Katzenstein et al. have called 'world political culture'. The AU's security architecture came into being at a time when the fundamental norms and institutions of the global polity – such as the institution of sovereignty, for example – were up for grabs. The global normative order is thus currently in flux and the fundamental rules of the game are being renegotiated. In this process of renegotiation, the concept of human security plays a central role in legitimizing the notion that states have a responsibility to protect their own citizens, and that the international community is entitled (and maybe even obliged) to hold states accountable for failure to live up to their sovereign obligations. Both the concepts of human security and R2P have become popular frames in discourses about legitimate statehood, they have sparked a burgeoning academic literature, and also inform the work of the UN Security Council, which increasingly incorporates civilian protection components in its peacekeeping mandates. Yet as noted earlier, despite R2P's rhetorical popularity, the military dimension of R2P continues to be highly contested, which means that R2P is far from crystallizing into a norm of customary international law. While the 'softness' of a concept may facilitate pruning, lack of precision also means that norm internalization cannot occur, because if there is no intersubjective consensus regarding the standard of appropriate behaviour dictated by a concept, how are states going to develop a consistent practice which would contribute to the concept's hardening into a norm of customary international law? Currently, R2P is simply too opaque to prevent different actors from invoking the concept to legitimize the pursuit of particularistic agendas in the name of allegedly 'universal' interests. The African approach to R2P, for instance, continues to reflect an agenda which is partly anti-colonial and emancipatory, but at times also repressive and backward-looking.

Secondly, on the regional level of analysis, we find a continental organization which is constantly torn between emulating Western standards of legitimate statehood and good governance on the one hand,[2] and trying to emancipate itself from the West by devising African solutions to African problems on the other hand. A major impetus for the founding of the OAU and its successor the AU was the idea that Africa should be able to solve its own problems in order to prevent foreign powers from exploiting Africa's internal weaknesses; at the founding of the OAU Ethiopian Emperor Haile Selassie urged 'We need an organization which will facilitate acceptable solutions to disputes among Africans' (Selassie 1963: 285). He further elaborated:

> Let us . . . create a single institution to which we all belong, based on principles to which we all subscribe . . . secure in the knowledge that the decisions there will be dictated by Africans and only by Africans and that they will take full account of all vital African considerations. (ibid: 285)

This notion of African emancipation from Western tutelage is a core part of the AU's emerging security culture. The AU's nascent regional identity is constructed around the ideology of Pan-Africanism, which in turn is premised on the assumption that

> . . . all Africans have a spiritual affinity with each other and that, having suffered together in the past, they must march together into a new and brighter future. In its fullest realization this would involve the creation of 'an African leviathan in the form of a political organisation or an association of states'. (Emerson 1962: 280)

Central to the ideology of Pan-Africanism are the concepts of Negritude and the idea of the African personality (ibid: 281), which define

Africanness among other things via that which it is not, thus invoking difference in order to create in-group cohesion. This is called 'othering' – a central concept in postcolonial thinking, where it is employed as a discursive frame 'in order to resist the Eurocentric, condescending assumptions of international law that were utilized to foster the colonial subjugation in Africa' (Gathi 1998/1999: 72). A sense of developing world identity and agency is thus asserted which was denied by the colonial powers and which is used as a rallying device to put up a united African front against Western domination. In this perspective, the creation of an African continental security architecture is, among other things, an attempt to balance the hegemony of the West, which in turn has significant implications for the African approach to R2P. The general African tendency towards rejecting hegemonic interference explains, for instance, why various African governments tend to support the ICISS's suggestion for establishing a code of conduct for the P5 members of the UN Security Council in situations involving mass atrocities. The veto power wielded by the P5 is anathema to many African states, who view the Security Council as a hegemonic body where Africans have no voice. Africa's mistrust of the UN Security Council also explains the AU's peculiar interpretation of the relationship between R2P and the principle of non-intervention. While Art. 4h of the AU Constitutive Act provides for a right to humanitarian intervention and hence at first glance seems to reject the principle of non-interference, it is important to note that the right to intervene belongs to the AU only. In relations between Africa and the outside world, the non-intervention principle continues to reign supreme. Thus, the AU has developed a very peculiar interpretation of R2P which includes a pruning of the non-intervention norm in favour of a right to intervene which is borne by the AU, but not the international community at large, as suggested by the ICISS. According to the AU's understanding of R2P, the primary duty-bearers are nation-states themselves; but if the former fail to live up to their responsibility, responsibility devolves to the continental organization. Prior authorization by the UN Security Council is seen as desirable; it is not, however, considered as a *conditio sine qua non* for the AU to launch a humanitarian intervention (Ladnier 2003: 53). The African version of R2P is obviously at odds with Art. 2(4) of the UN Charter, which posits that al member states 'shall refrain in their international relations from the threat or use of force against the territorial integrity or political independence of any state'. Art. 103 of the Charter in turn establishes the primacy of the Charter over other international treaties (including the AU Constitutive Act). The African R2P doctrine hence cannot be reconciled with the norms of the UN Charter.

A final variable from the regional level of analysis is the type of security challenges faced by a regional organization. As the African continent continues to be haunted by fundamental threats to human security such as state failure, civil war and the risk of mass atrocities, it seems only logical for the AU's regional security culture to reflect an interventionist posture. The urgent need for effective responses to these challenges also explains why Africans have adopted a rather pragmatic stance regarding the necessity of seeking a UN mandate for interventions led by regional and subregional organizations, and refuse to be bothered with legal niceties such as the incompatibility of Art. 4(h) of the AU Constitutive Act with Art. 2(4) of the UN Charter. The genocide in Rwanda made it painfully clear to Africans that the United Nations cannot be relied upon to protect African civilians; 'One clear and lasting lesson has been that the international community's interest in Africa is fickle in nature, and the costs of being dependent on others for action can be unacceptably high' (ibid.: 30). It was partially this realization which prompted the AU to adopt a security doctrine which is more interventionist than any other regional security culture in the world.

Third, we must look to the sub-regional level of analysis in order to understand the status of R2P in the AU's security culture. At the state level, the fear of neo-colonialism under the guise of humanitarian concerns continues to inform African leaders' attitude towards R2P. Many African governments are still strongly attached to traditional sovereignty norms, which has frequently led to a privileging of regime security over human security:

> For the newly independent states, sovereignty is the hard won prize of their long struggle for emancipation. It is the legal epitome of the fact that they are masters in their own house . . . Once they have achieved independence and reacquired sovereignty, they are very reluctant to accept any limitation of it. (Abi-Saab 1962: 103f)

Unsurprisingly then, the AU at times acts as a mutual preservation club of autocratic leaders, who maintain a strong sense of loyalty towards one another – witness the AU's reaction to the Bashir and Gaddafi arrest warrants. The arrest warrants issued against incumbent heads of state obviously made many authoritarian African leaders fear for their political survival; they viewed the indictments as the 'beginning of a trend against which they must unite' (Abdulai 2010). Consequently, atrocities occurring in AU member states are frequently 'swept under the carpet, and rationalized according to the outdated doctrine of territorial integrity and sovereignty concerns' (ibid.). In Africa a political culture persists which has been characterized as neopatrimonial, that is, based on clientelism and nepotism which operate 'behind a façade of ostensibly rational state bureaucracy' (Taylor and Williams 2008: 137). Hence, a genuine commitment to R2P as part and parcel of the African security culture is 'doomed to be theoretical rather than practical as long as its members are primarily interested in preserving regime security and their exclusive access to the state's resources' (ibid.: 145).

The prevalence of neopatrimonial regimes in turn means that variables from the societal level of analysis are less salient in Africa than in regions which are primarily composed of mature democracies. With regard to the role of R2P in the AU's security culture, the implications of this assumption are somewhat ambiguous; on the one hand, one could hypothesize that African citizens are less likely to stymie intervention on behalf of human rights than their casualty-averse counterparts in Western democracies. Yet on the other hand, in cases where the magnitude of human suffering outweighs the reluctance of a society to sacrifice its own soldiers, public pressure *in favour* of humanitarian intervention will probably not suffice to prompt African governments to intervene in the internal affairs of a neighbouring state, because many African leaders will frequently privilege their loyalties to fellow autocrats over the preferences of their own constituencies.

Overall, the AU's interpretation of R2P is conditioned by various, and at times conflicting, factors such as the influence of world political culture, the soft law character of R2P, the experience of colonialism, the desire to balance Western influence, the types of security challenges faced by the regional organization, the prevalence of neopatrimonial regimes and a corresponding privileging of regime security over human security. The interplay of these variables has led the AU to prune R2P to fit its needs, keeping the elements of R2P that are compatible with its own norms and preferences, and jettisoning the rest. The next section analyses how the AU's peculiar security culture informed its behaviour in the Libyan crisis.

The AU and the crisis in Libya

The crisis in Libya shows that even though organizations like the AU, the Arab League, NATO, the EU and others employ the same vocabulary – that of protecting civilians against an irresponsible sovereign – they strongly disagree over the scope of the mandate and the appropriate means for attaining this overarching goal. The following narrative focuses on some of the most contested aspects of the debate over the military realization of human security, namely issues of proportionality, right intention and selectivity which were at the heart of the ICISS's discussion of the legitimacy of military intervention, and which emerged as major objects of controversy during the Libyan crisis. The intervention in Libya also underscores that as long as there is no settled consensus on these crucial dimensions of R2P, the concept will not consolidate into a norm of international law.

In 2011, Libyans rose against Colonel Gaddafi, the 'Butcher of Sirte' (Kituyi 2011), prompting Gaddafi to initiate a bloody campaign of repression against his own people. A week into the carnage, the AU Peace and Security Council (PSC) issued a statement condemning the violence and calling upon the Libyan government to ensure the protection of its citizens. The statement moreover expressed sympathy for the aspirations of the Libyan people for democracy and political reform, but also highlighted the need to preserve the territorial integrity of Libya. The UN Security Council in turn sprang into action rather swiftly, adopting Resolution 1970 on 26 February, which referred the situation in Libya to the ICC. The resolution was greeted as 'historic', as a test case for the international community's commitment to implementing the R2P doctrine (Cotler and Genser 2011). Remarkably, the Council voted unanimously. Its three African members – South Africa, Nigeria and Gabon – who had previously sided with other African governments in frustrating the ICC proceedings against Al-Bashir – not only did not veto the resolution, but even cast an affirmative vote.

Yet the AU did not want to leave the resolution of the crisis to extra-continental powers alone, and therefore issued another statement on 10 March on the establishment of an Ad Hoc High Level Committee tasked with seeking a diplomatic solution to the conflict. The AU PSC moreover expressed its conviction that urgent African action had to be taken to reach a cessation of hostilities and the adoption of political reforms. This formula was seen as sufficiently flexible for leaving open the possibility of further engagement with the Gaddafi regime in pursuit of a diplomatic solution. When the UN Security Council – encouraged by the Arab League's request to establish a no-fly zone over Libya (Leiby and Mansour 2011) – upped the ante on 17 March by authorizing 'all necessary measures' to protect civilians and end the bloodshed, its African members voted in favour, even though the AU PSC had previously rejected any foreign military intervention. The onset of NATO's bombing campaign frustrated the AU's High Level Committee's diplomatic mission, however, because the eminent personalities could not even get into the country – which left the AU with a bitter sense of marginalization and further exacerbated tensions between the AU and the Western powers (Onyango-Obbo 2011). These tensions persisted throughout the intervention which culminated, as is well known, in the toppling of the Libyan regime and Gaddafi's death at the hands of Libyan rebels.

What does the AU's role in the crisis tell us about the organization's commitment to human security and R2P? In the following, I will show that the AU's interpretation of R2P's constituent principles such as proportionality, necessity, right intention and so on is frequently at odds with other (Western) actors' interpretation of these principles; that this difference is explicable with reference to the AU's peculiar security culture; and that the AU's commitment to human security is wavering when realizing human security comes at the expense of regime security – especially when the regime is one which has long played a leading role in the continental organization.

Initially, various African leaders tried to downplay the carnage – with Zimbabwe's Mugabe predictably treating the Libyan uprising as merely a 'domestic hiccup' (ibid.) and Uganda's Museveni defending Gaddafi as a 'true nationalist' (Museveni 2011). While admitting to Gaddafi's often lunatic posturing, Museveni nonetheless emphasized that 'Gaddafi has also had many positive points objectively speaking' (ibid.). He lauded the dictator as an independent spirit who never missed an opportunity to defy the West:

> I am not able to understand the position of Western countries which appear to resent independent-minded leaders and seem to prefer puppets. Puppets are not good for any country . . . Muammar Gaddafi, whatever his faults, is a true nationalist. I prefer nationalists to puppets of foreign interests . . . Therefore, the independent-minded Gaddafi had some positive contribution to Libya, I believe, as well as Africa and the Developing world. (ibid.)

At a time when Gaddafi was slaughtering his own people with the entire world watching, Museveni's defence of the Libyan dictator as a 'true nationalist' must have sounded like the purest form of irony to most non-Africans; yet in Africa this kind of anti-Western reasoning apparently continues to strike a chord with some of the continent's autocratic and pseudo-democratic leaders. For a long time, many of these despots were rulers by the grace of Gaddafi, who generously funded their political ambitions (Kituyi 2011). Unsurprisingly then, some of Gaddafi's former vassals were rather reluctant to turn against their long-time benefactor.

Despite lingering African sympathies towards the Libyan tyrant, in the end, however, the majority of African leaders were apparently convinced that 'Brother Leader' Gaddafi had become politically untenable (Bakata 2011). This realization notwithstanding, the AU feared that Resolution 1973 had left too much leeway for 'powerful Western states with a notorious track record of invasion and occupation' (D'Almeida 2011). Instead of supporting regime change from the outside, the AU believed that it was up to the Libyan people to initiate a process of political reform:

> The [AU High-Level Ad Hoc] Committee considers that it should be left to Libyans to choose their leaders and that international actors should refrain from taking positions or making pronouncements that can only complicate the search for a solution. The role of the international community should be to help Libyans achieve their legitimate aspirations, in a nationally-owned and nationally-led process. (African Union 2011)

The AU thus clearly did not think that forcible democracy promotion from the outside was a legitimate means to ensure the effective protection of civilians. NATO's expansion of its target list to include Gaddafi's compound in Tripoli, for instance, fuelled African fears of mission creep and hidden neo-colonial agendas (AllAfrica 2011; Oluka 2011). The AU High Level Committee therefore reminded the intervening party to strictly adhere to the provisions of Resolution 1973.

Admittedly, however, the terms of Resolution 1973 left room for debate over what means are conducive to ensuring the effective protection of endangered civilians, and whether, under a teleological reading of that resolution, regime change could be considered a necessary and proportionate way of living up to the international community's 'responsibility to protect'. As pointed out earlier, the ICISS report leaves some room for interpretation for assessing the necessity and proportionality of any particular military action aimed at protecting civilians. Hence, Resolution 1973 could be read as at a minimum not explicitly ruling out regime change. Interestingly, however, Gareth Evans, one of the drafters of the ICISS report, strongly argued against using R2P as a pretext for regime change in Libya, arguing that democratization could only be achieved by the Libyan people itself:

> The international military intervention in Libya is not about bombing for democracy or Muammar Gaddafi's head – let alone keeping

> oil prices down or profits up. Legally, morally, politically and militarily it has only one justification; protecting the country's people from the kind of murderous harm that Gaddafi inflicted on unarmed protesters . . . And when that job is done, the military intervention will be done. Any regime change is for the Libyan people themselves to achieve. (Evans, 2011)

According to this view, limited military action aimed at destroying Gaddafi aircraft taking off in the no-fly zone, strikes targeting anti-aircraft batteries or missile launch sites, as well as targeting troop columns advancing on rebel-held towns, would have been necessary and proportionate to discharge the R2P mandate. Evans does not believe, however, that the R2P doctrine covers assassinating Gaddafi, fighting on behalf of the rebels to ensure their victory, or forcible democracy promotion (ibid.). He concludes unequivocally that once the threat to the civilian population has been contained, military action must end (ibid.). Yet again, the question arises as to whether a murderous regime such as Gaddafi's – as long as it is in power – ever ceases to pose a threat to the civilian population, and whether, in this particular case, the only way of effectively living up to the international community's responsibility to protect would be to remove Gaddafi from power, which is what NATO and Libyan rebel forces ultimately did.

Apart from the controversy over the necessity and proportionality of military action to protect Libyan civilians, the criteria of right intention and non-selectivity were equally disputed among the various diplomatic players in the crisis. As we recall from the ICISS report, right intention can be measured on the basis of three indicators; multilateral action, popular support and the consent of other states in the region. While NATO's action (at least initially) had the blessing of the Security Council, the Libyan people as well as the Arab League, African leaders remained ambivalent. Even though the three African members of the UN Security Council voted in favor of Resolution 1973, the AU PSC rejected foreign military intervention in Libya. This rejection was partly based on suspicions of double standards in the application of R2P and of hidden agendas pursued by the West. Why, for example, did NATO intervene in Libya but not Yemen and Bahrain? The obvious answer is that these two countries are close US allies and therefore do not have to fear being held accountable for their failure to protect their own peoples (Bajoria 2011; Oluka 2011). Another suspicion was that the West's real motive for intervening in Libya was not the protection of civilians, but rather to secure Libya's vast oil supply (AllAfrica 2011).

While the AU's criticism of the West's selectivity in applying R2P was certainly justified, the AU's own image has also been tarnished by the crisis and serious doubts have been cast on the organization's commitment to applying R2P in a non-selective, impartial fashion. In the opinion of one commentator, the Libyan crisis not only exposed the lack of determined leadership at the regional level, but also highlighted the highly ambivalent commitment of many African governments to the notion of human security, especially when human security and regime security clash:

> If the African Union has gone further in its Constitutive Act than any organization in the institutional framing of norms about R2P civilians, these are still to find concrete expression in the actions of AU member states. As a result of its own contradictions, the AU has been lacking in political will and courage to deal with state-sponsored abuses of civilian right holders in member states, including Libya. To want to lead the mediation now is a little too late and a face-saving exercise for an institution without political resources and the will to solve such a complex impasse. (Hengari 2011)

The AU High Level Panel was criticized as an ineffective gathering of complacent, self-congratulatory African leaders who were ultimately forced to watch from the sidelines while NATO tried to bomb Gaddafi into compliance with the relevant Security Council resolutions (ibid.). In particular, the AU's credibility to act as an honest broker in the conflict was called into question, considering Gaddafi's central role as a prime financier of the continental organization (Sudan Tribune 2011). In light of the significant financial but also ideological and political influence Gaddafi wielded for so long in the OAU and later AU, it is thus rather questionable whether the AU itself fulfilled the criterion of right intention in implementing R2P in Libya. Note, however, that the AU is not a monolithic bloc, and that there is currently no unified approach to R2P on the African continent. Some African leaders such as Rwanda's Paul Kagame, for instance, openly criticized the AU's tepid response to the bloodshed in Libya; 'From the African perspective there are important lessons to learn, the main one being that we as the African Union need to respond faster and more effectively to situations such as these' (Kagame 2011). Some African media commentators judged the AU even more harshly:

> The circus of African inadequacy plays out even more glaringly in the case of Libya. With the exception of Rwanda and The Gambia,

African states have been very slow in their responses to the criminal violence Col Muammar Gaddafi has visited upon his own people. (Kituyi 2011)

Conclusions

The Libyan crisis has thrown into sharp relief the continuing disagreement over the scope of the obligations flowing from the concept of R2P, with different diplomatic players putting forward differing interpretations of what it means for the international community to exercise its responsibility to protect endangered civilians. At the outset I noted that the opaqueness of the notion of R2P has made it possible for different actors to make it congruent with their respective political agendas. The application of the principles of proportionality, necessity, just authority and right intention in particular continues to be strongly contested. The AU's interpretation of these principles – and thus its response to the crisis in Libya – was informed by its emerging security culture, which is in turn the product of a confluence of factors from different variables of analysis. First, regional security cultures are certainly not impervious to global discourses about human security, good governance and responsible sovereignty – a fact which is reflected in the repeated invocations of these concepts in the relevant statements and resolutions adopted by the AU throughout the crisis. Yet if 'world political culture' had been the only variable of interest, the AU's response would have been much more determined. In reality, however, the AU's role was rather ambivalent, and in order to understand this ambivalence, other explanatory variables must be taken into account. These include regional factors such as the significant financial and ideological influence wielded by Gaddafi in the continental organization, but also the AU's chronically underfunded peace and security architecture, which forced it to rely on diplomatic means for addressing the crisis. Third, variables from the nation-state level equally played a role, such as the (historically founded) fear of African governments that the West might use humanitarian arguments for the pursuit of a neo-colonial agenda. Another important explanatory factor is the undemocratic nature of many African regimes, which tend to extend solidarity to their fellow autocrats and often continue to privilege regime security over human security.

In sum, the present case study underlines the utility of the concept of regional security culture for understanding the responses adopted by regional organizations in the face of threats to international security. However, as a single-case study in an under-theorized field of research this chapter does not purport to be more than an 'exploratory drilling,' that is a first plausibility probe. More research – for instance case studies using cross-regional comparisons – is clearly necessary to fine-tune the notion of regional security culture. Future research will have to identify more precisely the interaction between the various causal factors sketched in this chapter and will also have to address the feedback loop from regional security cultures to norm development at the global level.

Notes

1. See, for example, A/RES/60/1, 24 October 2005; A/RES/63/308, 14 September 2009; S/RES/1674, 28 April 2006; S/RES/1706, 31 August 2006; S/RES/1856, 22 December 2008; S/RES/1857, 22 December 2008.
2. See, for example, Art. 3(g), 3(h), 4(h), 4(m), 4(o), and 4(p) of the African Union Constitutive Act, *supra* note 1.

References

Abi-Saab, G. M. (1962) 'The Newly Independent States and the Rule of International Law: An Outline', *Howard Law Journal*, vol. 8, pp. 95–121.

Abdulai, E. S. (2010) 'Looking to Kampala: The Challenges of International Justice in Africa', 10 March. Available online at: www.fljs.org/uploads/documents/Justice_in_Africa.pdf [Accessed February 2012].

Acharya, A. (2004) 'How Ideas Spread: Whose Norms Matter? Norm Localization and Institutional Change in Asian Regionalism', *International Organization*, vol. 58, no. 2, pp. 239–75.

African Union (2005) 'The Common African Position on the Proposed Reform of the United Nations: "The Ezulwini Consensus"', 7–8 March. Available online at: www.africa-union.org/.../Ext%20EXCL2%20VII%20Report.doc [Accessed August 2012].

African Union (2011) 'Report of the Chairperson of the Commission on the Activities of the AU High Level Ad hoc Committee on the Situation in Libya', PSC/PR/2(CCLXXV), 26 April. Available online at: www.peaceau.org/uploads/275reportonlibyaeng.pdf [Accessed August 2012].

AllAfrica (2011) Ambiguities over the Interpretation of UN Resolution 1973 Causing Global Consternation, 23 March 2011. Available online at: http://allafrica.com/stories/201103230883.html [Accessed February 2012].

Anderson, B. (1983) *Imagined Communities: Reflections on the Origin and Spread of Nationalism* (New York: Verso).

Bajoria, J. (2011) 'Libya and the Responsibility to Protect', 24 March. Available online at: http://cfr.org/libya/libya-responsibility to protect/p24480 [Accessed February 2012].

Bakata, S. (2011) 'Why Africa Abandoned "Brother" Gaddafi', *AllAfrica*, 26 March. Available online at: http://allafrica.com/stories/201103280137.html [Accessed February 2012].

Commission on Human Security (2003) 'Human Security Now'. Available online at: www.humansecurity-chs.org/finalreport/index.html [Accessed February 2012].

Cotler, I. and J. Genser (2011) 'Libya and the Responsibility to Protect', *New York Times*, 28 February. Available online at: www.nytimes.com/2011/03/01/opinion/01iht-edcotler01.html [Accessed February 2012].

CNN.com (2011) 'African Union: Members Will Not Cooperate with Gadhafi Warrant', 3 June. Available online at: http://articles.cnn.com/2011-07-03/world/libya.war_1_libyan-leader-moammar-gadhafi-libyan-people-arrest-warrant?_s=PM:WORLD [Accessed February 2012].

D'Almeida, K. (2011) 'Regional Support Erodes for Air War', *AllAfrica*, 21 March. Available online at: http://allafrica.com/stories/printable/201103220005.html [Accessed February 2012].

Dembinski, M. and T. Reinold (2011) 'Libya and the Future of the Responsibility to Protect: African and European Perspectives'. Available online at: www.hsfk.de/fileadmin/downloads/prif107.pdf [Accessed February 2012].

Deng, F. M., S. Kimaro, T. Lyons, D. Rothchild and I. W. Zartman (1996) *Sovereignty as Responsibility. Conflict Management in Africa* (Washington, DC: Brookings Institution).

Emerson, R. (1962) 'Pan-Africanism', *International Organization*, vol. 16, no. 2, pp. 275–90.

Evans, G. (2011) 'UN Targets Libya with Pinpoint Accuracy', *Sydney Morning Herald*, 24 March. Available online at: www.smh.com.au/opinion/politics/un-targets-libya-with-pinpoint-accuracy-20110323-1c6pc.html [Accessed February 2012].

Gathi, J. T. (1998/1999) 'Representations of Africa in Good Governance Discourse: Policing and Containing Dissidence to Neo-Liberalism', *Developing World Legal Studies*, vol. 15, no. 4, pp. 65–108.

Haacke, J. (2003) *ASEAN's Diplomatic and Security Culture. Origins, Development and Prospects* (London: Routledge).

Haacke, J. and P. D. Williams (2008) 'Security Culture, Transnational Challenges and the Economic Community of West African States', *Journal of Contemporary African Studies*, vol. 26, no. 2, pp. 119–36.

Hengari, A. T. (2011) 'Africa: The African Union Struggles to Exist on Libya', *The Namibian*, 25 March. Available online at: www.namibian.com.na/index.php?id=28&tx_ttnews[tt_news]=79586&no_cache=1 [Accessed February 2012].

Hurrell, A. (2006) 'Hegemony, Liberalism and Global Order: What Space for Would-be Great Powers?', *International Affairs*, vol. 82, no. 1, pp. 1–19.

ICISS (International Commission on Intervention and State Sovereignty) (2001) *The Responsibility to Protect* (Ottawa: International Development Research Centre).

Jaye, T. (2008) 'The Security Culture of the ECOWAS: Origins, Development and the Challenge of Child Trafficking', *Journal of Contemporary African Studies*, vol. 26, no. 2, pp. 151–68.

Johnston, A. I. (1995) *Cultural Realism: Strategic Culture and Grand Strategy in Chinese History* (Princeton: Princeton University Press).

Kagame, P. (2011) 'Rwandans Know Why Gaddafi Must Be Stopped', *AllAfrica*, 24 March. Available online at: http://allafrica.com/stories/201103240033.html [Accessed February 2012].

Katzenstein, P. J. (1996) 'Introduction: Alternative Perspectives on National Security', in P. J. Katzenstein (ed.), *The Culture of National Security: Norms and Identities in World Politics* (New York: Columbia University Press).

Katzenstein, P. J., R. L. Lepperson and A. Wendt (1996) 'Norms, Identity, and Culture in National Security', in P. J. Katzenstein (ed.), *The Culture of National Security: Norms and Identities in World Politics* (New York: Columbia University Press).

Kituyi, M. (2011) 'Libya, Côte d'Ivoire Burns as Africa Runs in Circles', *AllAfrica*, 26 March. Available online at: http://allafrica.com/stories/201103280161.html [Accessed February 2012].

Ladnier, J. (2003) *Neighbors on Alert. Regional Views on Humanitarian Intervention* (Washington, DC: Fund for Peace).

Leiby, R. and M. Mansour (2011) 'Arab League Asks UN for No-Fly-Zone Over Libya', *Washington Post*, 12 March. Available online at: www.washingtonpost.com/world/arab-league-asks-un-for-no-fly-zone-over-libya/2011/03/12/ABoie0R_story.html [Accessed February 2012].

Murithi, T. (2009) 'The African Union's Transition from Non-intervention to Non-indifference: An Ad Hoc Approach to the Responsibility to Protect?', *Internationale Politik und Gesellschaft*, no. 1, pp. 90–106.

Museveni, Y. (2011) 'Reflections on the Libyan Crisis', *The Herald*, 24 March. Available online at: www.herald.co.zw/index.php?id=5717:reflections-on-the-libyan-crisis&option=com_content&catid=39:opinion&Itemid=132 [Accessed February 2012].

Mwanasali, M. (2008) 'From Non-interference to Non-indifference: The Emerging Doctrine of Conflict Prevention in Africa', in J. Akokpari, A. Ndinga-Muvumba and T. Murithi (eds), *The African Union and its Institutions* (Auckland Park: Fanele).

Oluka, B. H. (2011) 'Uganda: Museveni Attacks West over Libya', *The Monitor*, 22 March. Available online at: http://allafrica.com/stories/201103220261.html [Accessed February 2012].

Onyango-Obbo, C. (2011) 'How AU Dropped the Ball in North Africa', *The East African*, 28 March. Available online at: http://allafrica.com/stories/201103280160.html [Accessed February 2012].

Printer, N. G. (2003) 'The Use of Force Against Non-state Actors Under International Law: An Analysis of the US Predator Strike in Yemen', *UCLA Journal of International Law & Foreign Affairs*, vol. 8, p. 331.

Reinold, T. (2010) 'The Responsibility to Protect: Much Ado About Nothing?', *Review of International Studies*, vol. 36, no. 1, pp. 55–78.

Reinold, T. (2011) 'State Weakness, Irregular Warfare, and the Right to Self-defense Post-9/11', *American Journal of International Law*, vol. 105, no. 2, pp. 244–86.

Reinold, T. (2012) *Sovereignty and the Responsibility to Protect: The Power of Norms and the Norms of the Powerful* (London: Routledge).

Selassie, H. (1963) 'Towards African Unity', *The Journal of Modern African Studies*, vol. 1, no. 3, pp. 281–91.

Sudan Tribune (2011) 'Libya: African Union Absent From 2nd Meeting on Libya as Its Chief Pleads for Funds', *Sudan Tribune*, 29 March. Available online at: www.sudantribune.com/African-Union-absent-from-2nd,38430 [Accessed February 2012].

Taylor, I. and P. D. Williams (2008) 'Political Culture, States Elites and Regional Security in West Africa', *Journal of Contemporary African Studies*, vol. 26, no. 2, pp. 137–49.

Williams, P. D. (2007) 'From Non-intervention to Non-indifference: The Origins and Development of the African Union's Security Culture', *African Affairs*, vol. 106, no. 423, pp. 253–79.

6
The Use – and Misuse – of R2P: The Case of Canada

Kim Richard Nossal

In the heated debate that has emerged over whether the Libyan intervention of 2011 advanced the entrenchment of the norm of the Responsibility to Protect (R2P), there is one facet of the Libyan case that both R2P celebrationists like Alex Bellamy and Paul Williams (2011; also Bellamy 2011), Thomas Weiss (2011), and Ramesh Thakur (2011c) and sceptics like the editors of this volume (Murray 2011; Hehir 2012) agree: the Libyan case was unusual. Indeed, Tim Dunne and Jess Gifkins (2011) have gone so far as to use the 'perfect storm' trope to describe the interconnected set of permissive conditions that allowed the use of force against the regime of Muammar Gaddafi. These unusual conditions included both domestic and internal elements. First, and most importantly, Gaddafi was willing to openly threaten his opponents with slaughter, and his televised claims that his opponents were 'rats' and 'cockroaches' (Ford Rojas 2011), the latter characterization explicitly evoking the word used by Hutu *génocidaires* in Rwanda to describe their victims. Second, although relations between Libya and the West had improved since 2001, it was relatively easy to re-demonize both Gaddafi and his regime simply by recalling a string of past misdeeds: the 1988 bombing of Pan Am flight 103 over Lockerbie, Scotland; the 1986 bombing of a discotheque in Berlin; or the 1984 murder of a British police officer by a sniper shooting from the premises of the Libyan embassy in London. Third, the willingness of the Arab League to support an international armed response was a crucial component of success, without which it is unlikely that Resolution 1973 would have passed without a veto being cast. Last, it was unusual that the People's Republic of China and the Russian Federation were willing to acquiesce in the passage of Resolution 1973 by abstention rather than express their traditional concerns about intervention via the veto.

But there is another unusual feature of the Libyan mission that has not been widely examined in the scholarly debate: the degree to which this mission was discussed, and often justified politically, as though it *was* a case of R2P when, as a number of scholars and others have pointed out (for example, Murray 2011; Hehir 2012), it was not. However, the inappropriate invocation of the R2P norm was not corrected in the dialectics of national debates: those who argued that Libya was a case of R2P were allowed to invoke the norm without contradiction or denial. It can be argued that this phenomenon – the inappropriate application of the language of R2P, and the unwillingness of participants in the policymaking process to correct the error – had an important impact on the process of norm consolidation.

This chapter looks at how R2P was used, and misused, in such a way in one particular country that contributed to the armed intervention in Libya in 2011. It examines the rhetoric used to debate the mission by the political parties in the Canadian House of Commons: the governing Conservatives; the Liberals, who were the Official Opposition until the May 2011 elections; the New Democratic Party (NDP), which replaced the Liberals as the Official Opposition in May 2011; the Bloc Québécois; and the Green Party, which was represented in the House of Commons by a single Member of Parliament.

I will show that Canadian political discourse on the Libyan mission was consistently marked by confusion about R2P on the part of all of the opposition parties. The Liberals, the NDP, the Bloc, and, after the May 2011 elections, the lone Green MP, all consistently took the view that the Libyan mission was driven by the Responsibility to Protect. And support for R2P appeared to generate considerable support among the opposition parties for the Canadian mission. By contrast, the Conservative government never allowed the phrase 'Responsibility to Protect' to appear in official discourse, a refusal that, as we will see, was criticized by the opposition parties. But at the same time, however, the Conservatives never openly corrected the opposition insistence that Canada was engaged in a humanitarian intervention rather than an R2P exercise. While there were important political reasons for the Conservative refusal to be pedantic, I will argue that one possible longer term consequence of the Canadian debate will be to make it more likely that the armed intervention in Libya in 2011 will be a unique event in contemporary global politics.

Canada's Libyan mission

The government in Ottawa was one of the eighteen countries that contributed armed forces to the enforcement of United Nations Security

Council Resolutions 1970 and 1973.[1] Once an international coalition began to take shape in response to the increasing use of violence by the Libyan authorities, Canadian Prime Minister Stephen Harper and his Conservative government were early enthusiastic supporters of the Libyan mission; Canada was quick to commit armed forces to the coalition that emerged to enforce UNSCR 1970 and 1973.

The first part of the mission began with Operation MOBILE, the deployment of aircraft in late February to evacuate Canadians and others from Libya. On 1 March, Harper announced that HMCS *Charlottetown,* a Halifax-class frigate, was being despatched to the Mediterranean, as part of the effort to impose an arms embargo on Libya in accordance with Security Council Resolution 1970 of 26 February 2011. With the passage of UNSCR 1973, Op MOBILE was transformed into a combat mission on 19 March, when Canadian CF-18 fighters were deployed to participate in air operations being conducted by the United States under the American operation in Libya, Operation ODYSSEY DAWN. And when the North Atlantic Council accepted responsibility for conducting both the naval and air operations under Operation UNIFIED PROTECTOR as of 31 March, Canada's forces were reassigned to that operation. In addition, the Harper government agreed to the appointment of a Canadian officer, Lt. Gen. Charles Bouchard, as the Combined Joint Task Force Commander of Operation UNIFIED PROTECTOR.

Between March and the conclusion of combat operations on 31 October, Canada's overall military contribution at its peak included 655 members of the Canadian Armed Forces, seven CF-18 Hornet jet fighters, two CF-150 Polaris refuellers, three Hercules and two CP-140 Aurora maritime patrol aircraft from the Royal Canadian Air Force. RCAF aircraft flew 1,539 sorties, including 946 Hornet sorties that dropped 696 bombs on Libyan targets. The Royal Canadian Navy deployed HMCS *Charlottetown* in theatre from 1 March to 18 August, when it was relieved by HMCS *Vancouver*. Canadian Forces suffered no casualties or loss of equipment during the mission (Canada, National Defence 2011; Pigott 2011; Davis and Berthiaume 2012).

Justifying the mission

Canada's political elites engaged in considerable discussion and debate about the mission. The prime minister and key members of his cabinet – the minister of national defence and the minister of foreign affairs and international trade – provided a number of public justifications for the mission from the outset. The intervention was also debated in the

House of Commons. Although constitutionally Canadian governments are not required to seek the formal approval of the Parliament for the foreign deployment of Canadian combat troops (Nossal et al. 2011: 264–5), the Harper government, like previous governments, sought to maximize the legitimacy of foreign deployments of combat units by seeking the approval of the House of Commons.

In the case of Libya, Members of Parliament debated the mission three times in 2011. The first debate occurred on 21 March, in the wake of Resolution 1973 passed by the Security Council on 17 March. The resolution 'taking note' of the Canadian military contribution that was already underway was passed unanimously (Canada, Parliament of 2011a: 19h35).

The second debate occurred on 14 June, when the Harper government sought parliamentary approval for a three-month extension. The Conservatives, however, were no longer in a minority position in the House of Commons as a result of the general election of 2 May. The elections resulted in a majority, with 166 seats of 308, up from 143 at dissolution. Support for both the Liberals and the Bloc Québécois collapsed. The Liberals went from 77 seats at dissolution to 34 seats, and the Bloc from 47 to just four seats. Both the Liberal leader, Michael Ignatieff, and the BQ leader, Gilles Duceppe, went down to defeat in their own ridings. The New Democratic Party vaulted from 36 seats at dissolution to 103 seats, becoming the official opposition. In addition, the Green Party of Canada elected one member: the party leader, Elizabeth May, was elected to the British Columbia riding of Saanich–Gulf Islands. However, the dramatic shift in party fortunes did not affect the Libyan mission: the government's motion was approved 294–1, receiving almost unanimous approval of the House; only Elizabeth May voted against the motion (Canada, Parliament of 2011b: L 19h05).

The third debate was held on 26 September, when the government sought a further three-month extension (Canada, Parliament of 2011c). On this occasion, however, the New Democratic Party was no longer in favour of continuing a military role. On the grounds that Gaddafi was no longer in power, it argued that Canada should withdraw its forces from Operation UNIFIED PROTECTOR and focus instead on a post-conflict role with a humanitarian focus. However, the government's motion was supported by both the Liberals and the Bloc Québécois, and passed easily 188–98.

Given the unanimity of support for the initial commitment of Canadian forces to the international coalition that emerged to enforce the two United Nations Security Council resolutions, and the near-unanimity of the June vote, it should not be surprising that the justifications offered for the mission by the various political parties did not diverge markedly. However, on one issue – the Responsibility to Protect – there was considerable difference, with the governing Conservatives taking one line and all the opposition parties taking another.

The initial justificatory positions on Canada's role emerged in the context of the unfolding situation in Libya itself. The government was relatively slow to become engaged on the Libya file. While Ottawa issued a number of condemnations of the initial outbreaks of violence, these tended to be brief, pro forma, and more focused on offering advice to Canadian citizens. On 21 February, Harper declared that he found 'the actions of the government firing upon its own citizens to be outrageous and unacceptable' (Harper 2011a). But it was not until 25 February, eight days after the 'Day of Rage' on 17 February that marked the first large-scale massacre by pro-Gaddafi forces, that the Canadian position hardened significantly.

On 25 February, the minister of national defence, Peter MacKay, happened to be giving a speech to the annual meeting of the Conference of Defence Associations in Ottawa, and took the opportunity to speak about Libya. 'Simply put,' he said, 'the outrageous and insidious abuse of government power in Libya must stop, and we in Canada stand united with like-minded, peaceful nations in support of the legitimate aspirations of the people of Libya' (MacKay 2011a). Over the course of the day, there was considerable diplomatic activity on the part of Western countries, including a phone call to the foreign minister, Lawrence Cannon, by the US Secretary of State, Hillary Rodham Clinton, to discuss a common Western approach to the unfolding crisis. That evening, the prime minister also spoke at length on what was happening in Libya. In a prepared statement, he asserted: 'The international community must send a very clear message: the killing of innocent civilians – the citizens of its own country – constitutes a gross violation of human rights and must carry serious consequences.' Claiming that 'Those responsible for ordering and carrying out atrocities against the Libyan people must be held accountable', he suggested that the perpetrators of such atrocities would be referred to the International Criminal Court. He noted that Canadian officials had been instructed to prepare a list of measures that Canada could take, unilaterally or in associated with other states, and declared that 'no options have been ruled out' (Harper 2011b; Alberts and Kennedy 2011; Clark 2011).

From this initial justificatory line – that Canadian policy on Libya was being driven by a deep concern for the protection of civilians against a human-rights-abusing regime – Harper and his ministers did not stray over the course of the intervention. From the prime minister's initial statement on 25 February until his speech at the ceremony held in Ottawa on 24 November 2011 to honour those members of the Canadian Armed Forces who had served in the intervention in Libya, Harper was consistent in his characterization of the mission. On all of the occasions that he spoke, formally or informally, about Canadian participation in the Libyan mission, he stressed the same essential elements: that the regime in Tripoli, often characterized in highly negative ways, was engaging in unjustifiable uses of force against its own citizens; that it was important to take measures to stop that use of force; and that there was multilateral approval for such an action.

Thus, for example, when the prime minister announced on 18 March 2011 that Canada was committing six CF-18 fighters to enforce a no-fly zone over Libya in accordance with UNSCR 1970, he characterized Canada's contribution in these terms: 'One either believes in freedom or one just says one believes in freedom. The Libyan people have shown by their sacrifice that they believe in it. Assisting them is a moral obligation upon those of us who profess to believe in this great ideal' (Fitzpatrick 2011).

Likewise, following the ouster of Gaddafi, Harper visited Canadian forces stationed in Trapani, Italy, in September. In a speech to Canadian Armed Forces personnel, he claimed that the mission was 'the best of Canada's military tradition'. The Canadian military, he said, had contributed to freedom in Libya: 'Because you held the ring while Libyans fought their own fight with their oppressor, the Libyan people are now free to choose' (Harper 2011c; Payton 2011).

One of the clearest statements of how the prime minister saw the intervention came at the conclusion of the mission. The government organized a ceremony in Ottawa on 24 November 2011 to honour those members of the Canadian Armed Forces who had served in the NATO intervention in Libya. Harper's speech on this occasion touched on all the key elements (often recycling tropes from earlier speeches): the claim that Canada's participation in that intervention had been 'undertaken for a noble and admirable purpose: to safeguard the lives of millions of innocent Libyan civilians'. Harper characterized the Gaddafi regime as a 'brutal and psychotic' dictatorship whose forceful response to opposition had been an 'invitation to genocide'. Harper repeated the line he had used earlier about Canadian forces 'holding the ring' while 'the Libyan people were able to lift Gaddafi's yoke from their necks'.

And, as in previous speeches, he cast the mission in broad human rights terms:

> So let no-one ever question whether Canada is prepared to stay the course in defence of what is right. For we believe that in a world where people look for hope and cry out for freedom, those who talk the talk of human rights must from time to time be prepared to likewise walk the walk. (Harper, 2011d)

Similar themes, not surprisingly, were echoed by the ministers of foreign affairs and national defence. Lawrence Cannon, minister of foreign affairs until the 2 May 2011 general election, and John Baird, his successor, consistently focused on the protection of civilians as the primary reason for Canada's use of force. Peter MacKay, minister of national defence, also stressed the theme of protecting Libyan citizens, defending 'Canadian values on the world stage' (MacKay 2011b), and 'bring[ing] about the dawn of a new democratic age' in Libya (MacKay 2011c). MacKay was also more prone to characterize the Gaddafi regime in negative terms than his foreign affairs counterparts, referring to Gaddafi as a 'brutal and maniacal dictator' (MacKay 2011c). He was not at all hesitant about embracing the idea of regime change, celebrating Canada's role as 'a critical component of a UN-mandated, NATO-led mission fighting to end the regime of a mad dictator who ruled Libya as the head of a brutal and violent regime' (MacKay 2011b), conveniently re-interpreting UNSCR 1973, which clearly did not authorize regime change.

What is noteworthy about Canadian government statements on Libya was that there was no reference made to the doctrine of the Responsibility to Protect, either the expansive version of the doctrine that was originally outlined by the International Commission on Intervention and State Sovereignty (ICISS 2001), or the much more restrictive version adopted by the United Nations in its 2005 World Summit Outcome Document, particularly articles 138 and 139, the two key articles dealing with the 'responsibility to protect populations from genocide, war crimes, ethnic cleansing and crimes against humanity' (United Nations 2005). Rather, the only 'responsibility to protect' mentioned by ministers was what they characterized as Canada's 'responsibility' to act to 'protect' civilians targeted by their own government. As Baird put it during the House of Commons debate on the Libyan mission in June:

> We have a responsibility to act when we can, when our objectives are right, when our objectives are clear, to protect and to assist those

> who share the values and would share the institutions for which many of our ancestors gave up their lives so that we could enjoy the benefits. (Canada, Parliament of 2011b: 10h25)

The idea that intervening to protect citizens openly threatened with death by their own leader was a Canadian duty, a responsibility, or an obligation, suffused official justificatory rhetoric throughout the Libyan mission. To be sure, the qualification that such action needed United Nations authorization was frequently added, in recognition of the unusualness of the Libyan case and the abstentions that made UNSCR 1973 possible.

By contrast, the rhetoric of the opposition parties in the House of Commons drew heavily on the doctrine of the Responsibility to Protect as their justification for approving the initial deployment of Canadian forces under United Nations Security Council Resolution 1973. A number of MPs from all opposition parties invoked R2P, often assuming that UNSCR 1973 authorizing the no-fly zone, asset freeze, arms embargo, and 'all necessary measures' (United Nations 2011b) was invoking the Responsibility to Protect doctrine approved by the General Assembly in 2005 (United Nations 2005). It is true that UNSCR 1970 mentioned the responsibility of Libyan authorities to protect its population (United Nations 2011a) and UNSCR 1973 explicitly mentioned the protection of civilians and 'civilian populated areas' (United Nations 2011b). But neither resolution invoked the Responsibility to Protect doctrine; rather, UNSCR 1973 stated unequivocally that the Security Council was acting under Chapter VII of the UN Charter.

The explicit language of the resolution indicating that Resolution 1973 was taken under Chapter VII rather than R2P did not stop opposition MPs from asserting that the Libyan intervention was an R2P operation. The Harper government introduced a resolution in the House of Commons on 21 March 'taking note' of the Canadian contribution to the intervention, giving the House an opportunity to debate and vote on that contribution. Bob Rae, the Liberal foreign affairs critic, took the lead in arguing that the UN Security Council resolutions demonstrated that the tenets of Westphalian sovereignty were in the process of changing, and that the doctrine of the Responsibility to Protect gave those changes 'real meaning'. Rae paid tribute to Michael Ignatieff, the Liberal party leader and Leader of the Official Opposition, who as an academic at Harvard University in the late 1990s had participated in the International Commission on Intervention and State Sovereignty to create 'new rules' that were then adopted by the United Nations (Canada, Parliament of 2011a: 15h55).

A number of other Liberal MPs followed Rae's lead. Mario Silva (Lib: Davenport), asserted that by adopting UNSCR 1973, the Security Council 'has again confirmed the doctrine is a right that comes with responsibility. One cannot have sovereignty in the absence of responsibility and the doctrine of responsibility to protect'. In his view, 'The Westphalia definition of state sovereignty no longer applies', and he applauded the Security Council for taking such a step (Canada, Parliament of 2011a: 18h25).

Likewise, Jim Karygiannis (Lib: Scarborough–Agincourt) claimed that he found 'a lot of comfort that the R to P, the work we are doing right now, has the United Nations resolution [sic]'. He noted, however, that other situations should be treated the same way: 'We cannot play around with people, and if people of one country are having [sic] R to P, then other countries should be given the same thing' (Canada, Parliament of 2011a: 17h30). His Liberal colleague Borys Wrzesnewskyj (Lib: Etobicoke Centre) lauded former Liberal prime minister Paul Martin for having introduced the Responsibility to Protect doctrine 'that provides us with the mandate' in Libya (Canada, Parliament of 2011a: 17h40). Larry Bagnell (Lib: Yukon) also praised Martin and applauded the Security Council for acting under R2P: 'It was a great move by the United Nations, but it had to be put into practice. I applaud the members of the Security Council who let this go through. It is a beginning for the world' (Canada, Parliament of 2011a: 18h25). The most extended discussion of R2P among Liberal MPs was contributed by Irwin Cotler (Lib: Mount Royal), the party's human rights critic, who delivered a long speech devoted to the nature of the Responsibility to Protect doctrine, and the path-breaking nature of UN Security Council Resolutions 1970 and 1973. He concluded that 'The situation in Libya is a test case of our commitment to the R to P doctrine and of our responsibility to protect the Libyan people' (Canada, Parliament of 2011a: 19h25).

MPs from the other opposition parties also invoked R2P. Claude Bachand (BQ: Saint-Jean), the party's national defence critic, cited R2P as a 'relatively new' development in international law that underwrote the military intervention in Libya: unlike in Bosnia, 'I think that, this time, the responsibility to protect was really taken into consideration and we intervened quickly' (Canada, Parliament of 2011a: 17h55). For its part, the New Democratic Party embraced the Libyan mission because of R2P. Jack Harris (NDP: St John's East), the party's national defence critic, noted that 'the responsibility to protect is what we are talking about. It is not exactly a doctrine but more of a norm that has found its way, through the assistance of Canada, into international law.

However, it only becomes part of international law when it is used and we have seen a remarkable coming together by the Security Council with unanimous resolution 1970, which is part of the process' (Canada, Parliament of 2011a: 18h50).

This pattern repeated itself in both the June and September debates: the justifications offered by the Conservatives did not mention R2P, while all of the opposition parties grounded their position on Canada's role in the intervention on R2P. In the June debate, R2P was invoked by the NDP, now the official opposition, with three MPs mentioning it specifically. The defence critic, Jack Harris (NDP: St John's East), reprised his March arguments about R2P. The critic for international cooperation, Hélène Laverdière (NDP: Laurier–Sainte-Marie), a former foreign service officer, noted that R2P was 'particularly dear to my heart since I was able to help promote it in a former life' and argued that UNSCR 1973 was 'a good example' of the responsibility to protect doctrine (Canada, Parliament of 2011b: 12h05). Joe Comartin (NDP: Windsor–Tecumseh) also noted that R2P is a debate about 'when does the international community have a responsibility to step in and to say to a sovereign nation, because obviously the regime in Libya is at this point, that it does not have a right to put down peaceful protest, democratic rights of assembly or freedom of speech with the use of violence' (Canada, Parliament of 2011b: 17h30).

In the June debate, all the minor parties raised R2P in their justifications for their positions. Three Liberals – John McKay (Lib: Scarborough–Guildwood), Scott Simms (Lib: Bonavista–Gander–Grand Falls–Windsor) and Francis Scarpaleggia (Lib: Lac-Saint-Louis) – argued that the mission was a case of R2P, though Bob Rae (Lib: Toronto Centre), who had assumed the leadership of the Liberal Party following Ignatieff's defeat in the May election, did not raise R2P in the June debate (Canada, Parliament of 2011b: 11h20). Jean-François Fortin (BQ: Haute-Gaspésie–La Mitis–Matane–Matapédia), the Bloc's foreign affairs and defence critic, also based his party's support for a continuation of the mission on R2P (Canada, Parliament of 2011b: 17h00).

Even the lone MP who voted against the continuation of the mission invoked R2P as the reason for her vote. Elizabeth May (GP: Saanich–Gulf Islands) argued that the mission was properly an exercise in R2P, but had suffered from 'mission creep', changing from protection to regime change. Thus, she said, had she been in the House in March, she would have voted in favour of the use of force by Canada; but given the change from R2P, she would have to vote no (Canada, Parliament of 2011b: 17h15).

May's objection in June was actually embraced by the NDP in the September debate. R2P was one of the reasons that the NDP voted against the extension being sought by the Harper government. As the party's defence critic, Jack Harris (NDP: St John's East), put it,

> We have grave concerns that this be done right and that in the future the responsibility to protect ought not to be used as a cover for regime change or other interventions. This is a very careful issue that I am sure will be debated by international legal experts for some time to come. However, I do not want to get into that too much as a justification for our position. [The main justification was that] 'Canada has done more than its share militarily and should now refocus its efforts on the other aspects of rebuilding of Libya. (Canada, Parliament, 2011c, 11h45)

This justification for the shift in the NDP position brought a withering attack from Bob Rae. Calling the NDP position 'preposterous' and 'absurd', Rae argued that the 'great revolution in international law' that R2P represented required an intensification of engagement, not a withdrawal (Canada, Parliament of 2011c: 12h10). Later in the debate, Irwin Cotler (Lib: Mont Royal) weighed in with a spirited defence of R2P as an integral part of the mission in Libya (Canada, Parliament of 2011c: 16h55–17h25).

Despite the centrality of R2P in the justificatory rhetoric of all the opposition parties in Canada, MPs on the government side never once in any of the three debates took the opportunity to correct the mistaken view that UNSCR 1973 was taken under the Responsibility to Protect doctrine. Neither of the foreign affairs ministers during this period, Lawrence Cannon nor John Baird, nor the minister of national defence, Peter MacKay, either mentioned R2P or engaged any speaker on this issue. And when Conservative MPs were asked directly about R2P, they simply dodged the issue. For example, Jean-Pierre Blackburn, the minister of veterans affairs, was asked by Borys Wrzesnewskyj (Lib: Etobicoke Centre) during the March debate whether Canada had 'done the right thing and invoked the responsibility to protect in this circumstance'. Blackburn's reply was simply that 'In voting for resolution 1973, the members of the United Nations assumed their responsibilities' (Canada, Parliament of 2011a: 17h45). Likewise, when Laurie Hawn, the parliamentary secretary to the minister of national defence, was asked by a Conservative back-bencher, James Lunney (CPC: Nanaimo–Alberni) to comment on R2P, Hawn appeared dismissive: '"responsibility to protect" are easy words. As I said in my remarks, we can talk about supporting freedom or we can act to support freedom. That is what we are doing along with our allies' (Canada, Parliament of 2011a: 18h10).

A good example of the degree to which those on the government side sought to avoid mentioning R2P is to be found in the appearance of Chris Alexander (CPC: Ajax–Pickering), the parliamentary secretary to the minister of national defence, at a symposium at the University of Ottawa on 4 November commemorating the tenth anniversary of the publication of the Responsibility to Protect. Appearing with Kofi Annan, the former Secretary-General of the United Nations, and Lloyd Axworthy, Alexander spent 100 minutes avoiding mentioning R2P, on occasion referring to 'this policy, this doctrine' (CIPS 2011: 1:15:26) rather than sounding it out. On only two occasions did R2P escape his lips: once in a response in French (1:16:51), and once in a reference to other doctrines that were developed at the same time as R2P (1:17:44). And when he was asked explicitly whether the Harper government was committed to R2P, he began by responding 'We are', but the rest of the sentence suggested an imaginative reinterpretation of what R2P involves (cf. Murray 2011): 'We are, but I think the way we put it these days is that we are recommitting ourselves to the fundamental values that brought about the existence of the United Nations, to human rights, to the Universal Declaration [of Human Rights], to that view of the world with the human being at the centre . . .' (1:34:30).

The fact that the Conservative government did not mention R2P in its justificatory rhetoric did not go unnoticed. In the March debate, for example, Mario Silva (Lib: Davenport) claimed that R2P was 'an important doctrine that has been recognized and used internationally by all governments. I have to say one thing. I try not to be partisan, but I am saddened by the fact that the government has refused to use the words "responsibility to protect" and the importance of that doctrine. The doctrine is something of which all Canadians can be very proud' (Canada, Parliament of 2011a: 18h30). Bob Rae acknowledged in the September debate that 'the government opposite is reluctant to talk about the responsibility to protect', and noted that the Liberals wanted to put the language of R2P into the parliamentary resolution (Canada, Parliament of 2011c: 12h10).

Explaining the Canadian debate

Two questions emerge from this portrait of the differences in justificatory discourse observed in the Canadian case. First, why were the opposition parties so keen, and the Conservative government so reluctant, to use the language of R2P? Second, why did Conservative MPs – ministers, parliamentary secretaries and ordinary backbenchers – so consistently refuse to take issue with the opposition's use of the language of R2P?

The enthusiasm for the language of R2P among the opposition parties likely stemmed from several sources. For all of the opposition parties, the R2P doctrine – at least as it was popularized – offered an attractive doctrinal alternative to the rhetoric of national interest and the muscular military policy favoured by the Harper Conservatives, and permitted self-declared 'parties of peace' to justify the use of military force for 'doing good'. Moreover, the normatively 'good' goals of R2P and the legitimacy of Security Council authorization fitted more closely the self-perception of these parties that Canada's proper role in the international system was as an internationalist, multilateral-minded peacekeeper and norm entrepreneur.

In the case of the Liberal party, there were two further attractions. The R2P doctrine provided a convenient way to overcome the deep divisions within the parliamentary caucus between the foreign policy 'realists' and the 'romantics' (for a discussion, see Gotlieb 2005). While these divisions had been evident over the course of the 1990s, they had flowered dramatically with the end of Liberal rule in 2006, and had seen the party badly split over the Afghanistan mission under the leadership of Stéphane Dion, and to a lesser extent Michael Ignatieff after Dion's ouster as leader in December 2008. R2P could be (and was) embraced by both realists and romantics in the party. In addition, Liberals could (and did) celebrate the fact that the R2P doctrine had been developed under the leadership of Lloyd Axworthy during the Liberal government of Jean Chrétien and embraced by the United Nations during the prime ministership of Paul Martin (even if many Liberals who celebrated the 2005 General Assembly decision appeared to believe that the version of R2P was the relatively robust version articulated by the International Commission on Intervention and State Sovereignty, not the watered-down version that appears in the 2005 World Summit Outcomes document).

The widespread invocation of the R2P doctrine by the opposition parties may also have been encouraged by the frequency with which op-eds by R2P celebrationists appeared in the press throughout the year. For example, Lloyd Axworthy joined with Alan Rock, a cabinet colleague during the 1990s and Canada's permanent representative to the United Nations during the 2005 World Summit, to write op-eds on R2P and the Libyan mission (Axworthy and Rock 2011a; 2011b). Likewise, Ramesh

Thakur, one of the members of the Commission on Intervention and State Sovereignty and a principal author of *The Responsibility to Protect*, contributed op-ed pieces to the *Toronto Star*, including one that claimed that the United Nations resolutions on Libya had 'breathed life' into R2P (Thakur 2011a; 2011b). Irwin Cotler, a Liberal MP and the party's human rights critic, also published in *The New York Times* (Cotler and Genser 2011). Roméo A. Dallaire, who had been the commander of the UN forces in Rwanda during the 1994 genocide, pressed his views about the importance of R2P in both English (Dallaire and Bernstein 2011) and French (Dallaire et al. 2011).

Why were Conservatives so hesitant to use the language of R2P? Some have suggested that the Harper government chose not to use the phrase in this context because of the sustained effort of the Conservatives to refuse to use foreign policy concepts that reminded voters of the Liberal era. That certainly was the view of Mario Silva (Lib: Davenport), who complained that the Conservatives were not using the language of R2P. The responsibility to protect 'is not a Liberal thing,' he argued. 'It is an international document in which Canada played a very important role, but we should not be afraid to use the language "responsibility to protect" and state the fact that this is very important international jurisprudence at the moment, in which Canada played a very important role' (Canada, Parliament of 2011a: 18h30). Lloyd Axworthy, during whose tenure as Canada's foreign minister R2P was developed, noted that while 'the name's not being used, the spirit is being applied' (Smith 2011). Jill Siskind, the president of Canadian Lawyers for International Human Rights, noted that the Conservatives were purposely avoiding language like R2P that was associated with the Liberals. According to Siskind (2011), it was this 'irresponsible partisanship' that explained the Harper government's refusal to use the language of R2P during the Libyan mission, 'muddying' what she claimed should be a 'point of pride' for Canada.

To what extent can we conclude that this is the explanation for the pattern of the Canadian government's justificatory rhetoric on Libya? On the one hand, there is clear evidence of orders from the ministers in Ottawa that certain language was not to be used in foreign policy discourse: in 2009 *Embassy Magazine* reported that among the 'forbidden phrases' were human security, public diplomacy, good governance and the responsibility to protect; 'preferred alternatives' were, apparently, human rights, the rule of law, democracy and democratic development (Davis 2009). And it is true that we can point to Peter MacKay's speech in September 2011 welcoming home HMCS *Charlottetown* from service in the Mediterranean, using precisely those 'preferred alternatives'. MacKay framed the Libyan mission as 'a visible and tangible demonstration of how military members continue to fight for the ideals Canadians hold dear: freedom, democracy, human rights and the rule of law' (MacKay 2011b).

Likewise, there can be no doubt that since coming to office in February 2006, the Harper government worked hard to distance itself from some of the main traditions in Canadian foreign policy that it associated with Liberal governments. We can see this most clearly in the Harper government's approach to the kind of liberal internationalism represented by R2P (Nossal 2012). Moreover, it is indeed unlikely, given the degree to which the Conservatives have used every foreign policy dossier, both major and minor, in an unabashed way for partisan electoral purposes, that the Harper government would have reached for a internationalist doctrine championed by its Liberal predecessors.

On the other hand, it is highly unlikely that in this case the Conservative government's well-established penchant for hyper-partisanship explains the refusal of Harper and his ministers to frame the Libyan intervention as an exercise in R2P. First, the ban on the mention of R2P was in fact lifted in 2009 by the minister of foreign affairs, Lawrence Cannon, in order to boost Canada's campaign to secure election to the Security Council (Davis 2009).

Second, and more importantly, there is a much more plausible explanation for the kind of justificatory rhetoric employed by the Canadian government in this case. If one compares the rhetoric of the other leading members of the Libyan intervention, one will see immediately that the rhetoric from Ottawa was *precisely* the rhetoric employed by Barack Obama, president of the United States; Nicolas Sarkozy, president of France; and David Cameron, prime minister of Britain. None of these leaders mentioned R2P in their public statements; all of these leaders stressed the protection of civilians, the murderous behaviour of the Gaddafi regime, and the responsibility to intervene to protect civilians (Obama 2011; Cameron 2011; Cameron and Sarkozy 2011; Sarkozy 2011). It is highly unlikely that the Harper government would have departed from what was a common script among the Western countries at the forefront of the intervention, a script that was designed in large part to avoid using the language of R2P precisely because of the concerns that the idea of R2P, especially in its robust form, had aroused in other countries, principally but not exclusively the Russian Federation and the People's Republic of China (Jones 2011: 53–7), that R2P could be used as a cover for legitimized military intervention to achieve regime change.

If the Conservative government had a powerful incentive to keep its language commensurate with what Gareth Evans, Australia's foreign minister from 1988 to 1996 and a member of the International Commission on Intervention and State Sovereignty, called the 'pinpoint accuracy' of the two Security Council resolutions (Evans 2011), why did Conservative speakers not move to correct or comment on the use of the language of R2P by opposition MPs? The answer is straightforward: in March, all of the opposition parties were in agreement with government policy on Libya; in June, after the election and the achievement of a majority, just one MP was opposed. Given this, there was no percentage for the Conservatives in raising any red flags that might have disrupted the near unanimity. The attitude seemed to be: 'Let the opposition claim that this is R2P if they wish; however, in everything that we say, we will use the agreed-upon coalition script that studiously avoids mention of R2P.'

Conclusion

While the Harper government's willingness to let erroneous claims about R2P slide can be readily understood from a short-term political perspective, it can be argued that there are longer-term implications of allowing the inaccurate portrayal of Libya as an R2P operation to persist. To the extent that others in the international system were paying attention to the terms of the Canadian debate over Libya, it is possible that Canadian discussions about their country's role in the armed intervention in Libya in 2011 contributed to the broader global view that the Libyan operation was indeed associated with R2P. And this, in turn, would surely have contributed to the increasing marginalization of R2P as a normative idea.

For one of the key ironies of Operation UNIFIED PROTECTOR is that the very success of the mission actually increased global opposition to the doctrine of R2P. In particular, those in the international system who had expressed most concern about the implications of R2P when the doctrine was first articulated – notably the Russian Federation and the People's Republic of China – had allowed UNSCR 1973 to pass in 2011 by abstaining on the vote, and then watched as the NATO-led mission engaged in what Jennifer Welsh has appropriately described as a 'creep towards partiality' (2011: 259) and produced the end that Russia and China were most concerned about: regime change. However, once bitten, twice shy: if R2P celebrationists used to use the slogan 'never again' to underscore the intent of the R2P doctrine to prevent the kind of mass atrocities that were so much a mark of the 1990s, it is likely that diplomatists in Moscow and Beijing – and many other capitals besides – will invoke that slogan before doing what they did in March 2011.

Note

1. The 18 governments were: Belgium (naval, air), Bulgaria (naval), Canada (naval, air), Denmark (air), France (naval, air), Greece (naval, air), Italy (naval, air), Jordan (air), Netherlands (naval, air), Norway (air), Qatar (air), Romania (naval), Spain (naval, air), Sweden (air), Turkey (naval), United Arab Emirates (air), United Kingdom (naval, air), United States (naval, air). In addition, beginning in March and April, the United States and the United Kingdom deployed intelligence operatives, military advisers and special forces into Libya.

References

Alberts, S. and M. Kennedy (2011) 'Canada Will Pursue Sanctions against Libya: Harper', *Postmedia News*, 26 February. Available online at: www.canada.com/news/Canada+will+pursue+sanctions+against+Libya+Harper/4349026/story.html

Axworthy, L. and A. Rock (2011a) 'World Leaders Must Call R2P What It Is', *Ottawa Citizen*, 2 March.

Axworthy, L. and A. Rock (2011b) 'A Victory for the Responsibility to Protect', *Ottawa Citizen*, 25 October.

Bellamy, A. J. (2011) 'Libya and the Responsibility to Protect: The Exception and the Norm', *Ethics & International Affairs*, vol. 25, no. 3, pp. 263–9.

Bellamy, A. J. and P. D. Williams (2011) 'The New Politics of Protection? Côte d'Ivoire, Libya and the Responsibility to Protect', *International Affairs*, vol. 82, no. 4, pp. 825–50.

Cameron, D. (2011) 'Prime Minister Statement on the UN Security Council Resolution on Libya', 18 March. Available online at: www.fco.gov.uk/en/news/latest-news/?id=568620282&view=PressS

Cameron, D. and N. Sarkozy (2011) 'Joint Statement by the PM and President Sarkozy', 28 March. Available online at: www.number10.gov.uk/news/joint-statement-on-libya-by-the-pm-and-president-sarkozy/ and www.archives.elysee.fr/president/les-actualites/declarations/2011/declaration-de-mm-nicolas-sarkozy-et-david.10987.html

Canada, National Defence (2011) 'Operation MOBILE'. Available online at: www.cefcom-comfec.forces.gc.ca/pa-ap/ops/mobile/index-eng.asp

Canada, Parliament of (2011a) *House of Commons Debates*, 3rd Session, 40th Parliament, edited Hansard, 145:145, 21 March. Available online at: www.parl.gc.ca/HousePublications/Publication.aspx?Language=E&Mode=1&Parl=40&Ses=3&DocId=5039495

Canada, Parliament of (2011b) *House of Commons Debates*, 1st Session, 41st Parliament, edited Hansard, 146:008, 14 June. Available online at: www.parl.

gc.ca/HousePublications/Publication.aspx?Language=E&Mode=1&Parl=41&Ses=1&DocId=5089492

Canada, Parliament of (2011c) *House of Commons Debates*, 1st Session, 41st Parliament, edited Hansard, 146:020, 26 September. Available online at: www.parl.gc.ca/HousePublications/Publication.aspx?Language=E&Mode=1&Parl=41&Ses=1&DocId=5132736

CIPS (2011) 'The Responsibility to Protect 10 Years On: Reflections on Its Past, Present and Future', panel discussion, Centre for International Policy Studies, University of Ottawa. Available online at: http://cips.uottawa.ca/event/the-responsibility-to-protect-10-years-on-reflections-on-its-past-present-and-future-2/

Clark, C. (2011) 'Canada Prepared to Impose Its Own Sanctions against Libya, PM Says', *The Globe and Mail*, 26 February, p. A12.

Cotler, I. and J. Genser (2011) 'Libya and the Responsibility to Protect', *The New York Times*, 28 February.

Dallaire, R. A. and J. Bernstein (2011) 'Does the World Belong in Libya's War? Yes. Now Let's Hope It's Not Too Late', *Foreign Policy*, 18 March. Available online at: www.foreignpolicy.com/articles/2011/03/18/does_the_world_belong_in_libyas_war?

Dallaire, R. A., F. Chalk and K. Matthews (2011) 'Responsabilité de protéger: 10 ans plus tard, tout reste à faire', *La Presse*, 23 October. Available online at: www.lapresse.ca/debats/votre-opinion/201110/21/01-4459662-responsabilite-de-proteger-10-ans-plus-tard-tout-reste-a-faire.php

Davis, J. (2009) 'Liberal-era Diplomatic Language Killed Off', *Embassy Magazine*, 1 July. Available online at: http://embassymag.ca/page/printpage/diplomatic_language-7-1-2009

Davis, J. and L. Berthiaume (2012) 'Canada Spent $25m Bombing Gadhafi Forces', *Postmedia News*, 18 April. Available online at: www.canada.com/Canada+spent+bombing+Gadhafi+forces/6480634/story.html

Dunne, T. and J. Gifkins (2011) 'Libya and R2P: Norm Consolidation or a Perfect Storm?', openDemocracy, 19 April. Available online at: www.opendemocracy.net/tim-dunne-jess-gifkins/libya-and-r2p-norm-consolidation-or-perfect-storm

Evans, G. (2011) 'UN Targets Libya with Pinpoint Accuracy', *Sydney Morning Herald*, 24 March. Available online at: www.smh.com.au/opinion/politics/un-targets-libya-with-pinpoint-accuracy-20110323-1c6pc.html

Fitzpatrick, M. (2011) 'Harper Heads to Paris Meeting on Libya', cbcnews.ca, 18 March. Available online at: www.cbc.ca/news/world/story/2011/03/18/pol-harper-libya.html

Ford Rojas, J. P. (2011) 'Muammar Gaddafi in His Own Words', 20 October. Available online at: www.telegraph.co.uk/news/worldnews/africaandindianocean/libya/8838644/Muammar-Gaddafi-in-his-own-words.html

Gotlieb, A. E. (2005) 'Romanticism and Realism in Canadian Foreign Policy', *Policy Options* (February), pp. 16–27.

Harper, S. (2011a) 'Statement by the Prime Minister of Canada on Recent Developments in Libya', Ottawa, 21 February. Available online at: www.pm.gc.ca/eng/media.asp?category=3&featureId=6&pageId=49&id=3980

Harper, S. (2011b) 'Statement by the Prime Minister of Canada on the Current Situation in Libya', Ottawa, 25 February. Available online at: www.pm.gc.ca/eng/media.asp?category=3&featureId=6&pageId=49&id=3990

Harper, S. (2011c) 'PM Thanks Members of the Canadian Armed Forces for Their Efforts to Protect Civilians in Libya', Trapani, Italy, 1 September. Available online at: www.pm.gc.ca/eng/media.asp?category=2&pageId=46&id=4322

Harper, S. (2011d) 'PM Pays Tribute to Troops who Served in Libya', Ottawa, 24 November. Available online at: www.pm.gc.ca/eng/media.asp?category=2&pageId=46&id=4507

Hehir, A. (2012) 'Syria and the Responsibility to Protect: Rhetoric Meets Reality', *e-International Relations,* 14 March. Available online at: www.e-ir.info/2012/03/14/syria-and-the-responsibility-to-protect-rhetoric-meets-reality

ICISS (2001) *The Responsibility to Protect: Report of the International Commission on Intervention and State Sovereignty* (Ottawa: International Development Research Council).

Jones, B. D. (2011) 'Libya and the Responsibilities of Power', *Survival,* vol. 53, no. 3, pp. 51–60.

MacKay, P. (2011a) 'Where We Are, Where We're Going', speech to the Conference of Defence Associations, Ottawa, 25 February. Available online at: www.forces.gc.ca/site/news-nouvelles/news-nouvelles-eng.asp?id=3816

MacKay, P. (2011b) 'Return of HMCS Charlottetown', Halifax, 2 September. Available online at: www.forces.gc.ca/site/news-nouvelles/news-nouvelles-eng.asp?id=3942

MacKay, P. (2011c) 'Return of Personnel from Op Mobile', Greenwood, NS, 4 November. Available online at: www.forces.gc.ca/site/news-nouvelles/news-nouvelles-eng.asp?id=4042

Murray, R. W. (2011) 'Libya Mission was Intervention, not R2P', *Embassy Magazine,* 16 November. Available online at: http://embassymag.ca/page/view/notr2p-11-16-2011

Nossal, K. R., S. Roussel and S. Paquin (2011) *International Policy and Politics in Canada* (Toronto: Pearson Education Canada).

Nossal, K. R. (2012) 'The Liberal Past in the Conservative Present: Internationalism in the Harper Era', in C. Turenne Sjolander and H. Smith (eds), *Canada in the World: Perspectives on Canadian Foreign Policy* (Toronto: Oxford University Press).

Obama, B. (2011) 'Remarks by the President in Address to the Nation on Libya', Washington, DC, 28 March. Available online at: www.whitehouse.gov/the-press-office/2011/03/28/remarks-president-address-nation-libya

Payton, L. (2011) 'Libya Mission Will Include Canada until End, PM Vows', *CBCNews.ca,* 1 September. Available online at: www.cbc.ca/news/politics/story/2011/09/01/pol-harper-libya-future.html

Piggot, P. (2011) 'Task Force Libeccio: Answering the Call', *FrontLine Defence,* vol. 8, no. 6, pp. 30–1. Available online at: www.frontline-global.com/downloads/Libeccio.pdf

Sarkozy, N. (2011) 'Nicolas Sarkozy Speech on No-fly Zone in Libya' [20 March]. Available online at: www.youtube.com/watch?v=QVMCe2SA6GM

Siskind, J. (2011) 'Canada and the Responsibility to Protect', *The Mark,* 19 October. Available online at: www.themarknews.com/articles/7072-canada-and-the-responsibility-to-protect

Smith, G. (2011) 'Explainer: What is Libya's "Responsibility to Protect" Its Citizens?', *The Globe and Mail,* 18 March.

Thakur, R. (2011a) 'We Have a Duty to Stop Libyan Slaughter', *Toronto Star*, 28 February. Available online at: www.thestar.com/opinion/editorialopinion/article/946306--we-have-a-duty-to-stop-libyan-slaughter

Thakur, R. (2011b) 'UN Breathes Life into "Responsibility to Protect"', *Toronto Star*, 21 March. Available online at: www.thestar.com/opinion/editorialopinion/article/957664--un-breathes-life-into-responsibility-to-protect

Thakur, R. (2011c) 'Has R2P Worked in Libya?' *Canberra Times*, 18 September. Available online at: www.canberratimes.com.au/opinion/editorial/has-r2p-worked-in-libya-20110918-1wqqb.html#ixzz1xIAlrLqd

Weiss, T. G. (2011) 'RtoP Alive and Well after Libya', *Ethics & International Affairs*, vol. 25, no. 3, pp. 287–92.

Welsh, J. (2011) 'Civilian Protection in Libya: Putting Coercion and Controversy Back into RtoP', *Ethics & International Affairs*, vol. 25, no. 3, pp. 255–62.

United Nations (2005) A/RES/60/1, 2005 World Summit Outcome Document, General Assembly. Available online at: http://daccess-dds-ny.un.org/doc/UNDOC/GEN/N05/487/60/PDF/N0548760.pdf

United Nations (2011a) S/RES/1970, 26 February. Available online at: http://daccess-dds-ny.un.org/doc/UNDOC/GEN/N11/245/58/PDF/N1124558.pdf

United Nations (2011b) S/RES/1973, 17 March. Available online at: http://daccess-dds-ny.un.org/doc/UNDOC/GEN/N11/268/39/PDF/N1126839.pdf

7

The (D)evolution of a Norm: R2P, the Bosnia Generation and Humanitarian Intervention in Libya[1]

Eric A. Heinze and Brent J. Steele

The March 2011 NATO intervention in Libya has been widely touted as evidence of a new international norm that has come about as a result of advocacy of the Responsibility to Protect (R2P) principle (Ban 2011; Gerber, 2011; Adams, 2011). Likewise, the Libya intervention has been characterized as an 'unprecedented moment' that is indicative of a new commitment and consensus by states that they have an obligation – indeed, a responsibility – to protect people who are being grossly abused by their own government (Williams 2011: 249). In contrast to the position that the Libya intervention is somehow groundbreaking or indicates the emergence of a new norm of humanitarian intervention that has been empowered by R2P advocacy, we argue that what enabled the Libya intervention is essentially an international normative environment that was brought about by precedents set during humanitarian interventions in the 1990s, while its proximate causes were the unique political and empirical circumstances that surrounded the Libya crisis. What supplemented this similarity in normative environments and confluence of political factors was a generation of policy analysts, advocates and practitioners who used the failures of the 1990s as a set of formative experiences that provided shortcut comparisons to springboard the Libya intervention. In other words, the Libya intervention does not indicate a departure from how humanitarian intervention was viewed and undertaken in the 1990s. We argue that this stems from practitioners interpreting the current international environment through the lens of their experiences during the broader practice and discourse of humanitarian intervention starting in the 1990s, attempting to address the wrongs of the past with what they consider to be a 'new approach' to human protection via R2P. Yet to the extent that

R2P has been a prominent feature of discussions about the Libya intervention, the conception of R2P embraced *by states* at the 2005 World Summit is actually a *reflection* of the norm of humanitarian intervention as it emerged from the 1990s – that is, as a permissive norm that allows states to undertake such interventions in response to gross human suffering, but at their own convenience, resulting in the continued selective, inconsistent and erratic practice of humanitarian intervention that persists today as it did in the 1990s.

This is not to downplay the fact that the Libya intervention was highly unexpected, nor is it to cast doubt on the moral desirability or strategic advisability of the decision to resort to force in this case. Indeed, coming off the heels of the 2000s, it is understandable how one might come to view this intervention as a significant step forward. That is, the 2000s were defined by the 9/11 terrorist attacks, fighting terror in Afghanistan, an unpopular war in Iraq with an unconvincing humanitarian pretext, and an extremely lethargic international response to what some called genocide in Darfur. Yet also in this decade we see an impressive amount of advocacy of the R2P principle and the emergence of a dense transnational network seeking to promote it as a new norm, resulting in the UN General Assembly endorsing *a version* of R2P at its 2005 World Summit. The coinciding of these events during the previous decade, and then the surprising and (to some) welcome actions of the United Nations Security Council in March of 2011 would make Libya seem even more so a revolutionary development.

What this story misses, however, are two factors. First, the international consensus about humanitarian intervention has not significantly changed during this time, while R2P, as endorsed by states in 2005, is a *reflection* of this consensus, not an evolution of it. What has changed and varied during these years, and thus led to the varied practice of humanitarian intervention, are the unique political circumstances surrounding each of these crises, leading to intervention in some instances but not others. In sum, the permissive normative environment for humanitarian intervention has been present since the 1990s. What is not always present are the circumstances that render such interventions politically feasible, which is why we see intervention in Somalia but not Rwanda, Kosovo but not Darfur, and Libya but not Syria. Second, and reinforcing this selectivity, is that interventions are contingent upon the perception of policy elites who interpret particular situations through generational paradigms. These paradigms shape the perception of the feasibility, and purpose, of an intervention. R2P is reflective of, rather than enabling, those paradigms. Yet far from seeing a progressive and linear logic whereby a 'norm' becomes internalized once and for all in the international community, different formative experiences lead to generational cycles, which help facilitate an ebb and flow to normative environments, including in this case the environment which promotes a 'responsibility to protect'. Put another way, different generations of policy elites will interpret a norm in different ways, again owing to their generation's own formative experiences.

This chapter proceeds in four sections. We first summarize the analytical framework we will utilize in this chapter – that of generational analysis – and address the key components assumed by the literature on generational paradigms, formative experiences and their influence on policy. We also identify here a group of policy elites who we call the 'Bosnia generation' – a term borrowed from George Packer – whose support for the Libya intervention can be traced to their formative experiences in previous decades (Packer 2002). We then examine these key periods and events that contributed to the development of the present norm of humanitarian intervention, paying particular attention to the roles and views of the 'generation' of policy elites who later supported and pushed for intervention in Libya. The second section provides a brief overview of the humanitarian interventions of the 1990s that culminated in the 1999 Kosovo intervention, wherein we argue that the loose consensus after Kosovo was that humanitarian intervention was a permissive, but not obligatory, norm – though one that requires the assent of the UN Security Council. We argue that the inconsistent practice of humanitarian intervention in the 1990s, as well as the perceived 'failures' of certain interventions, not only led to the initial effort to re-conceptualize humanitarian intervention into the broader R2P principle, but also heavily influenced the generation of elites that would later support the Libya intervention. Section three examines the international political realities that prevailed in the 2000s, which were scarcely conducive to humanitarian intervention, thus resulting in the recalcitrant international response to Darfur and the marginalization of those advocating a more forceful response. We argue that when states endorsed R2P at the 2005 World Summit, they effectively reiterated the same permissive norm that emerged in the 1990s. R2P served at most to streamline the interpretive (and discursive) process regarding intervention, but it did not present the bold transformation often assigned to it by advocates. Finally, we examine the Libya intervention in the context of these events, including the particular policy elites who pushed for it. We conclude that the intervention in Libya is not a result of a revolutionary new norm embodied in R2P, but rather a group of vocal policy elites who chose to utilize the 'permission' that the humanitarian intervention norm gave them to undertake/support it, which was informed by their collective experiences of failed interventions during the 1990s and 2000s and further supported by realities specific to the Libya case.

A generational take on the post-Cold War era

Part of the argument we pursue is that to understand some of the more recent global crises and the responses of the international community to those, we might examine the role of different generations of policymakers. There is, of course, much to be sceptical of regarding the notion of a generation. Age is a continuous variable, and individuals are born every second, rather than in 'chunks' of decades. As one recent study puts it: 'people are born continually, and boxing them together is a deliberate analytical exercise at best, or a sweeping reification at worst' (Herborth 2012: 72). Thus, the referent of a generation is in many ways a social construct, grafted into a population in seemingly arbitrary ways. Yet generational analysis is not focused on age per se – as individuals we indeed have an age that indexes the life 'stages' that formulate our social maturation process. What makes generational analysis possible is the cohort – and what brings a 'cohort' into existence is a set of collective 'coming of age' experiences which become cultural and political life lessons, internalized and drawn upon to formulate particular worldviews (Strauss and Howe 1991; Winograd and Hais 2008).

But generations do not just formulate these views vis-à-vis those experiences – they blame the previous generation, its outdated and intransigent ways of thinking, for the policy blunders which make possible the formative, and even collectively traumatic, experiences. The process, however, is not only demographic and emotional, it is also *intellectual*. Using Thomas Kuhn's framework on the rise and fall of scientific paradigms, Michael Roskin added the concept of a generation to understand the interventionist and non-interventionist 'swings' in US foreign policy over time. Roskin's basic argument was that 'each elite American generation comes to favor one of these orientations by living through the catastrophe brought on by the application *ad absurdum* of the opposite paradigm at the hands of the previous elite generation' (Roskin 1974: 563). Again, generations not only differ on worldviews, they add a causal story – *that* generation's way of thinking produced *this* catastrophe (Steele 2012: 39–40).

Roskin's important provision that 'because neither [of two competing paradigms] can be objectively verified in an indeterminate world [a] new foreign policy paradigm is merely *internalized*' (Roskin 1974: 566) means that the 'world out there' is hardly uniform, and in fact is subject to a variety of interpretations as it is dependent upon being filtered through a generation's lens. More than that, events going on 'now' have to be experienced through past, recalled events (again, configured in a particular way). Coupled with the work by Khong on the way in which historical analogies are appropriated (or misappropriated) to help simplify complex current foreign policy crises, this means that policy elites – and even political communities – are 'reliving' the past in the present as a basis for action (Khong 1992).

Who are we speaking about when it comes to 'a generation'? This is a methodological question as much as it is a question of ontology or substance. Although recent work has attempted to analyse the working of a generation in a more relational sense, mining the agent-structure problem for insights into how a generational cohort 'interacts' within the 'structure' of the nation-state (or in a transnational context more broadly; see Steele and Acuff 2012), the simpler and more ontologically and methodologically defensible strategy is to examine different national or transnational cohorts of generational *elites*, considering their smaller numbers but also greater access to institutional levers of power. Because worldviews are not only personal, but social, *elites* include not only policymakers but journalists, intellectuals and even academics. Information, perception and interpretation *circulates* across different fields of the generation. Nevertheless, in terms of how a worldview gets 'enacted', one must focus on the elites with the greatest access to institutions of power. This is the strategy used by Roskin, and in more recent studies by Youde and Acuff (see Youde 2012), and it is the one we use in this chapter as well.

This levels-of-analysis quandary touches upon some of the broader limitations, qualifiers and drawbacks of generational analysis, not all of which can be confronted here. Briefly, the main limitation to generational analysis is that it proves hard to say whether generations obtain in all or even most nation-states. Generations seem more evident in certain countries, such as Germany and the US, than in others. But related to this limitation, even if they did obtain in all national contexts, they seem difficult to identify in broader, transnational or global cohorts.[2] Some recent research has attempted to escape this 'methodological nationalism' (Beck and Beck-Gernsheim 2009; Carlson 2012), and based on the possibility, and even likelihood, that some formative events or experiences are *global* rather than only *international* or national in nature, certain transnational groups such as al-Qaeda seem to exhibit generational shifts as well (see Acuff 2011). And, even with all the credit given to social media as a key variable for the Arab Spring, demographic trends in that region of the world – and generational experiences based upon those – may have played just as large a role in those protests and revolutions (see Gelvin 2012).

Thus, following Peter Beinart, we surmise that the 'Bosnia generation', while largely US-based, extended to elites in other national contexts (and includes more than just Bosnia as the catastrophic reference point for those elites).[3] Finally, the qualifiers of the generation are that it is but one variable – a contextual one at that – shaping individuals and small groups in their political orientations. Other factors of identity such as ethnicity, economic and social class, and what Steele calls 'political-tribal' conditions can even counter a generational framework (Steele 2012: 38). Further, generations can and do overlap – even in the small group settings of policymaking individuals from different generational backgrounds all working together to 'create' policy, even if such work is marred by contention.[4]

What does this specifically imply for R2P as a developed *norm* of global politics and how it has affected the discourse and practice of humanitarian intervention? We will thread the argument throughout the following sections, especially when we discuss Libya, but for now several observations can be made regarding the application of the 'generation' to R2P, humanitarian intervention, and world politics over the past two decades (recognizing that the simplicity of these observations will be made more complex throughout the empirical review). First, the crises of especially the early 1990s in Somalia, Rwanda and Bosnia served as a set of formative experiences for generational elites who would play a role in the 2010s regarding the feasibility and normative purpose of humanitarian intervention, specifically in Libya. Often, these experiences could be captured with one key phrase or word – 'Srebrenica', 'Black Hawk Down', 'Rwanda' – which served to encapsulate each 'crisis' case. Successful operations, such as the no-fly zones in Iraq, combined with the 'catastrophes' of Somalia and (for the most part) Bosnia and Rwanda, served as 'data points' extrapolated by these generational elites regarding how to, and how not to, approach such crises in the future. In one article appearing in the run-up to the Iraq War, George Packer titled this group the 'Bosnian liberals' (Packer 2002).[5] Thus, these analogies would serve, in the following decade, as interpretive short-cuts for making sense of a complex world. Second, because of the multi-layered nature of these crises (involving not only states but international organizations like the UN Security Council and collective security institutions like NATO), they were national and internationally formative, and elites considered that resolutions to these crises, should they occur again, would involve a multi-faceted approach, which helps explain the development of R2P.

Third, the lesson regarding the failure to resolve these crises quickly and resolutely was likened both to international legal barriers as well as the *will* of particular nation-states; the latter were operating on an outdated realist perspective on the national interest – 'the cold language of interests', a relic of the Cold War that had dire consequences for the post-Cold War order. Yet, fourth, the 2000s and early 2010s, when this generation was ostensibly marshalling a new norm of *protection* into international society, were marked instead by the same sort of selective application of humanitarian intervention that defined the 1990s. Thus, while one could claim that the Libya intervention serves as the application of R2P and its consolidation as a norm of 21st-century international society, at worst if norms are truly 'identified by regularities of behavior among actors' (Hurrell 2002: 143) R2P does not qualify. At best, Libya suggests that norms are highly contingent upon the ability of generations, and other national and transnational cohorts, enacting them into practice via the recollection of past crises in the present, and the extent to which these past crises offer parallels to the specific realities of present-day crises.

Taken together, then, R2P was not the 'cause' of the 2011 Libyan intervention but rather was the partial effect of a generational transition occurring in a normative environment which was largely *static* (though permissive) throughout the 1990s and 2000s. Not being 'in power' prior to the late 2000s, these generational elites could only stand by and advocate from the sidelines particular foreign policy stance. Put another way, the particular elites who pushed for the intervention – people like Samantha Power, Susan Rice and Ann-Marie Slaughter in the United States, and Edward Llewellyn and Arminka Helic in the United Kingdom – had less access to the corridors of power in the early 2000s. But by the late 2000s and early 2010s this access changed, and they used catastrophes like Rwanda and Srebrenica as negative templates to enact the norm of R2P in Libya. Yet if our analysis is correct, then, the subsequent generations who have experienced and were shaped by the catastrophic policies of the 2000s and 2010s could be much *less* likely to use force for intervention or protective purposes when they come into power in the coming years, thus making R2P a highly contingent, rather than progressive, normative development, at least as it applies to humanitarian intervention.

Humanitarian intervention in the 1990s: the evolution of a norm

While the idea of humanitarian intervention has been around for centuries, and its earliest discussions are often linked to the writings of Hugo Grotius, the scholarly consensus is that humanitarian intervention only emerged as a potentially legitimate exception to the prohibition on the use of force in the immediate aftermath of the Cold War (Sandholtz and Stiles 2009: 270–87; see also Wheeler 2000). While numerous developments during the Cold War provide the normative underpinning for the idea of legitimate humanitarian intervention – such as the proliferation of human rights treaties and discourse – states did not generally view these developments as granting the right of humanitarian intervention. This general state of affairs changed when the Cold War ended. During this period, at least the following instances indicate an increased willingness on the part of states to consider forcible intervention into the internal affairs of other states to halt or avert large-scale human suffering to be permissible when authorized by the UN Security Council: the Nigerian-led ECOWAS intervention in Liberia in 1990, and again in Sierra Leone in 1997, the imposition of no-fly zones in northern Iraq in 1991 to protect the Kurds, the US/UN intervention in Somalia in 1992–3, the enforcement of UN-mandated 'safe areas' in Bosnia by NATO in 1993–5, the belated French-led intervention in Rwanda in 1994, the aborted US intervention in Haiti in 1994, the NATO intervention over Kosovo in 1999, and the Australian intervention in East Timor in 1999–2000 (see Heinze 2013). While space prevents us from a detailed analysis of each of these interventions, several items are worth noting about the collective effect of these interventions on prevailing state attitudes about humanitarian intervention.

First, each of these interventions, except for the Kosovo intervention, was authorized by the UN Security Council as a Chapter VII enforcement operation, while the ECOWAS interventions did not receive prior approval of the Council, it retroactively endorsed both of them (Henderson 2010: 233). Furthermore, regarding the willingness to condemn Iraq's repression of the Kurds in 1991 in Resolution 688, and perhaps more consequentially Resolution 794 pertaining to Somalia in 1992, the Council for the first time authorized coercive intervention for humanitarian purposes in response to an entirely *internal* situation that did not clearly present a threat to *international* peace and security. While this interpretation of the Council's authority to authorize humanitarian intervention occurred several more times during the 1990s, in some of these cases either the Council was much more hesitant to act (Rwanda, Kosovo), or states were reluctant to make full use of the Council's mandate (Bosnia), and those cases where intervention was more decisive and quicker (Haiti, East Timor) coincided with the more parochial interests of regional states.

The reluctance to act in both Rwanda and Bosnia was in no small part a result of the well-known public relations nightmare that resulted from the US involvement in Somalia, whereby the US mission to initially provide military protection for the delivery of humanitarian aid evolved into a mission to apprehend Mogadishu's most notorious warlord, Mohammad Aideed. This mission resulted in the well-known 'Black Hawk Down' incident, which caused the US to withdraw its forces from Somalia and withdraw its support of the UN mission there. As a result, the US in particular became exceedingly casualty-averse, which contributed to the overall reluctance to respond in a timely and decisive manner to imminent atrocities perpetrated in Rwanda and Srebrenica. In the Rwanda case, of course, there was a strong desire to avoid 'another Somalia' – that is, getting involved in a faraway African conflict where US interests are unclear at best. Pushing ahead with an intervention, US officials reasoned, would invite a disaster of the kind witnessed in Somalia a few months earlier ('Hearing . . .' 1994). US policy was therefore informed by the need to temper the unbridled UN ambitions that US officials believed brought about the debacle in Somalia. The national security team of the Clinton administration entrenched this view in the form of Presidential Decision Directive (PDD) 25, which reframed US national security interests into the more conventional realist understanding, which had prevailed for much of the Cold War (see Heinze 2007; Power 2002: 342).

A restrained logic also informed the reluctance to take quicker and more forceful action to prevent the infamous Srebrenica massacre of 1995 in Bosnia. In this case, NATO was to provide air support to UN peacekeepers on the ground in Bosnia protecting civilians inside safe areas from Serb assaults. In addition to NATO's own collective decision-making rules, however, there was a complex arrangement for authorizing airstrikes that required authorization from both UN civilian leadership and NATO authorities. This 'dual key' arrangement required that officials from both organizations agree on airstrikes, while both held veto power over when and where strikes could take place. As a result of this elaborate process, the full force of NATO airpower was stifled, and because no authorization was forthcoming under the dual key arrangement, NATO was unable to act when Serbs overran the safe area of Srebrenica and subsequently executed 7,000 men and boys (Chollet 2005: 8–9, 184–5; Power 2002: 392).

However, the arguably more successful and decisive interventions tended to occur when the international political climate was thought to be favourable for such interventions, or when the intervening state(s) in question had more self-serving reasons for wanting to intervene militarily. In Haiti, for example, it is widely known that Security Council Resolution 940, which authorized the use of force to remove the military junta whose pogroms were causing a refugee crisis, attracted US support precisely to stem the flow of refugees who were fleeing for US shores, while the Russians acquiesced in exchange for support for a Commonwealth of Independent States peacekeeping mission in Georgia, and the Chinese went along in exchange for US support of a World Bank loan (Chesterman 2002: 153–61). Likewise in East Timor, the Australian-led mission there was almost assuredly motivated by a desire to avoid a potential power vacuum on its doorstep and a subsequent refugee crisis on its shores (Wheeler and Dunne 2001; Chesterman 2002: 150).

But perhaps the most debated instance of humanitarian intervention of the 1990s was the Kosovo intervention undertaken by NATO in spring of 1999. In this case, as opposed to waiting until after large-scale crimes against humanity occurred before resorting to force, NATO intervened relatively early in the crisis as Serb forces were massing along the border with Kosovo, presumably preparing to cleanse the territory of Kosovar Albanians. The most striking feature about this intervention is that it went forward without Security Council authorization, as the Russians and Chinese were opposed to intervention and were poised to veto any resolution that authorized it. And while the intervention was widely supported in Western capitals, it was strongly condemned by the G-77 (Hehir 2010: 208). Furthermore, an international commission of experts who were convened to investigate the Kosovo crisis and the NATO intervention concluded that the intervention was technically illegal, but still legitimate (Kosovo Commission 2000: 4). It was illegal for not receiving prior Security Council authorization, but considered legitimate because it was undertaken by a multilateral alliance of liberal democracies as a last resort to rescue the Kosovar Albanians from the 'impending and unfolding humanitarian catastrophe' (ibid.: 163). It has also been suggested that there were few, if any, ulterior motives or particular interests on the part of the NATO states who intervened, while the memoirs of former President Bill Clinton indicate that the profound feelings of guilt he had for failing to act in Rwanda played no small part in his determination to not let it happen again in Kosovo

(Steele 2008: 133; Clinton 2009), while Britain's Labour party pinned much of their support for the Kosovo intervention as a *contrast* to the way in which the Conservatives had 'dithered for three years while Bosnia burned'.[6]

The lesson from these various interventions during the 1990s in terms of an emerging consensus about the legitimacy of humanitarian intervention is thus as follows: first, a variety of what we term the 'Bosnia generation' of policy elites, still emerging during this time, took from the Kosovo intervention the lesson that this limited use of force was feasible to stop abuses,[7] some even invoking it as a model for why the United States was justified four years later in 'going around the UN' (Slaughter 2003).[8] As a corollary, though certainly still controversial, the use of military force for the purpose of halting or averting large-scale and gross human abuse was considered to be legitimate under certain, highly restricted, circumstances. This is indicated, inter alia, by the Security Council's willingness to authorize such interventions in response to humanitarian catastrophes and the willingness of states to (sometimes) carry them out, even in the absence of such authorization, as in Kosovo. Third, while the precise conditions under which such action is permissible were (and are still) debated, the practice of the Council and discourse surrounding these interventions all suggest a vague agreement that only large-scale and severe human abuses are legitimate grounds for intervention, that it be undertaken multilaterally, as a last resort, using proportionate means, and have a reasonable prospect of success (Kosovo Commission 2000: 193–5; see also Danish Institute of International Affairs 1999; Fixdal and Smith 1998). Finally, and importantly, humanitarian intervention emerged as a *permissive* norm, rather than an *obligatory* one, meaning that the Council may at its discretion authorize such interventions, but is under no obligation to do so, as starkly evidenced by the belated or outright lack of such authorizations to prevent massacres in Srebrenica, Rwanda and Kosovo. Thus in practice, the humanitarian interventions of the 1990s were highly selective, very inconsistent, and their occurrence was predicated on a fortuitous convergence of both moral necessity and the more parochial interests of (powerful) states.

The response: R2P

In the debate about humanitarian intervention throughout the 1990s two broad positions emerged: one arguing that humanitarian intervention is an intolerable violation of state sovereignty, and the other advocating the notion of conditional sovereignty, whereby a state's sovereignty is a function of how it treats its citizens (Chopra and Weiss, 1992; Deng et al. 1996). The increased activity of the Council in the 1990s suggested that the emerging trend was in favour of the latter, yet as illustrated above, Council and state responses to humanitarian catastrophes were inconsistent and erratic, leading many observers concerned about human rights to conclude that this emerging consensus among states was highly problematic. As former UN Secretary-General Kofi Annan put it: 'if humanitarian intervention is an unacceptable assault on sovereignty, how should we respond to a Rwanda, to a Srebrenica, to gross and systematic violations of human rights that affect every precept of our common humanity?' (ICISS 2001: vii). *The Responsibility to Protect*, a report published by the ICISS in 2001, was an attempt to address this question.

The history and evolution of R2P is well-known (Evans 2008; Bellamy 2009a), and will not be recounted here in detail, but two points are worth emphasizing: first, R2P was initially created as a response to moral dilemmas having to do specifically with humanitarian intervention – most notably the unacceptable inconsistency of its practice throughout the 1990s, and the failure of the Council to come to a timely consensus on how to respond cases such as Rwanda, Srebrenica and Kosovo. Yet while most of the 2001 ICISS report is dedicated to the question of intervention ('the responsibility to react'), humanitarian intervention is only one of many possible strategies to protect vulnerable populations. Indeed, the Report also discusses 'the responsibility to prevent' and 'the responsibility to rebuild', but both are given less attention than the question of intervention. Furthermore, the primary responsibility to protect lays with the state in question, and this responsibility only transfers to the international community when the state in question is 'unwilling or unable' (changed in 2005 to 'manifestly failing') to discharge its responsibility. Nevertheless, the conflation of R2P with humanitarian intervention has proven to be an impediment to states widely endorsing it, given the contested nature of humanitarian intervention, so R2P advocates have gone to great lengths to decouple the two ideas.

Second, the use of the language of a 'responsibility to protect' was a deliberate speech act (on speech acts, see Onuf 1989: 82–7; Buzan et al. 1998: 23). That is, in order to correct what was perceived to be the morally problematic aspects of the emerging norm of humanitarian intervention, which was that it was a *permissive* norm to be invoked at the discretion of the Security Council, it was urgent to create a consensus around a new norm that would result in more consistent action by the Council in response to gross human rights violations. As a result, the ICISS deliberately sought to change the terms of the debate over humanitarian intervention by moving away from the language of the 'right to intervene', which captures the permissive nature of the humanitarian intervention norm as it had been developing throughout the 1990s. As Gareth Evans, co-chair of the ICISS, noted, 'the whole point of embracing new language of "responsibility to protect" is that it is capable of generating an effective, consensual response in extreme, conscience-shocking cases, in a way that "right to intervene" language simply is not' (Evans 2008: 293). R2P can therefore be considered a speech act intended to impel decisive action, or otherwise 'a label that can be attached to particular crises in order to generate the will and consensus necessary to mobilize a decisive international response' (Bellamy 2010: 159).

The devolution of a norm: Iraq, Darfur and the 2005 World Summit

Yet norms develop in fluid and contentious environments and their meanings are transformed and chastened by events that can even imperil their effectiveness. In the case of R2P, the events of 9/11 and subsequent US invasion of Afghanistan occurred as the ICISS was finishing up its work in the autumn of 2001, and while its Report received much attention, especially in academic circles, the primary international security concern of many states (especially the US) quickly shifted from ameliorating humanitarian catastrophes and protecting vulnerable populations to fighting global terrorism. Yet even though the US invasion of Afghanistan was clearly an act of self-defence by the US, and was justified as such, this did not prevent enterprising, yet thoughtful, discussions about the possibilities for alternative moral possibilities in this new international security environment. For instance, Nicholas Wheeler posited the possibility that in a post-9/11 world, '[m]ilitary interventions could be used to promote both counter-terrorist objectives. If what was lacking in the 1990s was a compelling security interest to motivate interventions in humanitarian emergencies, then does the threat posed by global terrorism supply the missing ingredient?' (Wheeler 2003: 193). Removing the Taliban regime from power in Afghanistan, at least in theory, could stand to contribute mightily to the human rights enjoyment of Afghans. Indeed, President Bush explicitly claimed that in addition to defending against future terrorist attacks, humanitarian goals would be also accomplished through the launching of Operation Enduring Freedom (see, for example, Moses et al. 2011).

A year later, however, the US began the drumbeat toward war with Iraq, which eventually occurred in March 2003, and was arguably one of the biggest setbacks to the idea of humanitarian intervention and to serious discussion of R2P by world leaders. Indeed, as George Packer identified in his aforementioned piece in the run-up to the Iraq war, what he termed the 'Bosnian consensus' had fallen apart. 'The argument that has broken out among these liberal hawks over Iraq is as fierce in its way as anything since Vietnam. This time the argument is taking place not just between people but within them, where the dilemmas and conflicts are all the more tormenting' (Packer 2002). Many of these divisions were encapsulated by those who would go on to work in the Obama administration. Some, like Susan Rice, were against the Iraq war even on humanitarian grounds.[9] Those 'for' the Iraq war on humanitarian grounds included Anne-Marie Slaughter, who would eventually publish an oft-cited article with co-author Lee Feinstein in the months following the initiation of the conflict with the conjecture that the 'biggest problem with the Bush preemption strategy may be that it does not go *far enough*' (Feinstein and Slaughter 2004).

While the reasons for the US invasion are still contested, the primary justification advanced by the Bush administration at the time was that it was a war of 'preemptive' (though actually 'preventive') self-defence. That is, the possibility that Saddam Hussein had or would otherwise develop weapons of mass destruction (WMD), and might either himself use them against the US or its allies, or give them to al-Qaeda terrorists to use, made his continued rule in Iraq an intolerable threat to the US. Supplementing this argument, of course, were the usual gestures to human rights and the fact that Saddam Hussein was a brutal tyrant who had massacred his own citizens in the past. Yet it was after the search for WMD had turned up empty when the humanitarian rhetoric was significantly ratcheted up by the administration. Eventually, the humanitarian argument became the *primary* reason justifying the invasion and continued US occupation of Iraq, once the primary justification of WMD and ties to terrorists turned out to be exaggerated if not outright false. Even so, Michael Ignatieff (an ICISS commissioner, incidentally) and other prominent proponents of humanitarian intervention supported the Iraq war on the basis of its potential for a positive human rights outcome (Ignatieff 2003).

Nevertheless, this argument was met by most members of the international community with extreme scepticism and was widely viewed as a cynical attempt to use humanitarianism as a pretext for an invasion whose original justification turned out to be faulty at best (Bellamy

2005; Roth 2004: 13–33). In the minds of many observers, the abuse of humanitarian arguments by the US in Iraq effectively made humanitarian intervention led by the US impossible (Kurth 2005). It effectively blunted the linear logic of a norm justifying intervention. In short, the *ex post facto* shift in the justification of the Iraq war not only severely undermined the credibility of the US, it had the net effect of delegitimizing humanitarian intervention as opposed to legitimizing the Iraq war, casting doubt upon the R2P doctrine, and caused many states to become suspicious that the West's humanitarian justifications simply mask neo-imperial ambitions (Thakur 2005; Bellamy 2004).

It has therefore become a common observation that these developments directly contributed to the general reluctance to take action to stop the ethnic killings in Darfur, Sudan, as that crisis began to reach a head in early 2004 (Williams and Bellamy 2005: 36). Interestingly, however, the Bush administration was very much engaged with the crisis in Darfur, owing to pressure from American evangelical groups who had seized upon Sudan's abuse of Christians in the North–South conflict, going even as far as officially declaring that the killings in Darfur constituted genocide (Heinze 2007: 368–72). What is noteworthy about this is the fact that almost exactly 10 years prior, the Clinton administration avoided characterizing the Rwanda killings as 'genocide' for fear that doing so may have obligated it to 'do something' about the killings there (Power 2002: Chapter 10). Furthermore, most indications are that the Bush administration had little desire to actually lead a humanitarian intervention in Darfur: the US military was stretched thin in Iraq and Afghanistan, and the administration had other competing goals in Sudan, most notably counter-terror cooperation and ending the North–South conflict. Yet it remained alone in its finding of genocide in Darfur, as the Arab League, European Union, numerous human rights and relief organizations, and even the UN International Commission of Inquiry on Darfur, all concluded that the killings in Darfur genocide were not genocide ('Sudan News Agency . . .' 2004; 'US Senate Leader . . .' 2004; 'Report of the International Commission . . .' 2005).

International opinion was likewise sceptical of the US position on Darfur. A widely referenced article in the British newspaper *The Observer* accused the US of 'hyping' genocide in Darfur, despite findings to the contrary by the UN Commission of Inquiry, AU and EU (Beaumont 2004). The framing of the crisis as 'Arab on African' violence was also not surprisingly opposed by prominent Arabs as yet another selective and unfair vilification of Arabs as *génocidaires*, particularly in a context in which the Western media routinely identify them as the instigators of terrorism (de Waal 2005: 200–1). Likewise, notable voices from the developing world – such as ICISS commissioner and staunch R2P advocate, Ramesh Thakur – openly disparaged Western 'humanitarians clamoring for another war', particularly in light of Iraq, arguing that any Western intervention in Darfur would 'be exploited as yet another assault on Arabs and Muslims' (Thakur 2004; see also 'Sudan Can't Wait . . .' 2004: 11). As Human Rights Watch's Michael Clough put it, 'the fact that the US was waging a globally unpopular war in Iraq without a UN mandate inevitably affected how other UN member states responded [to the US's genocide finding], particularly once the graphic images of . . . Abu Ghraib were broadcast around the world' (Clough 2005: 34).

The use of R2P to frame the Darfur crisis also could not overcome the reluctance of Western states to take decisive action, or of critics of humanitarian intervention from arguing that all the talk of humanitarianism was a pretext for Western imperialism. In the UN Security Council debates over Darfur, three positions emerged, although only the Philippines argued that international action was warranted on the basis of R2P. The position adopted by China, Pakistan and Sudan rejected the idea of international intervention, while Russia and Brazil were reluctant to even contemplate the possibility. Importantly, however, the position advocated by Western states was that it was the *Sudanese government* which still bore the primary responsibility to protect its own people (despite the fact that the UN had concluded that the Sudanese government itself was responsible for the atrocities), and referred to the AU as having the residual responsibility if Sudan should fail in its primary responsibility (Bellamy 2005: 42). There was thus extreme reluctance on the part of states at the Security Council to seriously consider humanitarian intervention in Darfur, and the international community's feeble response to this crisis suggests that R2P at this time had done little to change states' attitudes about humanitarian intervention.

Yet amidst the setbacks of the war on terror, the Iraq war and dithering over Darfur, the 2005 UN World Summit produced a supposedly remarkable endorsement of R2P, which was signed by all UN members' heads of state. Specifically, the World Summit *Outcome Document* contained two paragraphs (138 and 139) that endorse a heavily modified version of R2P (UN General Assembly 2005). The two paragraphs are worth quoting in their entirety:

> (138) Each individual State has the responsibility to protect its populations from genocide, war crimes, ethnic cleansing and crimes against humanity. This responsibility entails the prevention of such

> crimes, including their incitement, through appropriate and necessary means. We accept that responsibility and will act in accordance with it. The international community should, as appropriate, encourage and help States to exercise this responsibility and support the United Nations in establishing an early warning capability.
>
> (139) The international community, through the United Nations, also has the responsibility to use appropriate diplomatic, humanitarian and other peaceful means, in accordance with Chapters VI and VIII of the Charter, to help protect populations from genocide, war crimes, ethnic cleansing and crimes against humanity. In this context, we are prepared to take collective action, in a timely and decisive manner, through the Security Council, in accordance with the Charter, including Chapter VII, on a case-by-case basis and in cooperation with relevant regional organizations as appropriate, should peaceful means be inadequate and national authorities manifestly fail to protect their populations from genocide, war crimes, ethnic cleansing and crimes against humanity. We stress the need for the General Assembly to continue consideration of the responsibility to protect populations from genocide, war crimes, ethnic cleansing and crimes against humanity and its implications, bearing in mind the principles of the Charter and international law. We also intend to commit ourselves, as necessary and appropriate, to helping States build capacity to protect their populations from genocide, war crimes, ethnic cleansing and crimes against humanity and to assisting those which are under stress before crises and conflicts break out.

Almost immediately, advocates of R2P hailed this endorsement of R2P as a groundbreaking development of fundamental importance. Gareth Evans described the 2005 endorsement as 'the emergence of what can reasonably be described as a brand new international norm of really quite fundamental importance and novelty . . . that is unquestionably a major breakthrough' (Evans 2009: 16). Other commentators went even further to declare that this endorsement strengthened the legal basis for possible unilateral humanitarian intervention, and claimed that the Summit had essentially succeeded in establishing a new norm that legalized humanitarian intervention (Bannon 2006; Stedman 2007). And it does seem apparent that many members of the Bosnia generation invoked R2P at various points throughout the 2000s. For instance, Anne-Marie Slaughter described this and subsequent endorsements by the Security Council as 'an enormous normative step forward, akin to an international Magna Carta' (Slaughter 2011); and Susan Rice and Samantha Power also referenced R2P to justify US action in Darfur (Rice 2007). If the more prosaic appraisals of R2P were true, then this would be a significant normative as well as legal development, but such arguably hyperbolic appraisals of the significance of this document raise a couple of points.

First, it is now widely acknowledged among even R2P's most ardent supporters that the version of R2P endorsed by the General Assembly in 2005 'changed in important ways from the way it was originally conceived by the ICISS' (Bellamy 2009a: 195). In particular, while the ICISS doctrine says that the Responsibility to Protect transfers from the state to the international community in cases where the state is 'unable or unwilling' to protect its citizens, the World Summit *Outcome Document* amended this to cases where the state in question is 'manifestly failing' to do so – a clearly higher threshold for action. Second, the ICISS doctrine posits that military intervention will meet the just cause threshold in cases of 'serious and irreparable harm occurring to human beings, or imminently likely to occur', including 'large-scale loss of life' or 'large-scale ethnic cleansing', whereas the World Summit *Outcome Document* restricts these to the more limited circumstances of 'genocide, war crimes, ethnic cleansing, and crimes against humanity'. Third, the ICISS doctrine stipulates that the international community has a 'responsibility' to take action when the state in question fails, whereas the World Summit *Outcome Document* tempers this to say that the international community need only 'be prepared' to take action on a case-by-case basis. Finally, the ICISS report considers intervention without Security Council approval to be permissible in extreme cases, whereas the World Summit *Outcome Document* requires that any coercive action should be undertaken through the Security Council, and the idea of permanent members not using their veto in such situations was abandoned.

Thus, on a deeper look, what was endorsed in 2005 was actually reiteration of previously existing norms relevant to the human rights responsibilities of states and an endorsement of the Security Council and its long-standing and relatively uncontroversial powers to authorize coercive action to respond to extreme cases of grave human suffering. That is, the principle that states can no longer treat their people however they please and are obligated to treat them according to certain international standards has been around since at least the Universal Declaration of Human Rights was adopted in 1948, while the notion that the Security Council can authorize forcible humanitarian intervention on a case-by-case basis was a practice that began as early as 1992.

So as far as humanitarian intervention is concerned, what the UN essentially endorsed in 2005 was an institutional arrangement whereby the UN Security Council may, at its discretion, authorize military intervention in cases where human suffering has reached, or risks reaching, genocidal proportions, and when the state in question has 'manifestly failed' to act (or is itself the perpetrator). This is essentially the precedent the Council set in the 1990s described above when it authorized a series of military interventions in places such as Somalia, Bosnia and Haiti.

Second, the exaggerated claims about the impact of the *Outcome Document* led to what Alex Bellamy has called a 'revolt' against R2P by many countries – mainly Asian and Arab (Bellamy 2009b: 112, 117–18). This, according to Bellamy, was a result of the erroneous association of the broader R2P concept with the narrower and more controversial idea of humanitarian intervention. Specifically, the concern was that R2P would be used as a pretext that would be prone to abuse, which had been given a renewed impetus in light of the misuse of humanitarian arguments to justify the war in Iraq. States, therefore, seem to agree on the general principle that they have a responsibility to protect their citizens from genocide, war crimes, crimes against humanity and ethnic cleansing, and that they should be 'prepared to take collective action' in cases where a state 'manifestly fails' to do so. But they still disagree considerably about when this responsibility calls for military intervention, other than by letting the Security Council decide, which has been the prevailing practice for some time.

This is again the precedent the Council set in the 1990s in response to cases such as Iraq, Somalia, Bosnia and Haiti, and is largely reflected in state practice in the 2000s and early 2010s. As we argued above, there was no decisive intervention in Darfur to halt what were clearly large-scale crimes against humanity, if not genocide, except for a belated and restrictively mandated peacekeeping force under the auspices of the AU that was later folded into a broader UN operation. In fact, R2P was used as a basis to argue *against* humanitarian intervention in Darfur by claiming that the responsibility to protect still lay with the Sudan government and not with the international community. Compare this to the international response to the Libya crisis in 2011 (discussed below), which involved gross human rights violations, to be sure, though on a much smaller scale than in Darfur. The fact that states were scarcely criticized by their peers for failing to intervene to protect civilians in Darfur suggests that R2P as envisaged by the ICISS as a bona fide 'responsibility' is extremely weak at best, and most likely non-existent (Williams and Bellamy 2005: 42; Bellamy 2010: 161). Thus, R2P can only be said to be a norm in the sense that it reiterates previously existing norms about states' responsibility for protecting the human rights of their own citizens, as well as the previously existing norm of humanitarian intervention that emerged in the 1990s (and was reiterated in the 2005 *Outcome Document*) that gives states permission, but does not obligate them, to take decisive action under very circumscribed conditions.

The Bosnia generation and Operation Odyssey Dawn

The puzzle of US participation in the 2011 Libyan intervention has been subject to much conjecture-laden commentary. A popular thesis proffered at the beginning stages of Operation Odyssey Dawn was that the 'women' of the Obama administration, including Secretary of State Hillary Clinton, UN Ambassador Susan Rice, and Office of Multilateral and Human Rights Director Samantha Power (Avlon 2011), were the ones who pushed for the intervention. This proved to be a thesis which fitted into the overall genderizing of 'humanitarian action' as 'social work',[10] but it was not without its faults.[11] Others narrowed the analysis, from gender to the role of one individual in particular – Samantha Power (McKelvey 2011). Yet these commentaries, too, fell back into a gendered understanding of the intervention, referring to Power as the 'femme fatale' behind the intervention.

In between these two perspectives, and closer to the line of argument we make here, the NATO operation, and the US role in it, can be better examined via what Peter Beinart identified as the role of 'Bosnia' upon a generation of US (and European) elites. There is evidence that both Rwanda and Bosnia were invoked by policymakers and pundits – in discussions public and private – as an interest for Operation Odyssey Dawn. UK Prime Minister David Cameron pushed for an intervention because, according to one report, 'the prime minister told allies he did not want a repeat of Srebrenica, the infamous 1995 episode when blue-helmeted UN Dutch peacekeepers did not stop the massacre of 8,000 Bosnian Muslims' (Wintour and Watt 2011). And French President Nicholas Sarkozy remarked in Brussels in late March of that year that Benghazi would have been a 'second Srebrenica' without intervention.[12]

Beinart expresses almost verbatim in the language of generational analysis the way this transition played out:

> So why are we at war there? More than anything else, because of Bosnia. Ask most Americans about the Bosnian War and you'll get

> the kind of answers Jay Leno elicits when he asks passers-by who won the Battle of Britain. But foreign policymaking is generally an elite affair, and Bosnia *was the crucible in which a whole generation of American and European elites forged their view of the world.* It was Bosnia where Western liberals decided, 20 years after the fall of Saigon, that Western military intervention could be both moral and effective. It was Bosnia where civilian elites learned to distrust the Pentagon's warnings that limited war was impossible. It was NATO's success in Bosnia that convinced so many that the West could have intervened successfully in Rwanda, and which set the stage for the humanitarian war in Kosovo in 1999. (Beinart 2011: emphasis added)

Notice here that while Beinart focuses on a group of elites, he extends his argument outside of a US context, positing that the 'people who reportedly influenced their governments to back a no fly zone . . . [included] Samantha Power, who began her professional career reporting from Bosnia, [and] Bernard-Henri Lévy in France, who made a 1994 documentary urging military intervention against Slobodan Milosevic'. An *Economist* article written around the same time suggested that 'Europe's shameful failure to prevent genocide in the Balkans was a *formative experience* for a whole generation of British ministers . . . Some close observers of Balkan suffering now hold key posts in the present-day coalition government' ('The Crisis in Libya' 2011). The article identified two individuals pushing for Britain's role in the intervention – Ed Llewellyn, Prime Minister David Cameron's chief-of-staff who had previously worked for Lord (Paddy) Ashdown, a pro-interventionist MP, and Arminka Helic, a Bosnian Muslim who became a top aide to Foreign Secretary William Hague.

While the influence of the 'shadow' of Bosnia and Rwanda in these other contexts seems likely, it proves difficult to empirically validate so recently removed from that decision. In the US context, the connection is a bit clearer. Three individuals who helped shape the Obama Administration's stance leading up to the Libyan intervention invoked Bosnia and Rwanda. One, Anne-Marie Slaughter, who as we noted above likened the ICISS report to the 'Magna Carta', was just removed from her work in the Clinton-led State Department by only a few weeks when she 'tweeted' the following in late February 2011: 'The international community cannot stand by and watch the massacre of Libyan protesters. In Rwanda we watched. In Kosovo we acted' (Rogin 2011). Samantha Power is also integral here – not only writing a book detailing the ubiquitous malfeasance of US foreign policy in the face of genocide, but for her advocacy throughout the early 2000s on a more active US presence in halting the genocide in Darfur, and of course her work beginning in 2005 advising then-Senator Obama. Power's push to establish a US role in the Libyan intervention was highlighted by the US press leading up to Odyssey Dawn, although as one of these stories discussed, she maintained a 'low profile' (Stolberg 2011). The US ambassador to the UN, Susan Rice, invoked Libya as the counter-example to Rwanda, specifically asserting that the United States had fulfilled a 'Responsibility to Protect' in the former where it had failed in the latter: 'This time, the Security Council acted. And acted in time. Having failed in Rwanda and Darfur, it did not fail again in Libya. Within less than two days, American firepower played a decisive role in stopping Gadhafi's forces and saving Benghazi' (Garrison 2011).[13]

Further, we recall here how in generational analysis that elites do not define their perspective or worldview out of whole cloth, or even solely in reaction to past events, but also in *reaction* to another worldview it deems responsible for the negative (past) outcomes. Which worldview did the Bosnia generation define its view of 'interests' against? In this case, it was the views of the foreign policy realists who, as characterized by Samantha Power in *A Problem from Hell*, had prevented US action in Bosnia. These included individuals in the George H. W. Bush administration such as Secretary of State James Baker, National Security Advisor Brent Scowcroft and Chairman of the Joint Chiefs of Staff Colin Powell, all of whom represented the view, in Power's characterization, that '[t]he United States did not have the most powerful military in the history of the world in order to undertake squishy, humanitarian "social work"' (Power 2002: 261). Thus, while one may characterize the contest in the Obama administration as being between 'women' and 'men', it is more accurate to see the contest between Bosnia liberals like Power and Susan Rice (as well as Secretary of State Hillary Clinton, who also invoked Rwanda and Bosnia in her rationale for the intervention) (see Harris 2011) as running 'roughshod over the realists in the [Obama] administration' (Dreyfuss 2011). These realists included then-Defense Secretary Robert Gates, who was also the Deputy National Security Advisor and head of the CIA in the early 1990s. Gates notably stated during Operation Odyssey Dawn that Libya was *not* 'a vital national interest' (Hilsenrath 2011). Therefore, the debates between the Bosnian liberals and the realists in the Obama administration were as much generational as they were about foreign policy perspective.

We should not assume that this was the first and only opportunity for key international actors to reflect upon the failures of Bosnia and/or

Rwanda as a basis in formulating current policy. As discussed above, studies of Operation Allied Force, the NATO operation in Kosovo, have brought forth the role that both Bosnia and Rwanda played in the meaning-making of that intervention. Yet Libya was the first time that many of the Bosnia generation of elites were collectively in positions of power.

In addition, these elites were able to draw upon a number of exceptional factors in the Libya case that not only gave them much fodder to invoke the 'failures' of past responses to humanitarian emergencies, but lessened the overall political costs of the intervention. Thus, even supporters of R2P have conceded that Libya was highly exceptional and was enabled by a confluence of factors that are unlikely to be repeated in future interventions (Bellamy 2011: 266). First, as Bellamy has pointed out, is the extraordinary clarity of the threat of mass atrocities. Gaddafi indicated in no uncertain terms his intention to order the execution of anyone taking up arms against Libya, going so far as to state publicly that he had ordered his forces to 'purify' the region of these 'cockroaches', a term that has specific connotations associated with the Rwandan genocide of 1994, and facilitated numerous comparisons to that monumental moral failure (ibid.: 265; see also 'The Lessons of Libya' 2011). Second is the fact that the intervention was supported by regional actors, most notably the League of Arab States, the Gulf Cooperation Council, and the Organization of the Islamic Conference, without which it is almost assured that the Russians and Chinese would have vetoed the resolution that authorized the intervention (Bellamy 2011: 266). Thus, in contrast to Assad in Syria, Gaddafi had virtually no allies with a stake in his continued rule. Finally, one cannot ignore the fact that the Libya crisis took place in the context of the broader Arab Spring, where ostensibly liberal revolutions were on the march and there was much desire in Western capitals and elsewhere to see this momentum continue and succeed in Libya by effectively removing Gaddafi from power (see Juppé 2011: 8; Ramoin 2012).

All of this is to suggest that the NATO operation into Libya, and even the UNSC Resolution authorizing the no-fly zone, were not as groundbreaking or foundational moments as some may think, nor is it an indication of the emergence of a new international norm. It is indeed 'overdetermined' at first glance, but we aver that Libya was not 'caused' by R2P so much as it was made possible by: 1) a permissive normative environment that has been around since the 1990s; and 2) a generation of foreign policy practitioners who viewed Libya through the lenses of the experiences of the 1990s, a generation which attempted to frame it nevertheless in what they consider to be a new approach to 'protection' of endangered civilians (R2P), but one which recalled Rwanda and Bosnia as much or more as they invoked R2P.[14] The approach was essentially the same, which was that the Security Council responded in a highly selective fashion and the decisive factors that led to the intervention were the particular political circumstances surrounding Libya, not any 'new' international norm or commitment.

Conclusion

While R2P represents an impressive political and moral achievement, we have argued in this chapter that its *effects* on the consensus about humanitarian intervention are less clear, and in fact may be quite modest, both since its inception in 2005 and especially in the years that followed. We close here with one implication from the preceding arguments and findings for how one might approach future policy debates.

By using the aforementioned concept of the 'formative experience', the potential for an aging generation to invoke a generalized and out-of-date worldview suggests that policies which go to the well one too many times can be *destructive* of the norms they seek to uphold. That is, what tends to open up the critical space is a policy action which goes disastrously wrong, creating a rupture and an opening whereby a norm, and the generation invoking it, gets delegitimized. This occurs not only because of that action's consequences, but because of the generation's inability to see any fault in the worldview which led to the policy action. It is for these reasons, as Zack Beauchamp writes, that such an intervention – and a specific linking of it to R2P – would be problematic for both Syria and the 'norm' of R2P as well:

> Military intervention in Syria would not only be a misapplication of R2P, but would radically weaken the doctrine's role in building both a better Middle East and a better world. Our responsibility to protect both Syrians and the R2P doctrine itself demands that we stay out of it. (Beauchamp 2012)

And yet, one final note is that if one wishes to express further caution about the more liberal application of force, one must do more than bring up, in albeit the reasonable manner of Beauchamp's argument, some of the counterfactual problems which may arise in the case of a Syrian intervention. Some of these points made by Beauchamp would seem to conjure up the 'prudential' language of the Cold War-era generation of realists that the Bosnian liberals found to not only be incorrect, but *part of the problem*, in the 1990s. Note here the words of Roskin that generations with different worldviews will be incapable of compromise. Indeed 'the two different generations with their different assumptions talk past one another' (Roskin 1974: 567). If this is the case, then perhaps it is the best shortcut way to interrogating more strident proposals for 'protection'.

One might thus adopt a short-term strategy of invoking the very historical analogies that had been used to stimulate the use of force in Libya. Ann-Marie Slaughter, one of those noted above who pushed for the Libyan intervention by invoking the spectres of Rwanda and Bosnia in March 2011, penned an op-ed in late February of 2012, as the title suggested, on 'how to halt the butchery in Syria'. Slaughter posited that simply arming the Syrian opposition would be problematic, as would the additional steps of establishing 'no-kill zones' near the Turkish, Lebanese and Jordanian borders. The zones would then be slowly expanded over time as neighbouring countries, as well as 'possibly Britain and France' would 'offer tactical and strategic advice to the Free Syrian Army forces' (Slaughter 2012).

It was not long until critics invoked a data point from the failures of the 1990s (Srebrenica) and the idea of 'safe havens' as analogous to the model Slaughter was proposing (IRIN 2012). Yes, the analogy may be incomplete – all analogies are. But while the urge to analogize is somewhat absurd – as Lawrence Kaplan noted on the brink of the Libyan intervention in 2011 – it is also indelibly *human* (Slaughter 2012). Humans analogize all the time – it is how we simplify a complex world. Generations, especially, do this as well, reflecting over and over again on their own formative experiences as the primary comparative points for each unfolding event of the present. Challenging those who advocate, via R2P, interventions now and in the future with analogies may not prove ultimately successful. But such an invocation may be the best one can do, and it would at least be a moment where those embodying the R2P 'norm' for interventionary purposes acknowledge that something may be flawed in their approach, *before* the intervention takes place.

Notes

1. The authors would like to thank Helen Kerwin for her extremely helpful research and editorial assistance for this chapter.
2. Jon Acuff points out that Mannheim, who also theorized generations, asserted that 'generations developed as concrete domestic units, not generally as large scale, transnational movements' (Acuff 2012: 179).

3. Thus, this term is more of a metaphor for a *set* of formative experiences, including but not limited to Bosnia, with the experiences of Rwanda and other 1990s humanitarian disasters just as important.
4. Roskin includes an appropriate anecdote detailing the transition from the isolationist (wake of the First World War) 'Versailles' generation to the more interventionist Pearl Harbor one: 'The "isolationists" fought the growing interventionism every inch of the way. Strong emotions came to the surface. "I could scarcely proceed further without losing my self-control," wrote Secretary of State Cordell Hull of a 1939 confrontation with Senator Borah in which the latter disparaged State Department cables on an impending war in Europe. Other sources said that *Hull actually wept* at the meeting. It took the catastrophe at Pearl Harbor to squelch the obdurate bearers of the Versailles paradigm' (Roskin 1974: 577–8).
5. Packer wrote: 'Without the cold war to distort the debate, and with the inspiring example of the East bloc revolutions of 1989 still fresh, a number of liberal intellectuals in this country had a new idea. These writers and academics wanted to use American military power to serve goals like human rights and democracy – especially when it was clear that nobody else would do it. Many of them had cut their teeth in the antiwar movement of the 1960's, but by the early 90's, when some of them made trips to besieged Sarajevo, they had resolved their own private Vietnam syndromes. Together – hardly vast in their numbers, but influential – they advocated a new role for America in the world, which came down to American power on behalf of American ideals' (Packer 2002).
6. UK Foreign Secretary Robin Cook, in response to a question from Conservative leader Michael Howard, 19 October 1998 (see Steele 2008: 130–4).
7. See Power's chapter on Kosovo in *A Problem from Hell* (2003), Chapter 11, where she defends the US decision from a variety of both right and left-wing critics.
8. Anne-Marie Slaughter made this point in a *New York Times* opinion piece shortly after the United States had abandoned efforts to get diplomatic approval by the UN Security Council: 'By giving up on the Security Council, the Bush administration has started on a course that could be called "illegal but legitimate," a course that could end up, paradoxically, winning United Nations approval for a military campaign in Iraq – though only after an invasion. The relevant history here is from Kosovo. In 1999, the United States, expecting a Russian veto of military intervention to stop Serbian attacks on ethnic Albanians in Kosovo, sidestepped the United Nations completely and sought authorization for the use of force within NATO itself' (Slaughter 2003).
9. Susan Rice was quoted in early 2003 as stating: 'The problem is that many American people are not convinced that going to war against Iraq will actually make us in the United States safer. I think they fear reprisals and attacks and they think that our homeland is not yet secure and that with developments in the Middle East and al-Qaeda still very much on the loose there are many I think may fear that going to war against Iraq may in fact in the short term make us less secure, rather than more secure' ('Powell's Address . . .' 2003).
10. This is Michael Mandelbaum's term (Mandelbaum 1996).
11. Avlon's analysis was problematic for a whole host of reasons, not only with regard to the 'women' thesis, but with its understanding of the French

'reversing' their stereotypical aversion to force (Avlon 2011). Even casual observers of French foreign policy over the past three decades would note *many* occasions, including Lebanon in the early 1980s, and Bosnia in the mid-1990s, where the French preferred action over sometimes *strong* US opposition.

12. See the video of these remarks at: www.youtube.com/watch?v=MyyCw4De1Hk&feature=relmfu
13. Furthermore in reference to Rwanda, Rice felt she had a 'debt to repay', writing that 'I swore to myself that if I ever faced such a crisis again, I would come down on the side of dramatic action, going down in flames if that was required' (Power 2001).
14. Even Gareth Evans, in a defensive op-ed published during the Libyan intervention, invoked Bosnia and Rwanda as the reasoning *behind* the formation of R2P: '. . . the "responsibility to protect" doctrine . . . was unanimously endorsed by the world community in 2005 to try to end once and for all Cambodia, Rwanda and Bosnia-type mass-atrocity crimes' (Evans 2011).

References

Acuff, J. M. (2011) 'The Next Generation of Terror: Generational Analysis and the Strategy And Tactics of al Qaeda', paper presented at the 2011 International Studies Association annual meeting, Montreal, Canada.

Acuff, J. M. (2012) 'Generational Analysis and the Evolution of Military Doctrine and Strategy', in B. J. Steele and J. M. Acuff (eds), *Theory and Application of the 'Generation' in International Relations and Politics* (New York: Palgrave Macmillan).

Adams, S. (2011) 'R2P and the Libya Mission', *Los Angeles Times*, 28 September.

Avlon, J. (2011) 'Libya Airstrikes: the Women who Called for War', *The Daily Beast*, 20 March. Available online at: www.thedailybeast.com/articles/2011/03/20/libya-airstrikes-hillary-clinton-and-the-women-who-called-for-war.html

Ban Ki-Moon (2011) 'Statement by the Secretary-General on Libya', 17 March. Available online at: www.responsibilitytoprotect.org/index.php/crises/190-crisis-in-libya/3269-ban-says-historic-resolution-was-clearly-the-international-community-fulfilling-of-its-responsibility-to-protect

Bannon, A. L. (2006) 'The Responsibility to Protect: The UN World Summit and the Question of Unilateralism', *Yale Law Journal*, vol. 115, no. 5, pp. 143–70.

Beauchamp, Z. (2012) 'Syria's Crisis and the Future of R2P', *Foreign Policy*, 16 March, available online at: http://mideast.foreignpolicy.com/posts/2012/03/16/syrias_crisis_and_the_future_of_r2p

Beaumont, P. (2004) 'US "Hyping" Darfur Genocide Fear', *The Observer*, 3 October.

Beck, U. and E. Beck-Gernsheim (2009) 'Global Generations and the Trap of Methodological Nationalism: for a Cosmopolitan Turn in the Sociology of Youth and Generation', *European Sociological Review*, vol. 25, no. 1, pp. 25–36.

Beinart, P. (2011) 'Behind the Libya War', *The Daily Beast*, 20 March. Available online at: www.thedailybeast.com/articles/2011/03/21/libya-war-and-the-bosnia-hawks-on-the-obama-team-leading-the-charge.print.html

Bellamy, A. J. (2004) 'Ethics and Intervention: The "Humanitarian Exception" and the Problem of Abuse in the Case of Iraq', *Journal of Peace Research,* vol. 41, no. 2, pp. 131–47.

Bellamy, A. J. (2005) 'Responsibility to Protect or Trojan Horse? The Crisis in Darfur and Humanitarian Intervention after Iraq', *Ethics and International Affairs,* vol. 19, no. 2, pp. 31–52.

Bellamy, A. J. (2009a) *Responsibility to Protect: The Global Effort to End Mass Atrocities* (Cambridge: Polity).

Bellamy, A. J. (2009b) 'Realizing the Responsibility to Protect', *International Studies Perspectives,* vol. 10, no. 2, pp. 111–28.

Bellamy, A. J. (2010) 'The Responsibility to Protect – Five Years On', *Ethics and International Affairs,* vol. 24, no. 2, pp. 143–69.

Bellamy, A. J. (2011) 'Libya and the Responsibility to Protect: The Exception and the Norm', *Ethics and International Affairs,* vol. 25, no. 3, pp. 263–9.

Buzan, B., O. Waever and J. de Wilde (1998) *Security: A New Framework for Analysis* (Boulder: Lynne Rienner).

Carlson, J. D. (2012) 'Generational Analysis in IR Meets the World Values Survey', in B. J. Steele and J. M. Acuff (eds), *Theory and Application of the 'Generation' in International Relations and Politics* (New York: Palgrave Macmillan).

Chesterman, S. (2002) *Just War or Just Peace? Humanitarian Intervention and International Law* (Oxford: Oxford University Press).

Chollet, D. (2005) *The Road to the Dayton Accords: A Study of American Statecraft* (New York: Palgrave Macmillan).

Chopra, J. and T. Weiss (1992) 'Sovereignty Is No Longer Sacrosanct', *Ethics and International Affairs,* vol. 6, no. 1, pp. 95–117.

Clinton, W. (2009) 'Rwanda Guild Led to Kosovo Intervention', *Balkan Insight,* 2 November. Available online at: www.balkaninsight.com/en/article/clinton-rwanda-guilt-led-to-kosovo-intervention

'The Crisis in Libya: Bosnia's Long Shadow over British Foreign Policy' (2011) *The Economist,* 15 March. Available online at: www.economist.com/node/21016925

Clough, M. (2005) 'Darfur: Whose Responsibility to Protect?', *Human Rights Watch World Report, 2005* (New York: Human Rights Watch).

Danish Institute of International Affairs (1999) *Humanitarian Intervention: Legal and Political Aspects* (Copenhagen: Danish Institute of International Affairs).

Deng, F., S. Kimaro, T. Lyons, D. Rothschild and W. Zartman (1996) *Sovereignty as Responsibility: Conflict Management in Africa* (Washington, DC: The Brookings Institution).

de Waal, A. (2005) 'Who Are the Darfurians? Arab and African Identities, Violence, and External Engagement', *African Affairs,* vol. 104, no. 415, pp. 181–205.

Dreyfuss, R. (2011) 'Obama's Women Advisers Pushed War against Libya', *The Nation,* 19 March. Available online at: www.thenation.com/blog/159346/obamas-women-advisers-pushed-war-against-libya

Evans, G. (2008) *The Responsibility to Protect: Ending Mass Atrocity Crimes Once and For All* (Washington, DC: Brookings Institution Press).

Evans, G. (2008) 'Responsibility to Protect: An Idea Whose Time has Come . . . and Gone?', *International Relations,* vol. 22, no. 3, pp. 283–98.

Evans, G. (2009) 'From an Idea to an International Norm', in R. H. Cooper and J. V. Kohler (eds), *Responsibility to Protect: The Global Moral Compact for the 21st Century* (Basingstoke and New York: Palgrave Macmillan).

Evans, G. (2011) 'UN Targets Libya with Pinpoint Accuracy', *The Age*, 24 March. Available online at: www.gevans.org/opeds/oped110.html

Feinstein, L. and A. M. Slaughter (2004) 'A Duty to Prevent', *Foreign Affairs*, no. 136, January/February.

Fixdal, M. and D. Smith (1998) 'Humanitarian Intervention and Just War', *Mershon International Studies Review*, vol. 42, no. 2, pp. 283–312.

Garrison, A. (2011) 'Susan Rice in Libya and Rwanda for the US R2P', 25 November. Available online at: www.anngarrison.com/audio/susan-rice-in-libya-and-rwanda-for-the-us-r2p

Gelvin, J. (2012) *The Arab Uprisings: What Everyone Needs to Know* (Oxford: Oxford University Press).

Gerber, R. (2011) 'Beyond Libya: A World Ready to Respond to Mass Violence', *The Stanley Foundation*. Available online at: www.stanleyfoundation.org/resources.cfm?id=462

'Hearing of the International Security, International Organization and Human Rights Subcommittee of the House Foreign Affairs Committee', 17 May 1994.

Harris, E. (2011) 'Clinton Cites Rwanda, Bosnia in Rationale for Libyan Intervention', *ABC News*, 17 March. Available online at: http://abcnews.go.com/blogs/politics/2011/03/clinton-cites-rwanda-bosnia-in-rationale-for-libya-intervention/

Hehir, A. (2010) *Humanitarian Intervention: An Introduction* (New York: Palgrave Macmillan).

Heinze, E. A. (2007) 'The Rhetoric of Genocide in US Foreign Policy: Rwanda and Darfur Compared', *Political Science Quarterly*, vol. 122, no. 3, pp. 359–83.

Heinze, E. A. (2013) 'Humanitarian Intervention', in Z. P. Messitte and S. Grillot (eds), *Understanding the Global Community* (Norman: University of Oklahoma Press), pp. 66–100.

Henderson, C. W. (2010) *Understanding International Law* (Malden: Wiley-Blackwell).

Herborth, B. (2012) 'Toward a Sociology of Generational Change', in B. J. Steele and J. M. Acuff (eds), *Theory and Application of the 'Generation' in International Relations and Politics* (New York: Palgrave Macmillan).

Hilsenrath, J. (2011) 'Gates Says Libya Not Vital National Interest', *The Wall Street Journal*, 27 March. Available online at: http://online.wsj.com/article/SB10001424052748704308904576226704261420430.html

Hurrell, A. (2002) 'Norms and Ethics in International Relations', in W. Carlsnaes, T. Risse and B. A. Simmons (eds), *Handbook of International Relations* (New York: Sage Publications).

Ignatieff, M. (2003) 'I Am Iraq', *New York Times Magazine*, 23 March.

International Commission on Intervention and State Sovereignty (ICISS) (2001) *The Responsibility to Protect* (Ottawa: International Development Research Centre).

IRIN (2012) 'Briefing: Why Humanitarians Are Wary of 'Humanitarian Corridors', *IRIN*, 19 March. Available online at: www.irinnews.org/Report/95101/Briefing-Why-humanitarians-wary-of-humanitarian-corridors

Juppé, A. (2011) 'The Arab Spring: Hopes and Challenges', The Brookings Institution, 6 June, available online at: www.brookings.edu/~/media/events/2011/6/06%20arab%20spring%20juppe/20110606_arab_spring_juppe.pdf

Kaplan, L. (2011) 'Failed Analogy', *The New Republic*, 17 March. Available online at: www.tnr.com/article/crossings/85355/libya-obama-iraq-vietnam-foreign-policy

Khong, Y. F. (1992) *Analogies at War* (Princeton: Princeton University Press).

Kosovo Commission (Independent International Commission on Kosovo) (2000) *The Kosovo Report: Conflict, International Response, Lessons Learned* (Oxford: Oxford University Press).

Kurth, J. (2005) 'Humanitarian Intervention after Iraq: Legal Ideals vs. Military Realities', *Orbis*, vol. 50, no. 1, pp. 87–101.

'The Lessons of Libya' (2011) *The Economist*, 19 May. Available online at: www.economist.com/node/18709571

Mandelbaum, M. (1996) 'Foreign Policy as Social Work', *Foreign Affairs*, January/February, pp. 16–32.

McKelvey, T. (2011) 'Samantha Power's Case for War on Libya', *The Daily Beast*, 22 March. Available online at: www.thedailybeast.com/articles/2011/03/23/libya-war-samantha-power-and-the-case-for-liberal-interventionism.html

Moses, J., B. Bahador and T. Wright (2011) 'The Iraq War and the Responsibility to Protect: Uses, Abuses and Consequences for the Future of Humanitarian Intervention', *Journal of Intervention and Statebuilding*, vol. 5, no. 4, pp. 347–67.

Onuf, N. G. (1989) *World of Our Making: Rules and Rule in Social Theory and International Relations* (Columbia: University of South Carolina Press).

Packer, G. (2002) 'The Liberal Quandary over Iraq', *The New York Times*, 8 December. Available online at: www.nytimes.com/2002/12/08/magazine/08LIBERALS.html?pagewanted=all

'Powell's Address to the United Nations: Reaction' (2003) National Public Radio, 6 February. Available online at: www.npr.org/templates/story/story.php?storyId=980412

Power, S. (2001) 'Bystanders to Genocide', *The Atlantic Magazine*, September. Available online at: www.theatlantic.com/magazine/archive/2001/09/bystanders-to-genocide/4571/

Power, S. (2003) *'A Problem from Hell': America and the Age of Genocide*, 3rd edn (New York: Harper Perennial).

'Report of the International Commission of Inquiry on Darfur to the United Nations Secretary General' (2005) United Nations, Geneva, 25 January.

Ramoin, F. E. (2012) 'Why Intervention in Libya Was Justified', *e-International Relations*, 25 January. Available online at: www.e-ir.info/2012/01/25/why-intervention-in-libya-was-justified

Rice, S. (2007) 'The Genocide in Darfur: America Must Do More to Fulfill the Responsibility to Protect', The Brookings Institution. Available online at: www.brookings.edu/research/papers/2007/10/24darfur-rice-opp08

Rogin, J. (2011) 'Anne-Marie Slaughter Calls for Intervention in Libya', *Foreign Policy*, 24 February, available online at: http://thecable.foreignpolicy.com/posts/2011/02/24/anne_marie_slaughter_tweets_call_for_intervention_in_libya

Roskin, M. (1974) 'From Pearl Harbor to Vietnam: Shifting Generational Paradigms and Foreign Policy', *Political Science Quarterly*, vol. 89, no. 3, pp. 563–88.

Roth, K. (2004) 'War in Iraq: Not a Humanitarian Intervention', in *Human Rights Watch World Report 2004: Human Rights and Armed Conflict* (New York: Human Rights Watch), pp. 13–33.
Sandholtz, W. and K. Stiles (2009) *International Norms and Cycles of Change* (Oxford: Oxford University Press).
Slaughter, A.-M. (2003) 'Good Reasons for Going around the UN', *The New York Times*, 18 March. Available online at: www.nytimes.com/2003/03/18/opinion/good-reasons-for-going-around-the-un.html
Slaughter, A.-M. (2011) 'A Day to Celebrate, but Hard Work Ahead', *Foreign Policy*, 18 March. Available online at: www.foreignpolicy.com/articles/2011/03/18/does_the_world_belong_in_libyas_war?page=0,7
Slaughter, A.-M. (2012) 'How to Halt the Butchery in Libya', *The New York Times*, 23 February. Available online at: www.nytimes.com/2012/02/24/opinion/how-to-halt-the-butchery-in-syria.html?_r=1
Stedman, S. J. (2007) 'UN Transformation in an Era of Soft Balancing', *International Affairs*, vol. 83, no. 5, pp. 933–44.
Steele, B. J. (2008) *Ontological Security in International Relations: Self-identity and the IR state* (New York: Routledge).
Steele, B. J. (2012) 'Never Trust Anyone who Remembers Jerry Rubin: The Promise of Generational Conflict', in B. J. Steele and J. M. Acuff (eds), *Theory and Application of the 'Generation' in International Relations and Politics* (New York: Palgrave Macmillan).
Steele, B. J. and J. Acuff (2012) 'Introduction: The Evolution of Generational Analysis and International Theory', in B. J. Steele and J. M. Acuff (eds), *Theory and Application of the 'Generation' in International Relations and Politics* (New York: Palgrave Macmillan).
Stolberg, S. G. (2011) 'Still Crusading, but Now on the Inside', *The New York Times*, 29 March. Available online at: http://www.nytimes.com/2011/03/30/world/30power.html?_r=3&ref=samanthapower
Strauss, W. and N. Howe (1991) *Generations: The History of America's Future, 1584 to 2069* (New York: Morrow).
'Sudan Can't Wait' (2004) *The Economist*, 31 July. Available online at: www.economist.com/node/2963177
'Sudan News Agency on MSF's "Categorical Rejection" of Powell's Darfur Remarks' (2004) *BBC Monitoring Middle East – Political*, 16 September.
Thakur, R. (2004) 'Western Medicine is No Cure for Darfur's Ills', *Australian Financial Review*, 31 August.
Thakur, R. (2005) 'Iraq and the Responsibility to Protect', *Global Dialogue*, vol. 7, nos 1–2, p. 16.
United Nations General Assembly (2005) '2005 World Summit Outcome', UN Doc. A/RES/60/1, 24 October.
'US Senate Leader Insists 'Genocide' Underway in Darfur, Despite EU Statement' (2004) *Agence France Presse*, 10 August.
Wheeler, N. J. (2000) *Saving Strangers: Humanitarian Intervention in International Society* (Oxford: Oxford University Press).
Wheeler, N. J. (2003) 'Humanitarian Intervention after September 11, 2001', in A. F. Lang, Jr. (ed.), *Just Intervention* (Washington, DC: Georgetown University Press).

Wheeler, N. J. and T. Dunne (2001) 'East Timor and the New Humanitarian Interventionism', *International Affairs,* vol. 77, no. 4, pp. 805–27.

Williams, P. D. (2011) 'The Road to Humanitarian War in Libya', *Global Responsibility to Protect,* vol. 3, no. 2, pp. 248–59.

Williams, P. D. and A. J. Bellamy (2005) 'The Responsibility to Protect and the Crisis in Darfur', *Security Dialogue,* vol. 36, no. 1, pp. 27–47.

Winograd, M. and M. D. Hais (2008) *Millennial Makeover* (Camden: Rutgers University Press).

Wintour, P. and N. Watt (2011) 'David Cameron's Libya War', *The Guardian,* 2 October. Available online at: www.guardian.co.uk/politics/2011/oct/02/david-cameron-libyan-war-analysis

Youde, J. (2012) 'The Generational Shift in South African Policy', in B. J. Steele and J. M. Acuff (eds), *Theory and Application of the 'Generation' in International Relations and Politics* (New York: Palgrave Macmillan).

8
The UN Security Council on Libya: Legitimation or Dissimulation?

Tom Keating

Introduction

On 17 March 2011 the United Nations Security Council (UNSC) approved Resolution 1973. The Resolution empowered national governments acting alone or through regional organizations to 'take all necessary measures' to protect civilians and enforce a no-fly zone over Libya. Within 48 hours, armed forces from the United States, France, Britain, Canada and a handful of others launched aerial bombing raids against military and intelligence operations in Libya. These attacks would continue on a daily basis for the next eight months until the regime of Muammar Gaddafi collapsed and the leader himself was killed by insurgents. Ostensibly the Resolution and the no-fly zone were intended to protect civilian populations in the city of Benghazi that had been threatened by the Libyan president in response to rebel uprisings that had been taking place in the area since mid-February. The resolution marked a further escalation in the UNSC's response to the deteriorating situation in Libya as it followed UNSC Resolution 1970 that had condemned the use of violence against civilian populations.

These resolutions marked an important development in the Security Council's approach to civilian protection and Council members' reference to the principle of the Libyan government's responsibility to protect (R2P) its citizens. The UNSC's response to the crisis in Libya has been viewed as an example of R2P in practice (Tharoor 2011). There are, however, many reasons to question such an account. A closer examination of the politics surrounding the Council's decision reveals considerably less than wholehearted support for the R2P norm. Much like previous Security Council resolutions, 1973 was less a matter of elaborating and implementing international norms than it was the result of a political compromise among Council members, especially the permanent five (P5) members and some key colleagues. Indeed one could reasonably ask whether the politics at play in Council decisions are ever primarily engaged in debates and decisions over norms, which raises questions about the relationship between normative principles and national interests on the UNSC. Most noteworthy on UNSC 1973 was the abstention of five significant member governments – Russia, China, India, Brazil and Germany. While the abstention of the last of these appears to have been primarily a matter of domestic politics, these abstentions send a message as to the role of the Council, the degree of support for the use of force, and the principle of R2P equally as important as that of the ten states that voted in favour of the Resolution.

This chapter explores the politics surrounding the Council's decision to approve Resolution 1973, the Resolution that endorsed a no-fly zone, but also permitted 'all necessary measures' and enabled NATO governments to launch air strikes against the Gaddafi regime. UNSC 1973 cited the responsibility of the Libyan government to protect its civilian population and its approval demonstrated the Council members' willingness, once again, to allow member governments to intervene to protect civilian populations at risk. The abstention of five key Council members, while allowing the resolution to pass, reflected reservations over intervention, the use of force and indicated at best limited support for R2P. Most significantly, the abstentions were not an endorsement for the air assault that ensued or the regime that followed, let alone for any future actions. Abstaining governments repeatedly raised concerns over the implementation of the resolution, concerns that became more vocal and urgent as a resolution designed to protect civilian populations at risk was transformed into a licence for an aerial assault on the Gaddafi regime, the most effective weapon in the rebels' arsenal, and the lever that secured regime change in Libya. This was neither anticipated nor intended among those who abstained and left them feeling somewhat betrayed or hoodwinked. Their concerns also suggest that UNSC 1973 is unlikely to serve as a precedent for future actions. What for some was a legitimation of R2P and a template for future interventions, was for others a dissimulation for the violation of Libyan sovereignty and the pursuit of selected national interests in North Africa. Since the 1990s, UN Security Council resolutions that enabled interventions and the use of force have not been designed as precedent-setting, but as discrete agreements to address specific conflict situations. Indeed as was seen in the debates and vetoes on resolutions over Syria since Libya, the likelihood of future support from the Council for interventions to protect civilians is never certain and has quite likely been jeopardized by the manner in which member governments implemented the resolution on Libya.

The chapter begins with a brief review of the recent evolution of the Security Council's approach to intervention in civil conflicts and delegation of power to national governments and regional organizations, including a discussion of the Council's role in legitimating the interventionist practices of member governments and norms of international behaviour. It then proceeds to a discussion of the UNSC's response to the uprising in Libya and how this debate was informed by members' interests and their positions on intervention, the use of force, the role of the Security Council and R2P. The chapter concludes with an assessment of the implications of the Council's actions for the advancement of R2P and the Council's role in that process in the future. While the Resolution 1973 likely reinforced the role of the UN Security Council, its influence on R2P has been much more problematic.

The UNSC: intervention and the use of force

The UN Security Council has played an important role in managing the expanded mandate that has been placed before the organization since the end of the Cold War. Indeed the UNSC has become a prominent forum for many of the most significant debates and resolutions in addressing conflict in the post-Cold War period. Despite repeated suggestions that the UN has lost credibility, is unresponsive and unrepresentative, and can no longer serve the changing norms and practices that surround conflict resolution, member governments continue to turn to the Council as they respond to crises and conflicts. The demands on the UN increased significantly during the 1990s and the 2000s as the organization was asked by member governments to address a wide range of conflicts, crises and complex emergencies. In response numerous 'peacekeeping' operations have been established. The peacekeeping label itself has become less appropriate as most of these operations differ greatly from the peacekeeping missions of the Cold War era. The post-Cold War period has witnessed a number of significant developments in the arena of peacekeeping or what the UN describes as complex multidimensional emergencies. There has, for example, been a dramatic and persistent increase in the deployment of such operations, by the UN, but also by regional organizations, and in some instances ad hoc coalitions. The UN operations have varied greatly in size and scope and have also included Chapter VI, Chapter VII and Chapter VIII operations. Since the end of the Cold War, between 1989 and 2011, the UNSC dispatched more than forty new operations.

A significant development in the Council's approach to the increased demands being placed on the UN has been the Council's willingness to undertake activities under Chapter VII provisions and to authorize other parties to use force in implementing these Chapter VII resolutions. Prior to the end of the Cold War, the UNSC had authorized the use of force by other parties on two occasions; the first in Korea in 1950 and the second in Rhodesia in 1966. Other UNSC-sponsored operations during this period were more limited in their mandates and were also kept within the control of the UN itself. This was, in large measure, a reflection of the Cold War environment and the unwillingness on the part of any of the permanent members of the Council to allow other states or organizations to assume authority over how UNSC resolutions were to be carried out or to delegate to them an opportunity to deploy military force. The end of the Cold War changed that. Since the authorization of a naval blockade to monitor sanctions against Iraq following its invasion of Kuwait in 1990, the Security Council has approved 25 military operations by other parties over the next two decades. In some instances UNSC resolutions delegated authority to particular states or organizations. In other resolutions, including UNSC 1973, it was not explicitly stated, though perhaps assumed that a particular state or organization would take on the responsibility for using force in implementing the resolution. Over this period six of the operations were undertaken by the United States acting alone, another six were undertaken with the US acting through and alongside other NATO member states, four were undertaken by the European Union (EU), two by the African Union (AU), two by the Economic Community of West African States (ECOWAS), two by France and one each by Italy, Australia and Gabon. In taking on the use of force to implement UNSC resolutions, these states and organizations also took control over the nature, timing and frequently the scope of the operations. This practice reflects the changed circumstances in which the UN Security Council operated within post-Cold War international society; most importantly a society in which Western states and specifically the US held a preponderance of political and military power. Given the number of operations in which the US, NATO and the EU were the principals, it also demonstrates the willingness and capacity of Western powers to gain the support of the Council for undertaking military interventions.

Keeping in mind the expanded number and scope of all UN operations, there are a number of factors that help to account for the increased popularity of those operating under delegated authority. One consideration has been the nature of the conflicts that the UN has been called upon to address. The lack of control over combatants has created conditions in which UN forces faced increased risks of violent harm even in circumstances where there was some support from local authorities. Bosnia was perhaps the first such experience of this type. Contributing governments were often unwilling to operate under constraining UNSC mandates in these risky circumstances. Delegating responsibility also enabled the Council to allow particular states or organizations to take action in response to particular crises, such as for example Haiti or East Timor, that might have lacked a wider appeal among other UN members. The distribution of these delegated operations suggests that the US and selected European states were far more likely to press for the use of force and a degree of operational freedom when responding to crises. In this manner the UNSC was able to respond to the pressure for the use of force in an ad hoc manner without having to address in a direct way broader normative or Charter-based principles on the use of force and the principles surrounding armed intervention. Jennifer Welsh has noted that many of the UN resolutions authorizing these interventions 'were justified with appeals to "extraordinary" circumstances, illustrating the concern of key council members such as China about establishing precedents for future action that might infringe on the domestic jurisdiction of states' (2011:1199–1200).

Delegating responsibilities to member governments and other organizations also provided an alternative to further drains on the UN's scarce and vastly overstretched resources. As suggested, the last two decades have witnessed unprecedented demands on the resources and good offices of the UN. The organization has been challenged to make every effort to meet these demands both to shore up its own credibility but also to keep crisis management within a common framework. The substantial expansion in peacekeeping operations and their increased complexity challenged the administrative, operational and financial wherewithal of the organization. It led many to complain of the UN's lack of effective capacity and called into questions its credibility. Delegating operational responsibility to states and regional organizations has enabled the UN to have a continuing role in peace and security matters without having to exhaust its limited and heavily overtaxed resources. The lack of operational capacity has often been cited as one reason why member governments and regional organizations sought delegated authority that would enable them to operate free from UN constraints.

Many developed states seem to have less confidence in the command and control of the United Nations in robust peace operations than they do in regional frameworks such as the North Atlantic Treaty Organization (NATO). Part of the scepticism of troop contributors from NATO member states stems from the fact that they prefer detailed concepts of operation before they commit to participate. The UN develops a specific concept of operation much later in the mission-planning process than does NATO, to the chagrin of some Western troop contributors (Mikulaschek 2011: 39). Not incidentally, it also enabled those carrying out the operations to pursue options in the field that might otherwise have been prevented, or at least complicated, if they were compelled to operate under the collective management of formal UN command and control.

Finally, it bears mentioning that states and regional organizations have sought formal UNSC authorization for their actions as a way of gaining legitimacy for what they intended or were inclined to do regardless. Thus one can see the increased frequency of UNSC authorizations as a change not only in the organization, but in the foreign policy practices, specifically of Western governments. The prevalence of such operations and supportive UNSC resolutions is the result of the influence that these governments have been able to exercise on the Council and their willingness and capacity to use force to achieve their foreign policy objectives. It would seem that this has become more pronounced since the end of the Cold War. The tendency can even be found in the breach as US and British officials desperately sought and argued for a UN resolution before attacking Iraq in 2003, and after their failure to secure such a resolution, continued to argue that their actions were supported by previous resolutions.

There is little doubt, though, that the fact that military force was used in any case, by NATO in Kosovo and especially by the United States in Iraq, is an issue that still clouds discussions of force at the Security Council. The irony of the willingness of successive US administrations to use force absent Security Council authorization is that it has strengthened international attachment to that authorization (Jones 2011: 57). As a result, the UN Security Council has gained credibility as a source of legitimation for military interventions, but this legitimation has not been rooted in any specific set of legal or ethical norms.

UN approval provides many benefits for these states as they have attempted to deal with conflicts and complex emergencies that affect their interests. Malone, for example, concludes from his analysis of the UNSC's role in Haiti 'that the multilateral route for the promotion of

US national interests can be rewarding, helping to convince domestic opinion of the legitimacy of the strategy contemplated and also to defuse any regional opposition to it' (Malone 1998: 164) The interests of the US and other Western states in solidifying their power position and securing their dominance within selected states and regions alongside an interest in demonstrating their capacity to use force played a significant role in fostering interventions. The UN Security Council provided an important source of political support for these endeavours. As Roberts and Zaum discuss while there are any number of good reasons for delegating responsibility to other actors to carry out UNSC resolutions, such an approach carries significant risks for both the UN and member governments. It tends to encourage a perception that the enforcing parties are acting out of their own interests rather than serving the more general will of the organization. Additionally, it may lead to differences 'between members of the Security Council and the state or other body leading a coalition about the continuation and interpretation of an earlier mandate to use force' (Roberts and Zaum 2008: 46). The extensive use of delegated authority by the Security Council was thus a well-established practice by the time Libya came on to the agenda in late winter 2011. Its benefits for both the organization and member governments were clearly evident, but so too were the potential problems. These problems became magnified throughout the summer of 2011 and raised serious doubts about the liberal use of such practices in the future.

The UNSC and legitimacy

One of the persistent concerns surrounding interventions has been their legitimacy. As suggested by the above, the frequent use of the Security Council by the US and European governments since the 1990s, while proving helpful in creating a permissive environment for these interventions, has also been important in underpinning the legitimacy that a Security Council resolution provides. At the same time it has tended to reinforce the view that interventions in the absence of such approval lack legitimacy. Through this period the Security Council has seemingly been restored as the principal source of collective legitimacy for intervention and the use of force. The Council's role as the source of legitimacy for interventions stems in large measure from the UN Charter's prohibitions on the use of force in the absence of exceptional circumstances. The Charter does, of course, allow the Security Council to authorize the use of force. With the rare exceptions of self-defence, the Security Council is left as the primary source of authority in determining the legitimate use of force by states. The relationship between a UNSC resolution, legitimacy and the use of force remains a complicated one. The uncertain legitimacy of NATO's intervention in Kosovo was the primary motivation for the Canadian government to launch the International Commission on Intervention and State Sovereignty (ICISS) that subsequently proposed the Responsibility to Protect (R2P) principle.

The view that the UN Security Council should serve as *the* forum for legitimating the use of force by member governments has been considered for some time though it has never been free from debate. The debate on the Council's role reflects, in part, differences over whether the Council's legitimation role rests primarily on a political, legal or moral foundation. If one of the latter two, then the Council would serve as a forum for determining whether the acceptability, hence legitimacy, of any practice would be derived from the moral or legal principles on which it was based. Moral and legal arguments are, of course, different from political ones and despite arguments to the contrary are no less problematic or contested. They have also been the subject of considerable discussion in the Security Council. Advocates of R2P, for example, maintain that the moral principle of protecting civilians at risk should take precedence over legal principles, such as state sovereignty, as well as political interests. The emphasis on bringing the UN Security Council into the process of determining when and how R2P should be invoked, highlighted most prominently in the International Commission's 2001 report, suggests that the Council is the proper forum in which the moral principle would be deliberated. Such an approach is, as the Commission's report acknowledges, was seen as consistent with long-standing just-war principles invoking the importance of the proper authority. The idea of a proper authority also implicates the process by which decisions are made. It is this procedural aspect of sanctioning the use of force that is often viewed as the Council's primary role in legitimating the use of force regardless of the moral or legal issues considered. According to Thomas Franck, legitimacy is best viewed as 'a property of a rule or rule-making institution which itself exerts a pull towards compliance on those addressed normatively because those addressed believe that the rule or institution has come into being and operates in accordance with generally accepted principles of right process' (Franck 1990: 16). Whether the Security Council provides this 'right process' becomes one of the considerations in assessing its role in legitimating the use of force.

The UN Security Council is first and foremost a political forum and while moral and/or legal principles are often enshrined in its resolutions, political interests determine their adoption. Viewed in this light the substantive reasons for the decision are of secondary importance provided that the matter has been vetted and approved by the Council. The Council's composition demonstrates the importance of securing not just the support of any group of states through some sort of multilateral process, but of a particular collection of these states, because they represent critically important states in international society. In this case, the clear distinguishing feature is their relative power alongside some degree of regional representation as reflected in the non-elected members of the Council. The role of the five permanent members of the Council and their ability to veto proposed resolutions is the most critical component of the Council's structure. Even during the immediate post-Cold War period when the US might have been considered first among these unequals, the veto levels the playing field such that the views and interests of other members of the P5 cannot be ignored completely. It is also important to give some attention to the position of other key states, perhaps most notably India, Brazil, South Africa and key regional states. The support of these states may vary depending on the issue under discussion, representing as they do particular regional interests. While these states may not carry the same immediate influence as the P5, whose members are able to wield influence with their veto/s, they are important in providing additional political support for resolutions or in cases where such support is not forthcoming, suggesting reservations or opposition from broad segments of the globe's population. In thinking about the position of Council members both in general terms and in relation to the specifics surrounding UNSC 1973, it is important to keep in mind David Malone's view that 'Council actions are reviewed among the P-5 not only on their own merits but also as potential bargaining chips with each other' (Malone 1998: 167). If accurate, it provides further evidence that Security Council resolutions have less to do with the articulation and implementation of moral norms or legal principles than they do with political compromises among the P5 and other key member governments.

This suggests that the legitimacy of the Security Council is a political rather than moral or legal condition. As Inis Claude wrote in the midst of the Cold War: '[T]he process of legitimization is ultimately a political phenomenon, a crystallization of judgment that may be influenced but is unlikely to be wholly determined by legal norms and moral principles' (Claude 1966: 369). Erik Voeten confirms this interpretation which 'contrasts sharply with the view that IOs derive their legitimacy precisely from their ability to appear depoliticized', adding that 'the ability of the SC to legitimize the use of force stems from its function as a political meeting place' (Voeten 2005: 552). Legitimacy results from the fact that Council resolutions have been accepted by the most politically influential and representative collection of states as currently exists in any single forum. Viewed in this light it becomes more difficult to see the UNSC as adopting a role as a moral authority or judicial interpreter of legal doctrine and precedent. Indeed as the idiosyncratic rationales that have been used over the past two decades attest, it is difficult to see the Council as pursuing the development of a particular normative framework in support of human security, civilian protection, or R2P that would guide, let alone bind, the Council in the future.

As mentioned earlier, since the end of the Cold War, the UN and many regional organizations have adopted a more interventionist approach in response to civil conflicts and other domestic disturbances. Yet such decisions can best be seen as representing a collection of discrete political bargains that were made to reach a consensus for Security Council approval. These efforts, while intended to give more attention to local conditions and exceptional practices, also served to prevent a more permissive or inclusive set of principles that would endorse intervention. This would also ensure that the Council would retain a significant degree of freedom and flexibility in deliberating on future cases. The place of such norms as R2P rests more on their influence on the political interests of the member governments than they do on the current or past practice of the Council. A review of these interests and how they have influenced governments' position on R2P thus becomes a more important approach to considering if and how the Security Council might refer to R2P in the future.

The advent of a more interventionist set of practices and the concerted political effort to establish a set of guiding principles in support of such practices, as evidenced in the doctrine of Responsibility to Protect has generated a fairly consistent response from the P5 and especially from emerging powers – including some of those states that abstained on UNSC 1973. The R2P principle was primarily intended to highlight 'the rights of populations at risk to assistance and protection and the responsibility of outsiders to help'. Developed in the aftermath of the contested intervention in Kosovo in 1999, R2P was seen as way of bringing some degree of principle-defined procedure to the circumstances that would permit and trigger outside intervention. The debate on the R2P principle and its adoption by the UN provides a window on the views of the P5 and emerging powers and their attitudes toward this principle, the role of the UN, alongside their position on sovereignty and the use of force.

There is little indication that the Western states among the P5 have adopted a concerted approach towards R2P or that they share a substantially different view of the norm than that held by Russia and China or other emerging powers, specifically Brazil, India and South Africa. While these Western governments have repeatedly expressed their concerns for preventing or stopping genocide and crimes against humanity, they have been equally consistent in stating that such responses must be in accord with the international community and must work through the UN. The exception of Kosovo has, it would seem, only reinforced such a view. In a debate on implementing the R2P in 2009 Western governments indicated their support for implementation while identifying the need to work with the international community and through the UN.

The statements and policies of emerging powers while implying a lack of consensus surrounding interventionist practices, in light of their continued support for traditional principles of sovereignty, territorial integrity and limits on the use of force that have defined international order, have also been willing to support R2P. Yet such support is accompanied by support for a continued role for the UN and especially for the UNSC managing this implementation. It does reflect the fact that emerging powers want a larger say in defining international standards and practices and look to the UN and specifically the Security Council as a means for this.

Such countries as India have no desire to challenge the international system, as did other rising powers such as Germany and Japan in the 19th and 20th centuries. But they certainly wish to be given a place at the global high table. Without that, they would be unlikely to volunteer to share the primary burden for dealing with such issues as terrorism, climate change, nuclear proliferation and energy security – all of which concern the entire globe (Tharoor 2011).

It is also important to acknowledge that these states are not indifferent to the need for and the possibility of a more humane international order. The concern for human insecurities within states has been responsible for the limited support demonstrated by these states for such principles as R2P. This support, in turn, will likely encourage these states to continue along a more progressive view of aiding populations at risk. 'As a result, China's increasing participation in UN peacekeeping operations and more active international role may create a feedback loop that shapes China's worldview, with the result being that the Chinese government may no longer consider it conscionable or politically possible to fail to act in the face of mass atrocities or genocide' (Davis 2011: 281). The possibility of such feedback loops working effectively may very well depend on the willingness of others to be more attentive to some of the concerns raised by these emerging powers. There is some degree of support for interventions for humanitarian purposes, though the manner in which contributing governments dealt with Libya will make China and others much more diligent in trying to control the operational aspects of UNSC resolutions in the near term future.

What then does this entail for the Security Council's role in legitimating practices accompanied by normative principles? The debate over the implementation of UNSC Resolution 1973 can be viewed as a reminder of the Council's utility in reflecting the diversity of interests that continues to define the international community and the tentative nature of agreements on principles such as R2P. The resolution's passage and the subsequent fallout over its implementation also demonstrate the continued relevance of a political view of the Council's legitimation function. As Adam Roberts and Dominik Zaum remind us:

> . . . the Council is not intended to maintain the rule of law (or apply principles): it was intended to maintain international peace and security. That is a very different, and more limited, role. The Security Council is not a 'world policeman': it is an institutionalised process for managing international crises. (Roberts and Zaum 2008: 30)

The Council's efforts to manage the crisis in Libya are most instructive of how these political decisions develop.

The UNSC, Libya and R2P

The Security Council has been criticized frequently for its failure to act quickly and decisively in response to international crises and major threats to human security. Negotiations among Security Council members are seldom expeditious and the threat or use of the veto by one of the P5 imposes even more constraints on those interested in getting the organization to respond in a timely manner, as a successful resolution must have wide appeal lest it fall to the opposition of one or more of the permanent members. It was thus a pleasant surprise for many human security activists that the Council moved with what for it was alacrity in responding to the uprising that seized Libya in the first two months of 2011. It seemed clear from the outset that any action would require the support of the Security Council. Perhaps as a reflection of the Council's role in legitimating interventions, NATO's Secretary General Anders Fogh Rasmussen was quoted in February 2011 that NATO member governments had not yet discussed enforcing a no-fly zone, but went on to say 'that such a far-reaching approach would require a very clear international legitimacy and in particular a United Nations mandate' (Voice of America 2011). The Council expressed its concern over the violation of human rights and threats to civilians in mid-February and in quick succession approved resolutions 1970 and 1973 three weeks apart on 26 February and 17 March respectively. Resolution 1970 by a unanimous vote condemned the violence against civilians and called upon the Libyan authorities to exercise their responsibility to protect. Acting under Chapter VII it referred the actions of the Libyan government to the ICC and adopted an arms embargo, invoked a travel ban on selected Libyan authorities, froze the assets of these authorities held abroad, and called upon member states to provide humanitarian assistance to Libyans.

The failure of these measures to change the Libyan government's response to the uprisings, the continued violence on the ground, and most significantly the threats issued by Gaddafi to rebels in Benghazi, led to a second Resolution 1973 approved without a dissenting vote and five abstentions. Once again the Resolution condemned the violence, the threat to civilian lives and the Libyan government's responsibility to protect. It also recalled the condemnations of regional organizations, specifically the League of Arab States, the African Union (AU) and the Secretary General of the Islamic Conference. Acting once again under Chapter VII, the resolution called for a ceasefire and dispatched an envoy of the Secretary General alongside an envoy from the Peace and Security Council of the AU to seek a political settlement. The Resolution went on to authorize member states 'to take all necessary measures' 'excluding a foreign occupation force of any form on any part of Libyan territory' to 'protect civilians and civilian populated areas under threat of attack' in cooperation with members of the League of Arab States. The Resolution also established a no-fly zone and authorized member states to enforce compliance in coordination with the Secretary General and the League of Arab States and reinforced the arms embargo. 'US Ambassador Susan Rice was quoted as saying that: "I can't remember a time in recent memory when the Council has acted so swiftly, so decisively, and in unanimity on an urgent matter of international human rights"' (Dunne and Gifkins 2011: 522).

It is perhaps an indication of how frequently the UN Security Council had been allowed to delegate the use of force that the adoption of

Resolution 1973 was less eventful than some of those adopted in the early 1990s. At the same time, the Resolution marked yet another departure because it was the Council's first explicit reference connecting military action with at least one aspect of the R2P norm, that being a state's responsibility to protect its citizens. It also marked one of the first occasions where both Russia and China acquiesced in the practice of military intervention in the absence of the agreement of the local government. The Resolution and the consensus that allowed it to be passed was for these reasons unprecedented, but its approval reflected a very tenuous consensus. There were clear differences over means reflected throughout the debate on the Resolution and more explicitly once military operations were undertaken. For example, there was discussion over the value of and priority given to negotiations on a ceasefire and the value of a total arms embargo. But as noted by some, here was 'a non-liberal great power contesting the means rather than the ends of protective intervention' (Dunne and Gifkins 2011: 525). The means were, however, important and quickly became a source of contention.

The resolutions, though not their implementation, did suggest a close degree of adherence to the principles of R2P articulated in the original report of the ICISS, with the Security Council playing the role of the proper authority. The resolutions did provide, again in principle, some limited opportunity for an early end to the conflict through condemnation of violent practices, calls for a ceasefire and targeted sanctions. Resolution 1973, while putting in place the provisions that would allow for a more forceful intervention, also stressed the importance of envoys from the UN and the AU to work on a ceasefire. One could read this as moving to a military intervention as an instrument of last resort, the short timeline of which was being driven by conditions on the ground. The actual implementation of military operations so quickly after the resolution's adoption, however, raised questions about last resort, proportionality and the degree to which military operations were focused solely or even primarily on protecting civilian populations at risk. Thus while the resolutions suggest adherence to the principles of R2P, the ensuing military operation failed to do so, leading one Canadian group to conclude:

> The failure of the operationalization of Resolution 1973 through the military focus on inappropriate means and inappropriate ends creates an unfortunate precedent that has the potential to fatally weaken the concept of R2P for future acceptance and use by the International community. (Siebert 2011: 7)

The debate over Libya and the approval of these resolutions demonstrated the increased significance of regional organizations in shaping the attitudes of the permanent members of the Council. The support of the Organization of the Islamic Conference, the Council of the League of Arab States, and the Peace and Security Council of the African Union for the no-fly zone was critical on a number of fronts. It was instrumental in convincing the Obama administration to step forward with a more active diplomatic effort to secure approval for Resolution 1973. It was also instrumental in convincing China and Russia to refrain from using their vetoes to prevent the resolution's adoption:

> Both Russia and China place rhetorical emphasis on the importance of regional organisations, and to some extent their diplomacy backs their rhetoric; so the Arab League's call for action eased the pathway to abstention, a point made explicit in the Chinese explanation of their vote. (Jones 2011: 55)

China in particular had emphasized the importance of local input on deliberations over the implementation of R2P. The resolution makes explicit reference to the concerns expressed by these regional entities, further reinforcing their importance in determining the need for and scope of UN action on this issue. The significance of these regional organizations was subsequently noted by Edward Luck who viewed this as one of the critical differences between the Council's actions on Libya and its lack of action on Syria:

> I think if you compare what has happened or hasn't happened with Syria, for example, in the Security Council, and Libya, clearly the members of the Security Council listen to what regional organisations are saying. Regional organisations have not reacted the same way to the violence in Syria as they did to the violence in Libya. (Luck 2011)

The influence of these regional players on the permanent members of the Council suggests that the approach to R2P taken by local and regional actors may be of some importance in determining the level of support for implementing this norm in the future.

It has been suggested that there were few Western interests involved in the campaign against the Gaddafi regime in Libya and thus norms such as R2P must have influenced the behaviour of these Western governments. This is often mentioned in contrast to non-Western states who allegedly continue to be influenced by interests rather than these more virtuous alternatives. Such a reading seems to overlook the more than three decades during which the US and other Western governments sought to undermine the Gaddafi regime and the widespread support the US received from its Western allies when it bombed Libya in 1986. The more recent rapprochement between Gaddafi and these governments may have obscured this longstanding animosity, but it did not erase it. Further to this has been the ambivalence that these same Western governments displayed towards uprisings against those despots in the region who were friendly towards Western commercial and security interests. Support for regime change and interventions in support of rebel populations has, for example, been clearly absent in Bahrain, just as it was absent in Egypt earlier in 2011. Indeed in the case of the latter, the US, like their allies, seemed more than reluctant to let Mubarak go. Commentaries in the American press that emphasized the influence of values on US policy and the lack of interests in Libya eventually touched a nerve as, in a public address, US president Barack Obama offered a defence of American action on the basis of national interests (Obama 2011). Subsequently Anne-Marie Slaughter offered her own interest-based account of US support for intervention in Libya (Slaughter 2011). Slaughter argues that interests are not far from the values that are often articulated in their place and the connection is largely the result of the changed context in which global politics is now conducted. That context is one in which states and societies must be incorporated in the calculating of one's own national interests. The US can no longer operate in an exclusively inter-state system and must take into account societal elements in assessing its own national interests. Such an extended calculation requires American policymakers to take into account domestic societies in other countries and not limit their attention to their government counterparts. In this respect, American interests in the region rested on their ability to provide support for those societal interests leading political change within states rather than for the oppressive governments seeking to contain them. This becomes a matter not of abnegating national interests but of developing a fuller understanding and accounting of the multitude of factors that will affect one's national interests. The efforts to explain away rather than call attention to the force of the R2P norm and the very selective nature of American intervention make it difficult to argue that American support for intervention was driven by a commitment to R2P.

The French and British delegations led the call for intervention in Libya. Their reasons, like those of most states involved, were mixed, but also reflected in large part a concern over the need to respond in a more forthright manner to the wave of citizen rebellions that were demarcating the Arab Spring. Tentative responses to events in Tunisia and Egypt suggested a limited commitment to democratic reform and placed these and other governments (the US and Canada, for example) on the defensive both in the region and with their own domestic publics, including, in the French case, a sizable immigrant population from the region. There was considerable pressure to respond more constructively to the calls for reform in the region. Libya was an easier target than other candidates in the region, as the long history of difficult relations with the Gaddafi regime alongside significant economic interests (oil and arms for the French) made intervention in support of the rebels a more attractive option. French foreign policy under President Sarkozy had also developed a strong interest in deploying military force, according to some accounts, as a way of asserting French power within the European Union (STRATFOR 2011). Related to this, the French government was also anxious to develop its military cooperation with Britain and to see Europeans take the lead instead of following the Americans into yet another campaign. This view was not, however, shared by other European governments who were more interested in seeing NATO play a larger role. As *The Economist* reported: 'France has resisted giving NATO too prominent a role for fear that it will turn off Arab allies: Italy says the NATO label would be an attraction because it would put a straitjacket on the gung-ho French' (*The Economist* 2011). Given the level of support among Arab states, especially in the initial stages of the intervention, French concerns over NATO's involvement did not materialize.

The Obama administration in the United States was sympathetic to a European initiative although the press subsequently castigated the administration for 'leading from the rear'. Following the interventions in Afghanistan and Iraq, the Obama administration had refrained from taking the lead on additional military interventions without a clear indication of interest and commitment from others. The US became fully engaged once French and British support was clearly demonstrated and a decision was made to seek a UN resolution to authorize the intervention:

> From the moment Obama made the decision to go for humanitarian intervention, the US diplomatic machinery went into overdrive, with intensive contacts US diplomacy went into overdrive at the UN and telephone diplomacy to key capitals. This was particularly important

in Russia, as well as with South Africa, which was persuaded to vote in favour of the resolution. (Jones 2011: 55)

While US diplomacy might have swayed Russia to abstain, the Russian abstention can also be viewed in terms of both domestic politics and Russian–US relations alongside some commercial interests in Libya. In the context of the bilateral relationship, Libya looked to be an opportunity where Russia could, with minimal economic, strategic or political costs, allow the US and other Western interests to advance their humanitarian goals. Domestically, Russian President Dimitri Medvedev decided to adopt such an approach, thinking it might help his own chances to retain his post. This was despite the fact that his main rival, Vladimir Putin, saw any support as toeing the American line and thus open to the charge of undermining Russia's strategic interests, a view that won him some sympathy with Russian citizens. Russia's policy on Libya reflected this tension within the Soviet leadership and a clear difference in approach between Medvedev and Putin, with the latter making a principled defence of non-intervention alongside a harsh criticism of the US's tendency to resort to the early use of force and the former defending the abstention on the grounds of protecting civilians and working alongside the Arab League. Russia abstained from Resolution 1973, but was brought on board at the time of the G8 summit when the Libyan intervention seemed to be at impasse and Obama wanted someone to test Gaddafi's resolve with a diplomatic envoy. Medvedev signed up to the G8 communiqué that asked Gaddafi to give up power, thus supporting the revised policy objectives adopted by NATO but not endorsed by the Security Council.

The Chinese abstention suggested a broader set of considerations that are important in considering China's approach to R2P and to the UN Security Council. China has expanded its participation in UN operations quite significantly since the end of the Cold War. Suzuki has argued that such practices are a reflection of China's efforts to present itself as a responsible member of the international community and thereby lending support to international order and stability (Suzuki 2008). Foot and Walker, in their examination of China's approach to international order, provide a further interpretation of these activities. As the UN has expanded both the scope and nature of its interventions, the Chinese government's position has also changed. 'Generally, they have acquiesced in UN action but have been keen to claim that precedents have not been set, that host state consent has been sought and (mostly) given, and that regional states were supportive of the action'

(Foot and Walker 2011: 47). Jonathan Davis's review of China's policy on various post-Cold War interventions provides a similar view, but one that highlights the persisting importance of sovereignty. In his view, China has retained its commitment to sovereignty while moving some way towards accepting the significance of severe human rights violations and the need for these to receive international attention. Chinese authorities did so in a manner that gave preference to sovereignty, as reflected in their reaction to UNSC Resolution 1244 that established the organization's post-Kosovo War role 'In essence, the "human rights over sovereignty" theory serves to infringe upon the sovereignty of other States and to promote hegemonism under the pretext of human rights. This totally runs counter to the purposes and principles of the United Nations Charter. The international community should maintain vigilance against it' (cited in Davis 2011). Allen Carlson has argued that Chinese policy has not remained static on sovereignty. He quotes Chinese legal scholar Wang Tieya who described China's policy of the early 1990s: 'Strict adherence to the principle of the inviolability of sovereignty has become a distinctive feature . . . and is treated as the basis of international relations and the cornerstone of the whole system of international law', but goes on to argue that such views have been modified more recently (Carlson 2011: 92).

To some degree these changes have been reflected in the Chinese government's response to R2P. Its views on intervention and R2P were presented in its 2005 UN Security Council reform paper in which it supported international action to resolve humanitarian crises, but like Brazil, argued for strict control of such practices by the UN Charter and the Security Council. In perhaps the most significant signal of China's growing acceptance of R2P, Beijing included a section entitled 'The Responsibility to Protect' in its June 2005 position paper on UN reform. In that paper, China stated that '[e]ach state shoulders the primary responsibility to protect its own population' but it also explicitly acknowledged '[w]hen a massive humanitarian crisis occurs, it is the legitimate concern of the international community to ease and defuse the crisis'. The position paper also stated that international responses to humanitarian crises 'should strictly conform to the UN Charter' and should respect 'the opinions of the country and the regional organisation concerned'. The paper further reiterated China's position that decisions to intervene should fall to the Security Council alone, a position not at odds with the evolving doctrine of R2P (Chinese position paper cited in Davis 2011: 260–1).

While acknowledging the principles of constructive assistance by outside parties, at the UNGA debate on R2P in 2011 the Chinese government took the position that a response to any crisis 'should be accomplished within the UN framework . . . and the implementation of the Security Council resolution must be strict and accurate. Neither liberal interpretations of the [SC] resolutions nor action beyond the provision of the Security Council resolutions would be acceptable'. In this debate, occurring as it did in the midst of NATO operations against Libya, the Chinese statement also stated bluntly that: 'No party should engage in regime change or get involved in civil war in the name of protecting civilians' (cited in Davis 2011).

It is important to recognize that China did not reject the R2P idea out of hand, but they sought to ensure that it would be reined-in significantly:

> China signaled a growing willingness to accept the broad outlines of the R2P, albeit with strong caveats that any intervention must receive Security Council approval and that the Security Council should respond to humanitarian crises cautiously and on a case-by-case basis. The latter caveat indicated Beijing's preference that the Security Council's approach to humanitarian intervention should remain ad hoc and exceptional rather than become 'normalized'. (Davis 2011: 260–1)

One can also find in these comments that China, while securing R2P within the narrower confines of the UN Charter and the UN Security Council, had severely curtailed the more activist application of the doctrine as it was envisioned by many of its proponents. It was not, however, a wholesale rejection of the concerns at the root of this emerging norm.

China invariably insists that any international intervention in response to a humanitarian crisis is solely the province of the Security Council and that the legality of any intervention depends on authorization by the Security Council, after a determination that the situation constitutes a threat to international peace and security. China's position is best understood as rejecting claims to a unilateral right of humanitarian intervention while, in practice, acquiescing in the exercise of a multilateral right through the Security Council (Davis 2011: 273).

For many this might seem an emasculated Council. For China it is the Council playing the role that it was designed to play – a forum where great powers would negotiate the management of global order. On the one hand, China's position on R2P might offer evidence of China's sophisticated and adept diplomacy, allowing it to appear cooperative and conciliatory without ceding ground on its vital interest in preserving sovereignty and restricting interventionist claims. On the other, it demonstrates China's willingness to engage in new developments in UN peacekeeping despite its reservations, which so often fall on deaf ears or are presumed to be a recalcitrant rather than a divergent position.

China has adeptly avoided directly challenging what it perceives to be the Western normative order underpinning R2P in a manner that might threaten China's self-professed responsible engagement in UN peacekeeping arrangements. At the same time, China has leveraged its relationship with like-minded states to limit the prospect of R2P directly undermining its resistance to non-consensual intervention, or of utterly discrediting its commitment to enhancing civilian protection through political negotiations rather than enforcement measures (Teitt 2011: 299).

Brazil and India, while supporting human rights in principle, have been less willing to support the use of military force and outside interference as a means of protecting these rights. As such, their abstentions demonstrated reservations similar to those of China, reservations very much influenced by their historical experiences with outside interventions. As with China, there is also a strong commitment to reinforcing regional approaches to dealing with crises. Unlike China, however, whose permanent seat (and veto) are firmly in place, Brazil and India also have a strong interest in gaining a greater voice in the Security Council. The Brazilian government has expressed concerns over the R2P principle and particularly with the potential for its abuse by interveners. This approach to such practices would seem to be entrenched in Brazil's domestic politics as the former president, Lula da Silva, came under attack for abandoning the non-interventionist tradition of foreign policy in favour of peace enforcement in Haiti. In this light, Brazil's 'hesitant internationalism' could as well be described as seeking to influence developing norms in international society by contesting the Western powers' approach to such norms, in preference to an approach that is cautious about redefining core principles of the prevailing international order such as sovereignty and non-intervention. As Alex Bellamy noted in examining Brazil's response to the Libyan resolution:

> The Brazilian government for its part, made explicit its acceptance of the principle that states needed to look after their citizens and went on to reiterate the primary role that the UN must absolutely play in determining when, where, and how to advance on the principle. 'The protection of civilians is a humanitarian imperative. It is a

> distinct concept that must not be confused or conflated with threats to international peace and security, as described in the Charter, or with the responsibility to protect. We must avoid excessively broad interpretations of the protection of civilians, which could link it to the exacerbation of conflict, compromise the impartiality of the United Nations or create the perception that it is being used as a smokescreen for intervention or regime change. To that end, we must ensure that all efforts to protect civilians be strictly in keeping with the Charter and based on a rigorous and non-selective application of international humanitarian law. (Bellamy 2011)

Brazil's reservations were expressed in the concept paper presented to the UN in November 2011. The paper, entitled 'Responsibility While Protecting', urges caution in the rush to military force and regime change that seem to lie behind many proposals for implementing R2P. The paper reflects a view widely shared among the group of states reviewed here when it states: 'the world today suffers the painful consequences of interventions that have aggravated existing conflicts, allowed terrorism to penetrate into places where it previously did not exist, given rise to new cycles of violence and increased the vulnerability of civilian populations' (Brazil 2011). The paper recommended a much stronger application of the UN Charter and oversight by the UN Security Council to control the use of force in exercising the responsibility to protect.

Four of the five members of the Council who abstained on UNSC Resolution 1973 – China, India, Brazil and Russia – constitute the BRICs, that group of emerging powers identified in a Goldman Sachs report which highlighted their explosive rates of economic growth. While largely defined along economic grounds the group also represents in broader geopolitical terms a collection of emerging powers, each of which in turn has indicated its interest in the emerging international order and the role of the UN in that order. The group, along with South Africa (who with some initial misgivings supported UNSC Resolution 1973, in part to further its own interests on the continent), have also begun to meet in their own summit meetings. The common position of the BRICs on the Libyan resolution put the spotlight on the role of these states in international peace and security matters. An examination of the practices and policy statements of these emerging powers reveals a nuanced and evolving approach to intervention and R2P; one that urges caution in the advancement of interventionist norms and remains staunchly pluralist in its desire to protect state sovereignty while not completely abandoning some degree of concern for humanitarian protection. Their views also demonstrate a strong commitment to maintaining a prominent role for the UN, regional organizations and local states in a manner that allows for variations in the response to peace and security issues and, especially, seeks to limit the use of force in responding to such issues.

The debate over Libya brought to the forefront the role that these emerging powers were playing in the UN and their approach to the organization's expanded role in peace and security. It was also a demonstration of their attitudes towards the Responsibility to Protect norm. The common approach adopted by the BRICs was widely noted, especially in terms of the development of the R2P norm and the apparently more favourable approach to intervention being pursued through UNSC resolutions. Dunne and Gifkins are among those who took note of their position, describing it as a 'constructive abstention':

> Resolution 1973 must be viewed in the context of the normative development of R2P and the protection of civilians since the end of the Cold War. Many aspects of this resolution are unique and reflect the difficult lessons learnt during this period. Resolution 1973 is the first no-fly zone explicitly authorized for civilian protection purposes and the language used to do this is more expansive than prior examples. However, abstentions from two permanent members and other rising powers suggest that while a shift is evident it is not without contestation. (Dunne and Gifkins 2011: 522)

Other views were less favourable. The BRICs' failure to support UNSC 1973 led some observers to criticize the lack of support these states were willing to give to international order. Their abstentions were criticized on the grounds of national interests overriding the need to support international norms such as R2P. Wagner and Jackman expressed such a view and asked 'when the BRICS will be willing to step up to the plate and place idealism above self-interest' (Wagner and Jackman 2011). Such criticisms failed to account for the considerable compromise that such an abstention required, especially for China and Russia. Moreover, as Jones points out, 'the reasons for BRICs' caution in relation to (UNSC) 1973 are multiple and include reasonable concerns about the efficacy of force and a likely gap between the political intent and the kind of military actions that were suitable' (Jones 2011: 526). The implicit assumption here that supporters of UNSC 1973 were not guided by self-interest and had forsaken this interest in support of idealist objectives warrants further attention. There is a tendency to exaggerate the extent to which interests, as compared to purely normative considerations, influenced the position of the non-Western permanent members of the UNSC while assuming that self-interest is not involved in the support that other states have given to R2P. 'After all, in expressing ambivalence about the consequences of force in Libya, countries like India and Russia were taking essentially the same position as the US Department of Defense' (Jones 2011: 53).

The 'constructive abstention' quickly turned into a more critical reaction in response to the manner in which force was deployed and the shift in policy to one of regime change in Libya. Those abstaining 'did so because they believed that the resolution very narrowly circumscribed the kind of force that NATO would use. They expected civilian protection. What NATO became was the de-facto air force of Libyan rebels' (Goldberg 2012). Almost immediately criticisms appeared among not only those who abstained on Resolution 1973, but also among some proponents of the no-fly zone in the Arab League. For some, the Resolution was being abused as France, Britain and others were more interested in using this opportunity to overturn the regime rather than protect civilians. For others, regime change was the only way to protect civilians. Either way the issue for members of the Security Council was how Resolution 1973 was being interpreted and implemented. Interpretation issues came up again in debate on the protection of civilians in May 2011. The representative of India, for example, Manjeev Singh Puri, asked, 'Who watches the guardians?' and noted a 'considerable sense of unease about the manner in which the humanitarian imperative of protecting civilians has been interpreted for actual action on the ground' (cited in Bellamy and Williams 2011: 847). Likewise, China's representative Li Baodong opposed 'any attempt to willfully interpret the resolutions or to take actions that exceed those mandated by the resolutions' (cited in Bellamy and Williams 2011: 847). These concerns reflected not only particular problems with the interpretation of Resolution 1973 but much broader considerations about the use of force and the potential for interventions under the principle of R2P to be used to overturn regimes and undermine sovereignty.

Conclusion

Writing in *The Guardian*, Simon Tisdall reported: 'The war in Libya was a one-off. It established no new doctrine. Rather, it set a limited post-Iraq paradigm for selective, "do-able", feel good interventionism. For the seriously oppressed peoples of Syria, Burma, Belarus, Zimbabwe and North Korea, for example, it is a meaningless exercise' (Tisdall 2011). It is reasonable to conclude that the aftershocks from the implementation of UNSC Resolution 1973 will be felt not only in the future support given to the R2P doctrine, but also in that given to the role of the UN Security Council more generally in peace and security matters. The decision by a handful of states to abstain from supporting the resolution was an indication of their disquiet with the Council adopting such an interventionist stance in response to a civil conflict, yet it was also an effort to reaffirm the central role of the UN in managing a response. Abstaining, as opposed to voting against the resolution, attests to their interest in reinforcing the Council's role and perhaps was an attempt to determine if the organization could act in a manner that would support both protection of civilians and respect for state sovereignty. The end result speaks as much to the difficulty of doing this as it does about the role of the Council or the UN at large.

The UNSC's approach to the uprising in Libya and its decision to allow states to employ the use of force to support regime change in the country has once again raised concerns about the legitimacy of that organization. For some this stands as a testimony to the ability of the organization to respond effectively to support international norms such as the responsibility to protect, while others viewed it as an abuse of the UNSC's mandate by powerful states bent on pursuing their own specific interests under the guise of an international norm and under the cover of a UNSC resolution. Both accounts are somewhat misleading in assuming that the UNSC has ever been anything more than a political forum in which competing ideas and interests are considered, contested and, on some occasions, co-opted, allowing for concerted action. We see in the case of Libya that interests and ideas did indeed converge and enabled an undertaking the likes of which was neither anticipated nor fully supported by all of the parties involved. This suggests little more than that the convergence of interests and ideas in this particular case but not a substantive degree of agreement as to either interests or ideas. The result provides yet another reminder not to interpret UNSC resolutions as marking definitive directives or conclusive consensus on norms and practices. Instead Resolution 1973, like other UNSC resolutions, reflected a tentative and partial agreement in response to a very specific set of conditions. That the Resolution was subsequently employed to justify actions which some parties neither anticipated nor supported serves only as a reminder that resolutions may move states in different directions and urges a much greater degree of caution for the future.

This is in part what one sees in the response of Russia and China to resolutions on Syria.

What this means for the future of the UNSC's approach to R2P is uncertain. It is very likely that the Council will be unable to reach an easy agreement on its implementation in the near future as Russia and China and perhaps other emerging powers seek to rein in the possible use of force. It will also likely mean that future resolutions that seek to implement the principle will need to be more carefully constructed so as to remove the potential for using force. The efforts to develop such language proved unworkable in relation to Syria, at least to the point where some parties wished to force a vote that would expose the opposition of Russia and China to a possible intervention. It will certainly mean persistent selectivity as the UNSC encounters situations demanding a response from the international community. This is nothing new, though it is often disparaged by observers:

> The Security Council is not an impartial judicial body, but a deeply political organisation, to which a selective approach is more appropriate . . . Although selectivity is often viewed critically, its practice reflects the political realities within which the Council acts, whereby the permanent members and their right to veto, and the interests and policies of the wider membership of the UN, force the Council to act selectively. (Roberts and Zaum 2008: 20 and 8)

The Council is after all a political forum of very different states with varied and competing interests, where norms play a less prominent role. Any agreement reached among such a group is a considerable achievement. Nico Krisch is of the view that 'in most cases, Russian and Chinese accommodation of Western interests is more likely to be due to a general desire not to weaken the Council as an institution and also to maintain a positive relationship with the dominant powers' (Krisch 2008: 141–2). One might also see it as way of maintaining relationships with lesser powers that may be inclined to agree with the practices of Western states on some occasions.

It is important to recognize that all states, but especially great powers, have a somewhat schizophrenic relationship with the UN and thus with the authority of the Security Council. The Council has the potential to confer a dose of legitimacy on the actions of states. Great powers have the capacity and thus the potential to undertake actions independent of the UN and without the approval of the Council. As they do this, however, they run the risk of undermining that legitimacy which makes their activities much easier to carry out. The same set of considerations play out for those states more resistant to the sorts of undertaking desired by great powers. The veto can be invoked by other permanent members of the Security Council. The use of the veto, however, carries with it the risk that these states will simply move outside of the UN and carry out their actions independent/free from its control, acting in a manner that is not accountable to any other party outside itself. Such are the considerations that shape a great power's decision to work within or alternatively allow others to benefit from the legitimacy that UN-approved operations provide.

It would be wrong to read from these events that the aftermath of UNSC 1973 is the death knell for R2P or for the Security Council playing a role in managing the future implementation of this norm. The subsequent failure (to date) to secure resolutions to address the ongoing violence in Syria has without question been influenced by the manner in which events unfolded in Libya. This is not, however, the sole explanation for the lack of consensus on Syria among the members of the Council. Syria presents a different case with different interests involved, just as the Libyan case had its own particular features. 'Arguably, RtoP was born in an era when assertive liberalism was at its height, and sovereign equality looked and smelled reactionary. But as the liberal moment recedes, and the distribution of power shifts globally, the principle of sovereign equality may enjoy a comeback. If so, it could very well dampen the new climate of expectations around the responsibility to protect' (Welsh 2010: 425). A combination of particular events and distinct political choices resulted in a consensus sufficient to pass Resolution 1973. It is not inconceivable that some future situation would allow for a similar outcome, albeit probably for different reasons and guided by other choices. What these events do suggest is that the UNSC does not operate on the basis of moral or legal principles and the decision to adopt Resolution 1973 does not set any precedents in either area. These events also suggest that a number of states will continue to struggle to ensure that the UNSC remains the forum in which such decisions are reached, or not.

References

Bellamy, A. J. (2011) 'The Responsibility to Protect and the Problem of Regime Change', in *The Responsibility to Protect: Challenges and Opportunities in Light of the Libyan Intervention*. Available online at: www.e-ir.info/wp-content/uploads/RTOP.pdf [Accessed August 2012].

Bellamy, A. J. and P. D. Williams (2011) 'The New Politics of Protection? Côte d'Ivoire, Libya and the Responsibility to Protect', *International Affairs*, vol. 87, no. 4, pp. 825–50.

Burges, S. (2011) 'The BRICS and the UN: Coordination or Fragmentation?', e-International Relations, 21 October. Available online at: www.e-ir.info/2011/10/21/the-brics-and-the-un-coordination-or-fragmentation [Accessed August 2012].

Carlson, A. (2011) 'Moving Beyond Sovereignty?', *Journal of Contemporary China*, vol. 20, no. 68, pp. 89–102.

China (2005) 'Position Paper of the People's Republic of China on the United Nations Reforms'. Available online at: www.china-un.org/eng/xw/tl99101.htm [Accessed August 2012].

Claude, I. L. (1966) 'Collective Legitimation as a Political Function of the United Nations', *International Organisation*, vol. 20, no. 3, pp. 367–79.

Davis, J. E. (2011) 'From Ideology to Pragmatism: China's Position on Humanitarian Intervention in the Post-Cold War Era', *Vanderbilt Journal of Transnational Law*, vol. 44, no. 2, pp. 217–83.

Dunne, T. and J. Gifkins (2011) 'Libya and the State of Intervention', *Australian Journal of International Affairs*, vol. 65, no. 5, pp. 515–29.

The Economist (2011) 'Who Is In Charge Here?', 25 March.

Foot, R. and A. Walker (2011) *China, the United States, and Global Order* (Cambridge: Cambridge University Press).

Franck, T. M. (1990) *The Power of Legitimacy among Nations* (New York: Oxford University Press).

Jones, B. D. (2011) 'Libya and the Responsibilities of Power', *Survival*, vol. 53, no. 3, pp. 51–60.

Goldberg, M. L. (2011) 'The Illogic of a Nofly Zone for Libya', *UN Dispatch*, 9 March. Available online at: www.undispatch.com/the-illogic-of-a-no-fly-zone-for-libya [Accessed August 2012].

Goldberg, M. L. (2012) 'How Libya's Success Became Syria's Failure', *UN Dispatch*, 19 January. Available online at: www.undispatch.com/how-libyas-success-became-syrias-failure [Accessed August 2012].

Hulme, M. (2011) 'Chinese Sovereignty and the Structuration of the International Community', paper presented to the annual meeting of the Canadian Political Science Association, Waterloo, Ontario.

Kenkel, K. M. (2010) 'South America's Emerging Power: Brazil as Peacekeeper', *International Peacekeeping*, vol. 17, no. 5, pp. 644–61.

Krisch, N. (2008) 'Great Powers and the Council', in Vaughan Lowe, Adam Roberts, Jennifer Welsh and Dominik Zaum (eds), *The United Nations Security Council and War* (Oxford: Oxford University Press).

Luck, E. (2011) Interview with Edward Luck, Special Advisor to the UN Secretary-General. Available online at: www.un.org/apps/news/newsmakers.asp?NewsID=38 [Accessed August 2012].

Malone, D. (1998) *Decision-making in the UN Security Council: The Case of Haiti 1990–1997* (Oxford: Oxford University Press).

Mikulaschek, C. (2010) 'The United Nations Security Council and the Responsibility to Protect: Policy, Process and Practice', in H. Winkler, T. Reid-Larsen and C. Mikulaschek (eds), *The United Nations Security Council and the Responsibility to Protect*, 39th IPI Seminar, Vienna, Austria, Factiva Paper 1/2010, pp. 20–49.

Nasu, H. (2009) 'Operationalizing the "Responsibility to Protect" and Conflict Prevention: Dilemmas of Civilian Protection in Armed Conflict', *Journal of Conflict & Security Law*, vol. 14, no. 2, pp. 209–41.

Roberts, A. and D. Zaum (2008) *Selective Security, War and the United Nations since 1945*, Adelphi Paper 395 (London: International Institute for Strategic Studies).

Siebert, J. (2011) 'Libya and R2P: The Failure of Bombing Raids to Protect Vulnerable Civilians' (Waterloo, ON: Project Ploughshares).

STRATFOR (2011) 'France, UK Have Differing Motives for Intervening in Libya', *Forbes*, 29 March. Available online at: www.forbes.com/sites/energysource/2011/03/09/france-u-k-have-differing-motives-for-intervening-in-libya [Accessed August 2012].

Suzuki, S. (2008) 'Seeking "Legitimate" Great Power Status in the Post-Cold War International Society: China's and Japan's Participation in UNPKO', *International Relations*, vol. 22, no. 1, pp. 45–63.

Teitt, S. (2011) 'The Responsibility to Protect and China's Peacekeeping Policy', *International Peacekeeping*, vol. 18, no. 3, pp. 298–312.

Tharoor, S. (2011) 'Security Council Reform, Past, Present and Future', *Ethics and International Affairs*, vol. 25, no. 4. Available online at: www.ethicsandinternationalaffairs.org/2011/security-council-reform-past-present-and-future-full-text/ [Accessed August 2012].

Tisdall, S. (2011) 'Lessons from Libya: How Cameron and Sarkozy Got Lucky', *The Guardian*, 13 October. Available online at: www.guardian.co.uk/commentisfree/2011/oct/13/lessons-from-libya-obama-cameron-sarkozy [Accessed August 2012].

United Nations Security Resolutions 1970 and 1973, 2011. Available online at: http://daccess-dds-ny.un.org/doc/UNDOC/GEN/N11/268/39/PDF/N1126839.pdf?OpenElement [Accessed August 2012].

Vesel, D. (2004) 'The Lonely Pragmatist: Humanitarian Intervention in an Imperfect World', *Brigham Young University Journal of Public Law*, vol. 18, no. 1, pp. 1–58.

Voeten, E. (2005) 'The Political Origins of the UN Security Council's Ability to Legitimize the Use of Force', *International Organisation*, vol. 59, no. 3, pp. 527–57.

Voice of America (2011) 'EU, NATO, UN Discuss Intervention in Libya'. Available online at: www.voanews.com/content/eu-nato-un-discuss-intervention-in-libya-116931063/170508.html [Accessed August 2012].

Wagner, D. and D. Jackman (2011) 'BRICS Form Unstable Foundation for Multilateral Action', *Foreign Policy Journal*, 2 April. Available online at: www.foreignpolicyjournal.com/2011/04/02/brics-form-unstable-foundation-for-multilateral-action [Accessed August 2012].

Welsh, J. (2010) 'Implementing the "Responsibility to Protect": Where Expectations Meet Reality', *Ethics & International Affairs*, vol. 24, no. 4, pp. 415–30.

9

NATO's Intervention in Libya: A Humanitarian Success?

Alan J. Kuperman[1]

Introduction

On 17 March 2011, the United Nations authorized military intervention in Libya to protect civilians, responding to violence between government forces and opponents that had erupted the preceding month. Two days later, NATO initiated the intervention, including establishing a no-fly zone and launching aerial attacks on government forces. After seven months of NATO intervention, Libyan rebel forces conquered the country and killed the former authoritarian ruler, Muammar Gaddafi, in October 2011. Immediately, Western media and politicians praised the intervention as a humanitarian success for having averted a bloodbath in Libya's second largest city, Benghazi, and helping replace the dictatorial Gaddafi regime with a transitional council pledged to democracy. Based on this ostensible success, many experts now cite Libya as a model for implementing the so-called 'Responsibility to Protect' (R2P). Before embracing such conclusions, however, it is important to conduct a more rigorous assessment of the net humanitarian impact of NATO intervention in Libya.

This study starts by reciting the commonly accepted Western narrative of the 2011 conflict and intervention in Libya. Next, it documents two significant flaws in that narrative's qualitative portrayal: the nature of violence prior to NATO's intervention, and the eventual objective of NATO's intervention. Third, it conducts a counter-factual analysis to explore the likely outcome and human costs in Libya if NATO had not intervened. Fourth, it documents the actual outcome and human costs in Libya in the wake of NATO's intervention. Fifth, it explores whether the prospect of NATO's intervention in Libya actually fostered the rebellion that triggered civilian victimization, thereby escalating the type of violence that it was intended to prevent – via a 'moral hazard' dynamic. Sixth, it examines the post-war situation in Libya and surrounding countries to assess the longer-term benefits and costs of NATO's intervention. Seventh, it summarizes the net humanitarian impact of the intervention. Finally, the chapter infers lessons from the events in Libya to generate policy recommendations for future humanitarian intervention and implementation of R2P.

Common wisdom: a successful model of R2P intervention

The common Western narrative of the Libya conflict and intervention runs as follows. By early 2011, two successful, non-violent 'Arab Spring' uprisings in Tunisia and Egypt had lifted the veil of fear in Libya. Accordingly, in mid-February 2011, the Libyan people rose up in similar, nationwide, non-violent protests against their dictator Muammar Gaddafi, whose oppressive rule they universally detested. Gaddafi responded by ordering his forces to shoot the peaceful protesters, killing thousands of innocent victims in just three days, especially in the eastern city of Benghazi. Such brutal government violence compelled the peaceful protesters to take up arms in self-defence and launch a rebellion. Gaddafi counter-escalated criminally, deploying his ground troops to fire heavy weapons indiscriminately into residential areas and his air force to bomb civilians. The freedom fighters made progress for two weeks, gaining control of half the country by early March, but over the next ten days Gaddafi's forces pushed them back to their last stronghold of Benghazi. Gaddafi explicitly threatened to attack the civilians there, deployed his troops to the gates of the city, and prepared to commit an imminent 'bloodbath'.

At that moment, on 17 March 2011, the UN Security Council authorized a no-fly zone and all necessary means except occupation forces to protect Libya's civilians from Gaddafi's troops and air forces. This protection against criminal violence gradually enabled the freedom fighters, because of their nationwide support, to turn the tide of the conflict, overthrow Gaddafi, and pave the way for representative government. Overall, the NATO intervention – by protecting Benghazi and helping remove Gaddafi from power – averted a Rwanda-like genocide, restored human rights, fostered democracy and the rule of law, and helped sustain momentum for the Arab Spring. It did so quickly and without deploying ground forces, thereby establishing a new model for successful implementation of the emerging norm of R2P.

Indeed, this common wisdom has been endorsed in the world's leading journal of international affairs by no less than the top US military and civilian representatives to the trans-Atlantic alliance that led the intervention. The US Permanent Representative to NATO, and the Supreme Allied Commander Europe, authored the lead article in *Foreign Affairs*, which concluded as follows: 'NATO's operation in Libya has rightly been hailed as a model intervention. The alliance responded rapidly to a deteriorating situation that threatened hundreds of thousands of civilians rebelling against an oppressive regime. It succeeded in protecting those civilians' (Daalder and Stavridis 2012: 2).

Did Gaddafi target peaceful civilians?

The first problem with the common narrative is that it relies on two demonstrably false premises: that Gaddafi initiated the violence by targeting peaceful protesters, and that NATO's intervention aimed primarily to protect civilians. Contrary to most contemporaneous Western reporting, many Libyan protesters actually were armed and violent from the first day of the uprising, 15 February 2011, in Benghazi (BBC News 2011). Government forces initially responded with non-lethal force: rubber bullets and water cannon. Western media on that first day incorrectly reported that Gaddafi's forces had fired live ammunition at peaceful protesters, citing video posted on the internet. The BBC, to its credit, admitted the next day that 'subsequent inquiries suggested this was footage originally uploaded more than a year ago', but few other Western media corrected the error or acknowledged that they had fallen victim to anti-government propaganda (ibid.). Gaddafi's security forces refrained from deadly force until the protesters' violence escalated and spread during the following days.

In Benghazi, the protesters used firearms, Molotov cocktails, bulldozers and vehicle bombs to capture the army garrison in that biggest city of eastern Libya by 20 February, just three days after launching their 'Day of Rage' on 17 February. In all four cities initially consumed by the conflict, large-scale violence was initiated not by government forces but rather by the protesters. In Benghazi, on 15 February, protesters threw petrol bombs (ibid.). In Al Bayda, on 17 February, 'Witnesses told Amnesty International that in the evening they saw police defectors shooting at al-Gaddafi forces. From then on, the protests quickly escalated into violent confrontations' (Amnesty International 2011: 37). In the capital, Tripoli, on 20 February, protesters initiated the violence by burning government buildings, thereby prompting Gaddafi's forces to respond brutally. According to one eyewitness testimony, the protesters

> . . . kicked out the pro-Gaddafi people in the Square and burned the internal security center. They entered and burned it all, and I think the general security building overlooking the martyrs' square too . . . After the speech, suddenly cars came, the land cruisers, with people. They were far away so I can't tell you if they were Africans or Libyans or from Sirte. They gave us no chance. Heavy fire, like it was a war. (Alive in Libya 2011)

In Misurata, on 21 February, protesters attacked and seized weapons from police and army bases, triggering a spiral of violence. As the UN reported,

> Protests appeared to have escalated rapidly, however, with demonstrators attacking offices of the Revolutionary Committees, police stations and military barracks on 21 and 22 February 2011 and arming themselves with weapons found at these locations. The Qadhafi Government admitted to firing live ammunition at those who, it said, were involved in violent actions. (UN Human Rights Council 2012: 53)

Likewise, a former high-level Libyan military commander told a UN inquiry that 'only after demonstrators acquired arms did the Qadhafi forces begin using live ammunition' (ibid.: 52). Moreover, when government forces initially responded violently, notably on 17 February in Benghazi, they aimed to wound, not to kill. According to a French doctor working in a Benghazi hospital, on that day 'we had dozens of patients with bullet wounds in the abdominal area or in the legs' (AFPTV 2011). He reports that 'at first, the security forces shot people in the legs and abdomen' and only 'subsequently, in the chest and head' (Malye 2011). The government's escalation was undoubtedly rapid – from rubber bullets, to wounding shots, to deadly force, in about three days – but responded to the protesters' own escalation of violence. Admittedly, not all or even most of the protesters in the crowds of this initial uprising were armed, so the government's retaliation unavoidably hit many unarmed protesters, who were 'human shields' essentially for the rebels. But the image created by Western media of Gaddafi's forces initiating violence by attacking peaceful protesters was simply false.

After absorbing the first strike by armed protesters in these cities, government forces subsequently initiated the violence in several other cities where protesters had been peaceful. The regime apparently suspected, correctly, that the rebels aimed to militarize these other protests too, so it resorted to force preemptively in hopes of stemming the spread of rebellion – but failed. On 23 February, for example, the Libyan army's 32nd Brigade, commanded by Gaddafi's son Khamis, arrived in Zawiya near the capital and shot at protesters who had been conducting sit-ins for four days. Despite this, the city fell to the rebels just three days later (UN Human Rights Council 2012: 53).

Although the government did respond forcefully to the rebels, it never targeted civilians, nor resorted to 'indiscriminate' force, as Western media reported. Indeed, their early press accounts exaggerated the death toll by a factor of ten. This error can be traced partly to the French physician in Benghazi, who extrapolated wildly from the tiny sample in his hospital. Shortly after returning home on 21 February, he estimated to the press that 'more than 2,000 deaths' had occurred in Benghazi and its surroundings during his stay (Malye 2011). In reality, Human Rights Watch has documented only 233 deaths across all of Libya before he left the country (2011a).

The best evidence that Gaddafi did not use force indiscriminately, but rather targeted the rebels narrowly, comes from the city of Misurata, Libya's third largest, where the civil war had become most intense by March. During the first seven weeks of fighting, according to Human Rights Watch, 949 people in Misurata were wounded, of whom only 22 were women and eight children (2011b). This means that only about 3 per cent of the wounded were female, which indicates that government forces were very discriminate in targeting rebels, who were overwhelmingly male. If government forces had targeted civilian areas indiscriminately, the female percentage of wounded should have approached 50 per cent, rather than a mere 3 per cent. Moreover, Human Rights Watch reports that during this initial period, Misurata's medical facilities documented only 257 people killed – including rebels and government forces – in a city of 400,000. That means the proportion of the population killed during nearly two months of fighting in the war's most intense theatre was less than 0.0006 – which represents indisputable evidence that the government avoided using indiscriminate force. It should be noted that Human Rights Watch's report did also accuse the government of 'targeting civilians and civilian objects' in violation of international law. But the organization's own data demonstrate that any such use of force by the government was the rare exception, rather than the rule.

Similar evidence comes from the capital Tripoli, where the government used significant force during only two days prior to NATO's intervention, to suppress violent protesters who were burning government buildings. Libyan doctors subsequently told the United Nations that they observed more than 200 corpses in the city's morgues on 20–21 February. But according to the UN report, 'Almost all of the bodies received were male. [The doctors] could only recall the bodies of two women killed – one shot and one stabbed – during the period of the protests' (UN Human Rights Council 2012: 54). If women were only one per cent of the victims in the capital, it again suggests strongly that the government targeted its force quite narrowly at violent protesters, who were virtually all male, rather than indiscriminately at the civilian populace.

Also contrary to common wisdom, Gaddafi's regime never threatened or perpetrated revenge killings against civilians in areas that it recaptured from the rebels. The government did attempt to intimidate the rebels, by promising to be relentless in pursuing them. On 20 February, for example, Gaddafi's son, Saif Al-Islam, declared that 'we will fight to the last man and woman and bullet'. Two days later, Gaddafi warned that he would deploy forces to areas to 'sanitize Libya an inch at a time' and 'clear them of these rats', referring to the rebels (International Criminal Court 2011b: 10). But this rhetoric never translated into reprisal targeting of civilians. From 5 to 15 March, Libyan government forces retook all but one of the major rebel-held cities, including Zawiya, Bani Walid, Ras Lanuf, Brega, Ajdabiya and most of Misurata. In none of those cities did the regime target civilians in revenge, let alone commit a 'bloodbath' of them for their previous support of the rebels.

When the regime was poised in mid-March to recapture the last rebel-held city, Benghazi, it again threatened ruthless violence against rebels who stayed to fight, as widely reported at the time. But international media either failed to report or downplayed the regime's public reassurances that it would *not* target civilians, nor rebels who laid down their arms, nor rebels who fled, which the regime encouraged them to do. On 17 March, Gaddafi directly addressed the rebels of Benghazi: 'Throw away your weapons, exactly like your brothers in Ajdabiyah and other places did. They laid down their arms and they are safe. We never pursued them at all' (BBC Monitoring Middle East 2011).[2]

Was NATO's intervention to protect civilians?

It is possible that NATO's intervention was born of a desire to protect civilians, consistent with the UN Security Council authorization. But within a few weeks of launching the operation, the evidence shows that NATO's primary aim had become to overthrow Gaddafi's regime, even at the expense of increasing harm to Libya's civilians. If NATO had sought merely to protect civilians, in accordance with its authorization, the trans-Atlantic alliance would have enforced the no-fly zone, bombed forces that were threatening civilians, and attempted to forge a ceasefire.

Instead, NATO took actions that were unnecessary or inconsistent with protecting civilians, but which fostered regime change. Less than two weeks into the intervention, for example, NATO began attacking Libyan forces that were retreating and thus not a threat to civilians, who were far away (Fahim and Kirkpatrick 2011). At the same time, NATO started bombing forces in Gaddafi's hometown of Sirte, where they represented no threat to civilians because the residents supported the regime (Swami et al. 2011). The government immediately complained, according to the *New York Times*, that 'Western powers were now attacking the Libyan Army in retreat, a far cry from the United Nations mandate to establish a no-fly zone to protect civilians'. As evidence, a spokesman noted that Libyan forces 'were attacked as they were clearly moving westbound' (Kirkpatrick and Fahim 2011).

Rather than pursuing a ceasefire, NATO and its allies aided the rebels who rejected that peaceful path and sought instead to overthrow Gaddafi. This significantly extended the war, magnifying the harm to civilians, contrary to the intent of the UN authorization. On 4 March, the UK announced that it would deploy military experts to advise the rebels in eastern Libya, which the press characterized as 'a clear intervention on the ground to bolster the anti-Gaddafi uprising' (Wintour and Norton-Taylor 2011). In the middle of the month, US President Barack Obama signed an intelligence 'finding', authorizing covert aid to the rebels (Hosenball 2011). At the moment when the UN authorized the intervention, on 17 March, the United States already knew that Egypt was supplying arms to the rebels (Levinson and Rosenberg 2011). By 6 April, British military and intelligence officials in Benghazi were helping the rebels establish a command structure and defence ministry (Urban 2012). By mid-April, Qatar was shipping French anti-tank missiles to rebels in eastern Libya (Black 2012). Early the next month, France started air-dropping weapons to opposition forces in western Libya (Nakhoul 2011), who were being trained by operatives from the UK, Italy, and France – as these countries later admitted to a UN panel (Birnbaum 2011; Lynch 2012b). NATO ally Qatar was the most egregious in violating the UN authorization that had been explicit in 'excluding a foreign occupation force of any form on any part of Libyan territory'. Qatar's military chief of staff subsequently revealed that 'the numbers of Qataris on ground were hundreds in every region'. Qataris also were 'running the training and communication operations' for the rebels, he said. The leader of Libya's opposition concurred that Qataris had 'planned' and were 'a major partner in all the battles we fought' (Al Arabiya 2011).

NATO and its allies kept providing such military aid even as the rebels repeatedly rejected the government's ceasefire offers that could have ended the violence and thereby spared civilians. As early as 3 March, barely two weeks into the violence, Gaddafi embraced Venezuela's offer of mediation, but Mustafa Abdel Jalil, head of the Libyan opposition's umbrella Transitional National Council, 'totally rejected the concept of talks' (Al Jazeera 2011). On 11 April, Gaddafi accepted an African Union proposal for an immediate ceasefire to be followed by a national dialogue, but the rebels said they refused to consider any ceasefire while the Libyan leader remained in power (Kenyon 2011). On 26 May, Libya's government offered not merely a ceasefire, but negotiations towards a constitutional government and compensation to victims, yet the rebels again demurred in favor of war (Chulov 2011). It is impossible to know if Gaddafi would have honoured a ceasefire or the promise to negotiate a political transition. But if NATO had sought primarily to protect civilians, it would have conditioned its aid to the rebels on their sincerely exploring the regime's offers. Unfortunately, there is no evidence that NATO ever sought to use its leverage in this manner. To the contrary, all available evidence indicates that NATO's primary objective, starting early in the intervention, was to help the rebels overthrow Gaddafi, even if this escalated and extended the civil war and thereby magnified the threat to Libya's civilians.

What if NATO had *not* intervened?

To estimate the likely outcome if NATO had not intervened, it is essential to review the first month of the conflict, prior to intervention. Contrary to the portrayal by Western media of a nationwide peaceful protest against a dictatorial regime, the conflict actually started as an armed rebellion by tribal, regional and religious rivals of the regime. The regional aspect (see Figure 9.1) is demonstrated by the fact that from 15 to 19 February 2011, violent uprisings emerged only in eastern Libya – the historic, regional rival to Tripoli – in four cities: Benghazi, Al Bayda, Ajdabiya and Darna. By contrast, near the capital, protest was non-violent and confined to one city, Zawiya, during this time. The

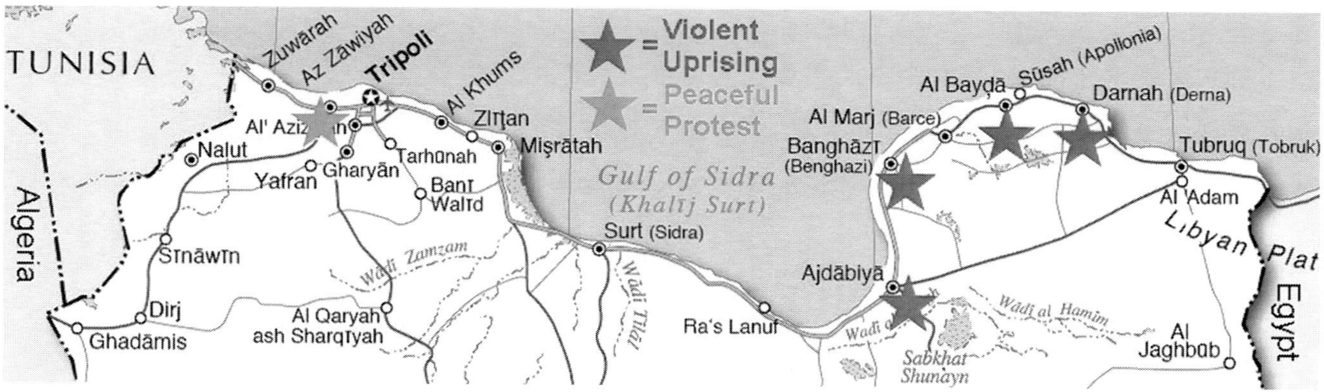

Figure 9.1 Rebellion in Eastern Libya: 15–19 February 2011
Source: Adapted from Nations Online Project.

tribal nature became clear on 20 February, when the rebellion spread to the first city outside the east, Misurata, a bitter tribal rival of the regime. Violent protest also erupted that day in the capital, but – without regional or tribal rivalry to sustain it – the Tripoli uprising was brutally suppressed by the following day.

Benefitting from surprise, the rebels made rapid progress over the next two weeks. They captured eastern Libya's entire coastline, from Egypt to Ras Lanuf, the port used for most oil exports. On the central coast, they gained control of Misurata and its surrounding towns. Just west of the capital, they took the cities of Zawiya and Zuwara, so that they now controlled six of Libya's nine biggest cities (see Figure 9.1). In the Nafusa mountains, southwest of the capital, they claimed Gharyan, Yafran, and Nalut. Indeed, by 5 March, the high point of the initial violent uprising, the rebels remarkably controlled at least half of the country's populated areas (see Figure 9.2).

But the rebels' progress was short-lived, as Gaddafi's forces commenced a massive counter-offensive on 7 March. Within two days, government troops had recaptured the main oil port of Ras Lanuf in the east, the biggest mountain town of Gharyan in the west, and Zawiya near the capital. By just one week later, Gaddafi had recaptured virtually all significantly populated areas west of the rebels' final stronghold of Benghazi (see Figure 9.3). A small part of Misurata remained contested, but the rebels there were doomed because they had no access to resupply, as Gaddafi now controlled both the sea and land lines of communication to the city.

With the rebels in abject retreat, and the government poised to attack their last stronghold of Benghazi, Gaddafi's son Saif al-Islam declared on 16 March: 'everything will be over in 48 hours' (*Daily Telegraph* 2011). Had the UN not authorized intervention the following day, enabling NATO to start bombing Libyan forces on 19 March, his prediction likely would have proved essentially right. In the preceding week, the rebels had not put up any real defence, given that they were neither equipped nor trained to do so. Instead, they retreated, typically within two days, from each successive town that the army targeted on its eastward march: Ras Lanuf, Brega and Ajdabiya. Based on this progression, government forces probably would have captured Benghazi by 20 March. The remaining small towns further east along the coast almost surely would have fallen within the next week, prompting the rebels to flee into Egypt for refuge. Without NATO intervention, therefore, Libya's rebellion, civil war and resulting endangerment of civilians likely would have ended by late March 2011, less than six weeks after the conflict started.

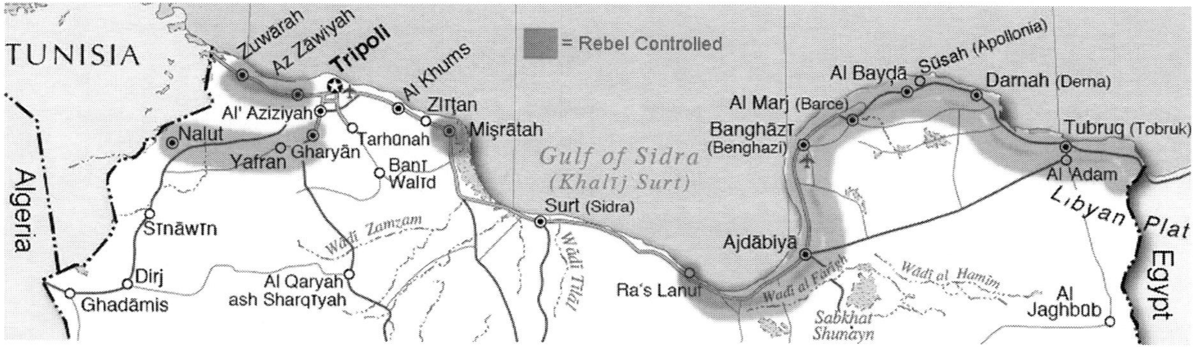

Figure 9.2 High point of initial rebellion: 5 March
Source: Adapted from Nations Online Project.

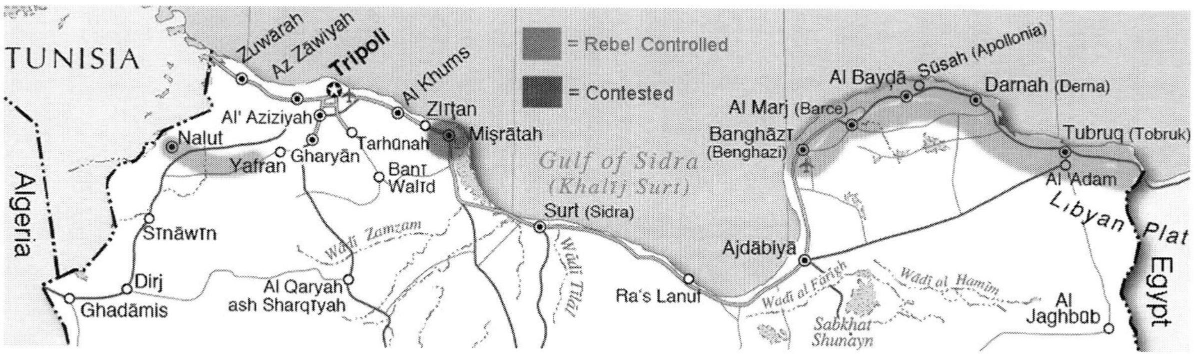

Figure 9.3 Rebels' retreat to Benghazi: 16 March
Source: Adapted from Nations Online Project.

It is impossible to project definitively how many Libyans would have died in the conflict if NATO had not intervened. But estimates should be based on the conflict's history and trajectory at the time of intervention. Starting from this evidence, the analysis below indicates that approximately 1,100 Libyans – including government forces, rebels, and non-combatants – likely would have died without NATO intervention.

Conflict-related deaths prior to the intervention were confined mainly to five areas of Libya, and likely would have remained so in the absence of NATO action. The bloodiest region was Benghazi and its surroundings in eastern Libya. In early March, a medical committee in the city reported, apparently based on counting corpses, that at least 228 residents had been killed since the start of the conflict (*Sydney Morning Herald* 2011). From that moment until NATO intervened, however, the city remained under rebel control and thus suffered few if any additional casualties. In all of eastern Libya, including Benghazi, medics estimated that at least 400 had been killed by 9 March, according to a press report, though the basis of this estimate is unknown (Lambroschini 2011).[3] Additional war-related deaths, perhaps a dozen or two, probably occurred when Ajdabiya was retaken by the government in mid-March. If not for intervention, Benghazi and towns to the east probably also would have suffered dozens of additional deaths when government forces recaptured them in late March. But there is no reason to believe that a 'bloodbath' would have occurred in Benghazi, considering that Gaddafi had not threatened to attack civilians there and had not perpetrated such violence in any of the other cities that his forces recaptured from the rebels (see Table 9.1). Accordingly, the best estimate is that without NATO intervention, about 500 Libyans in Benghazi and surrounding areas of eastern Libya would have died from the conflict over the course of six weeks.

Three other Libyan cities reportedly suffered significant casualties prior to NATO's intervention. In Misurata, as noted, 257 conflict-related deaths were documented by 10 April, after seven weeks of fighting that included three weeks of NATO's intervention (Human Rights Watch 2011b). Interpolation suggests that if the war had ended earlier, in late March without NATO's intervention, Misurata's death toll would have been somewhat lower, around 200, depending on when and how the rebels ceased fighting. In Tripoli, as noted, major violence during the early months of the conflict was confined to two days – 20 and 21 February – when the government attacked violent protesters for burning government buildings, leaving at least 200 dead, according to doctors at city morgues (UN Human Rights Council 2012: 54).[4] If the

Table 9.1 No 'bloodbaths' by Gaddafi forces

Ranking by size	City	Population	Date captured by rebels	Date retaken by government	Bloodbath when retaken?
1	Tripoli	1,150,989	–	–	–
2	Benghazi	650,629	20 Feb	–	–
3	Misurata	386,120	23 Feb	20 Mar	No
4	Tarhuna	210,697	–	–	–
5	Al Bayda	206,180	23 Feb	–	–
6	Al Khums	201,943	–	–	–
7	Zawiya	186,123	26 Feb	9 Mar	No
8	Zuwarah	180,310	23 Feb	14 Mar	No
9	Ajdabiya	134,358	26 Feb	16 Mar	No

Key: '–' city not captured by rebels or retaken by government prior to significant NATO intervention.
Population sources: www.worldcities.us/libya_cities and http://population.mongabay.com/population/libya
Note: In Misurata, government forces entered the city centre on 20 March but failed to control the entire city before retreating after NATO intervened.

war had ended in late March, without intervention, the toll in Tripoli probably would have remained at that level, given that the capital was firmly under government control. In Zawiya, after rebels were defeated in mid-March, doctors at the town's hospital were reported to have 'counted 175 people killed in battle' (Walt 2011).

The last area that likely suffered any significant casualties prior to NATO's intervention was Libya's central coast, where the cities of Brega and Ras Lanuf changed hands several times between the government and rebels, from late February through mid-March. With each attack, the cities were subject to fire from artillery, mortars, rocket-propelled grenades and additional small arms. But neither side appears to have put up a strong defence, instead retreating when faced with superior firepower. This would explain why control initially switched frequently and why no large-scale casualties were reported. Nevertheless, dozens of deaths probably resulted from such fighting before NATO intervened. By mid-March, however, the government controlled these central-coast cities, so without intervention the death toll there likely would have been capped at this relatively low level.

The International Criminal Court, in its June 2011 explanation of arrest warrants for Gaddafi and his inner circle, did allege that the regime had targeted non-combatants, but only during a brief period that ended at least two weeks prior to NATO's intervention. 'There are reasonable

Table 9.2 Estimated outcome if NATO had not intervened

• 6-week war	
• 1,100 deaths:	
o Benghazi & east:	500
o Misurata:	200
o Tripoli	200+
o Zawiyah	170
o Central coast	10s

grounds to believe that, as of 15 February 2011 and within a period of less than two weeks in February 2011, hundreds of civilians were killed by the Security Forces' (International Criminal Court 2011b: 13). The court has also cited more precise estimates, characterized as credible, 'that as the result of the shootings 500 to 700 persons died, only in February' (International Criminal Court 2011a: 4). The ICC allegations are consistent with the numerical estimates in this study, although the court downplays that many among the victims were armed and violent.

As summarized in Table 9.2, if NATO had not intervened, the estimate is that the conflict would have lasted six weeks and inflicted about 1,100 deaths. Of course, any retrospective prediction has some margin of error. It should be noted, however, that none of the sources for casualty estimates cited in this study was sympathetic to Gaddafi's regime or had any other obvious reason to underestimate the death toll prior to intervention.

What actually happened (with NATO intervention)

When the UN authorized intervention on 17 March 2011, and NATO started bombing two days later, Libyan government forces quickly halted their eastward offensive. As a result, Benghazi was not retaken by the government, the rebels did not flee to Egypt, and the war did not end in late March. Instead, the rebels in Benghazi reversed their retreat and launched a second westward offensive. Within barely a week, benefiting from NATO bombing of government forces, the rebels recaptured Brega and Ras Lanuf. But, in so doing, the ragtag rebels outran their supply lines, and the government was able to retake the cities two days later. Over the next four months, such cities on the central coast changed hands several more times as the region became a primary theatre of the war. Repeatedly, NATO bombed Libyan forces, the rebels advanced on populated areas, and the government then counter-attacked – all of which inflicted mounting casualties on both fighters and non-combatants.

In Misurata, too, intervention prolonged and escalated the fighting. On 19 March, Libyan government forces were just retaking the city's centre from the rebels, who without resupply routes were doomed to fall within days, roughly one month after the fighting had started there. But when NATO attacked both the government's ground forces near the city and its naval vessels off the coast, the rebels gained breathing room and reopened their supply lines. As a result, fighting in Misurata continued for another four months until the rebels eventually prevailed in late July, by which time the city's death toll had grown substantially, as detailed below.

In Libya's western mountains, the rebellion also revived, fostered by weapons and training from NATO member states. As a result, by late August 2011, rebels converged on Tripoli in a pincer from east and west (see Figure 9.4). Not surprisingly, government forces staged a fierce defence of the capital – magnifying several-fold the death toll of soldiers, rebels and civilians in an area that had been quiescent during the five preceding months – before the rebels captured it on 28 August. Gaddafi and some loyalists retreated southward to pro-government areas, where they continued the battle for nearly two more months. But on 20 October, rebels discovered Gaddafi, and then tortured and summarily executed him. Three days later, on 23 October, the regime's last remnants were defeated and the war ended.

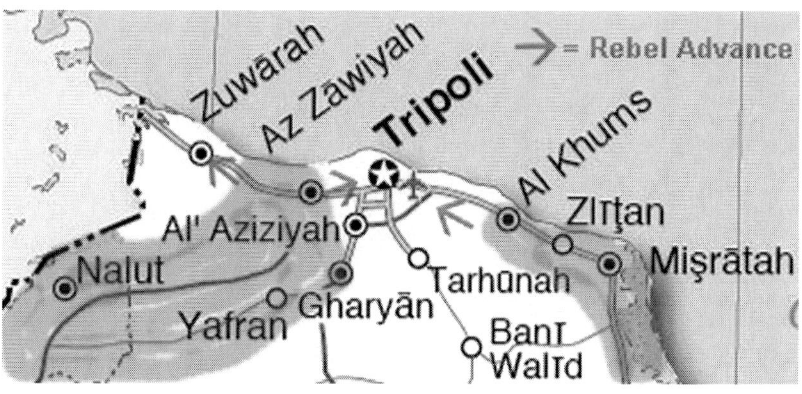

Figure 9.4 Rebels converge on Tripoli after five months of NATO intervention
Source: Adapted from Nations Online Project.

As the result of NATO's intervention, Libya's war lasted 36 weeks (eight months), rather than ending in about six weeks, as estimated above. There is no reliable count of the number killed, and claims vary wildly. Libya's new leaders established a Ministry for Martyrs and the Missing, which was supposed to conduct such a tally, but it had not done so six months after the war ended (Abrahams 2012). One US government official, at a closed-door conference in November 2011, estimated the final death toll at around 8,000 (O'Donnell and Vaïsse 2011; Vaïsse 2012). By contrast, the rebels' interim health minister asserted in September 2011, before the war even had ended, that 30,000 Libyans already had died in the conflict. A press report characterized this as the 'first detailed estimate of the high cost in lives of ousting former Libyan leader Muammar Al Qathafi from power . . . based in part on reports from hospitals, local officials and former rebel commanders' (*Tripoli Post* 2011). The minister estimated that half the dead were Gaddafi forces, while the rest were rebels and civilians (see Table 9.3). In Misurata, he reported that at least 2,000 rebels and civilians had been killed, in addition to government forces, a toll roughly ten times higher than if NATO had not intervened, according to the analysis above. In Tripoli, the minister estimated that the intense one-week battle for the capital, in late August 2011, by itself killed 1,700 rebels and 100 civilians, in addition to government troops – which suggests that in the capital too the eventual death count was multiplied about ten times by NATO intervention.

As for the overall death toll, the two vastly disparate estimates – by the US government and the Libyan rebels – conceivably may bound the actual number killed in the conflict. If so, and if the counter-factual analysis above is correct, then NATO intervention magnified the death toll in Libya by about 7 to 27 times. This would be consistent both with city-level data provided by the rebels, which indicates that the

Table 9.3 NATO intervention magnifies the toll

- 36-week war (8 months)
- 8,000–30,000 deaths:
  - 8,000 (US estimate, Nov 2011)
  - 30,000 (Libya estimate, Sep 2011)
    - –15,000 security forces
    - –15,000 others
      - → 2,000 rebels & civilians in Misurata
      - → 1,700 rebels, 100 civilians in Tripoli's fall

intervention multiplied the deaths in Tripoli and Misurata about ten-fold, and the fact that NATO's intervention broadened the geographic scope of fighting in the country. It also would confirm the speculation of knowledgeable observers, such as Seumas Milne, who opined at the war's end that 'while the death toll in Libya when NATO intervened was perhaps around 1,000–2,000 (judging by UN estimates), eight months later it is probably more than ten times that figure' (Milne 2011).

Did NATO foster the rebellion?

To measure the impact of NATO's intervention, the two most obvious metrics are those already discussed: the war's duration and death toll. But it is important also to consider whether the expectation of such intervention helped trigger or escalate the Libyan rebellion that provoked government retaliation and thereby endangered civilians. Such a potential dynamic is known as the 'moral hazard' of humanitarian intervention (Kuperman 2008).

Unfortunately, this question cannot be answered for the period prior to the rebellion, because the main players have yet to write or tell that history. However, less than two weeks into the rebellion, its leaders clearly viewed NATO intervention as essential. On 28 February, the head of the rebels' political wing, Mustafa Abdul-Jalil, during a television interview, called for international imposition of a no-fly zone. 'What we want is an air embargo to stop Gaddafi bringing in mercenaries' (Rossi 2011). Two days later, the rebels' military commander spoke by telephone to Britain's foreign secretary 'about planning for a No-Fly Zone' (UK Foreign and Commonwealth Office 2011). The next day, 3 March, British Special Forces and intelligence agents clandestinely attempted to meet with rebels in eastern Libya (Chulov et al. 2011). On 5 March, France formally praised the rebels' establishment of a national transitional council (NTC). Then, just five days later, French president Nicolas Sarkozy remarkably agreed to recognize the rebel council as Libya's legitimate government, during a meeting at his office with the rebels' top diplomat, Mahmoud Jibril (Erlanger 2011). On the same day, 10 March, with the rebels in abject retreat, their political leader appeared on CNN to plea again desperately for a no-fly zone: 'It has to be immediate action' (CNN 2011).

This evidence demonstrates that, by the third week of the rebellion if not sooner, the rebels were relying on a strategy that depended on NATO intervention, which they had good reason to expect. By early March 2011, the UK had provided the rebels with military advice and discussed with them the creation of a no-fly zone, while France had recognized them as Libya's new government. In light of such early and significant support from NATO countries, it is understandable that the otherwise feeble rebels dared to confront the government's superior forces. The crucial, counter-factual question is whether these Libyan militants would have dared to challenge Gaddafi without the expectation of NATO support. If not, then NATO's willingness to intervene not only escalated Libya's civil war and resultant civilian suffering, but possibly triggered it in the first place by encouraging the initial rebellion that provoked Gaddafi's retaliation. To answer this question definitively, however, would require evidence that is not yet available.

Post-war Libya

Although NATO's intervention was explicitly predicated on the short-term goal of protecting civilians, and apparently backfired in this regard, it is worth exploring whether the intervention produced any longer-term net benefit for Libyans. The most positive development in post-war Libya undoubtedly was the democratic election of July 2012, which brought to power a moderate, secular coalition government – a stark change from Gaddafi's four-decade dictatorship (Kirkpatrick 2012c). Less encouragingly, the country's first democratically elected prime minister failed to last even one month in office, being removed by a vote of no confidence, attributed to regional rivalries (Kirkpatrick 2012d). Other developments have been even more discouraging. In the immediate wake of victory, rebels perpetrated scores of reprisal killings, in addition to torture, beating and arbitrary detention of thousands of suspected Gaddafi supporters. A Human Rights Watch official characterized this as 'a trend of killings, looting and other abuses committed by armed anti-Gaddafi fighters who consider themselves above the law' (Lyons 2011; see also Lynch 2012a). Rebels also expelled 30,000 mostly black residents of Tawerga, burning or looting their homes and shops, on grounds that some of them had worked as mercenaries in the government's attacks on nearby Misurata (Fahim 2011). The ramifications of this racial violence have been nationwide: 'For the more than one million African guest workers who came to oil-rich Libya seeking their fortunes, it has meant terror . . . These innocent migrant laborers now find themselves singled out by ordinary Libyans and rebels who believe they are the enemy' (Wheeler and Oghanna 2011). Even six months after the war, in April 2012, Human Rights Watch reported that abuses around Misurata still persisted and 'appear to be so widespread and systematic that they may amount to crimes against humanity' (2012). Ironically, such racial or ethnic cleansing had never occurred in Gaddafi's Libya.

Indeed, during his final decade in power, Gaddafi had even significantly improved his overall human-rights performance. Amnesty International's 2010 annual report refers to major abuses only prior to 2000, observing that 'Hundreds of cases of enforced disappearance and other serious human rights violations committed in the 1970s, 1980s and 1990s remained unresolved'. The report does indicate that the 'Internal Security Agency (ISA), implicated in those [earlier] violations, continued to operate with impunity', but it does not allege any large-scale offences in the 2000s (Amnesty International 2010).

After the war, Libya's new government also has failed to disarm or bring under its control the dozens of militias that arose during the revolution, which has produced deadly turf battles between rival tribes and commanders, and a growing threat from radical Islamists. In small signs of progress, the government has succeeded in removing most militia checkpoints in major cities, and has retaken control of seaports, airports and border crossings. But according to a June 2012 NGO report,

> . . . in the provinces, the *thuwwar* [former rebels] largely rule the roost. Many a militia can outgun the army . . . Even in Tripoli, where the government's grasp on security is most advanced, rogue militias continue to occupy key military installations in defiance of NTC demands that they leave. (Pelham 2012; see also International Crisis Group, 2012)

The *Washington Post* likewise reported in April 2012 that 'rival militiamen, some of them intoxicated and most of them unemployed, battle over turf in the capital'. In the southern city of Sabha, skirmishes between rival tribes inflicted 147 deaths in March 2012 (Hendrix 2012).

In oil-rich eastern Libya, also known as Cyrenaica or Barqa, persistent regional rivalry has prompted demands for secession and independence, or at least substantial autonomy within a federal system. Militants have attacked electoral offices on grounds that the region is underrepresented in the new government (Hendrix 2012; Kirkpatrick 2012b; Umana 2012).

Radical Islamist groups, suppressed under Gaddafi, emerged during the revolution as some of the most competent rebels, and afterwards have refused to disarm. Their persistent threat was highlighted by the September 2012 attack on the US consulate in Benghazi, reportedly by the Ansar al-Sharia militia, which killed Ambassador Christopher

Stevens and three of his colleagues. According to a *New York Times* report on the attack, the militia 'holds that democracy is incompatible with Islam. It has paraded the streets with weapons calling for an Islamic state, and a few months ago its leader boasted publicly that its fighters could flatten a foreign consulate' (Kirkpatrick et al. 2012). Even prior to the consulate attack, the growing threat from Libya's radical Islamists had compelled many Western diplomats and NGOs to evacuate the country (Hauslohner and Londono 2012).

In light of this ongoing instability and insecurity, it is perhaps understandable that many Libyans are nostalgic for a strong leader like Gaddafi, who at least maintained order and provided a minimum level of social services. The country's first national survey after the war, conducted in late December 2011, reported that 54 per cent of respondents 'strongly agree' that the country needs 'a (single) strong Libyan leader' (Oxford Research International 2012: Q31A). Even when respondents were asked what kind of government Libya would need in the future – one year and five years hence – this response was the most popular (ibid. Q31B-C). These statistics may even underestimate Libyan support for a strong man like Gaddafi since some respondents presumably were inhibited from expressing such an opinion in a country now controlled by the victorious rebels, to interviewers perceived as pro-revolution. Indeed, the survey organizers downplayed these findings in their executive summary and presented the full survey results only on paper at a small public event, rather than posting them on the internet.[5]

Regional spillover

A final set of consequences that must be factored into any assessment of NATO's intervention in Libya is the effect on neighbouring states and the wider region. The most obvious negative impact has been on Mali, which previously was perceived as the region's peaceful and democratic exception. When Gaddafi was defeated, however, Malian ethnic Tuareg fighters in his security forces fled home with their weapons and launched a rebellion in their country's north, where they rapidly inflicted defeats on government forces (Nossiter 2012a). Malian army officers, frustrated by their losses, staged a coup on the grounds that the government had underequipped them. Making matters worse, the rebellion in the north quickly was hijacked by local Islamist forces (Ansar Dine) and elements of al-Qaeda in the Islamic Maghreb, who defeated the Tuareg, imposed Sharia, and declared their half of the country to be independent (Douthat 2012). All of this fighting, and the imposition of strict Islamic law, spurred massive displacement of hundreds of thousands of Malian civilians, creating a humanitarian emergency (Nossiter 2012b). Amnesty International characterized it, in May 2012, as 'Mali's worst human rights situation in 50 years' (2012). Meanwhile, the country's north has become a safe haven for radical Islamists (Cody 2012; Miller and Whitlock 2012). Mali's new troubles have also spread chaos to other countries, spurring deadly ethnic conflict in Burkina Faso (AP 2012; Zoubir 2012), and the growth of radical Islam in Niger (Raghavan 2012).

A second negative regional impact has been the leakage of weapons, liberated from Gaddafi's arsenal, to arms markets and radical Islamists. Of greatest concern are man-portable, surface-to-air missiles, also known as MANPADs, which in capable hands can readily shoot down civilian airliners in addition to military aircraft (Nordland and Chivers 2011). As many as 15,000 such missiles were still unaccounted for as of February 2012, according to a US State Department official cited in the *Washington Post*, because a $40 million buy-back effort secured only 5,000 weapons. Western intelligence sources say hundreds are loose in the region, including in Niger, where some have been obtained by Boko Haram, the radical Islamic group based in northern Nigeria (Ignatius 2012). A few dozen missiles also have been found in Algeria and Egypt (Stewart 2012). Al-Qaeda's North African branch is said to be using its 'money to stock up on weapons that have flowed out of Libya after dictator Moammar Gaddafi was overthrown' (Miller 2012). In October 2012, militants in the Gaza Strip fired one such missile for the first time, reportedly aiming at an Israeli army helicopter, and 'Israel believes that the weapons originated in Libya' (*New York Times* 2012). Illustrating the scope of the problem, Libyan MANPADs and sea mines have even surfaced in West African arms markets, where they reportedly have been snapped up by Somali buyers for use by Islamist rebels and pirates in northeast Africa (Reuters 2012).

Another potentially negative regional effect is more speculative – namely, that intervention in Libya exacerbated civil conflict in Syria. When NATO started bombing Libyan forces, in March 2011, Syria's uprising was overwhelmingly non-violent and its government's response – although criminally and unjustifiably violent – was relatively circumscribed, killing dozens per week. After NATO's intervention helped Libya's rebels turn the tide of war against Gaddafi by summer 2011, however, Syria's uprising turned violent, provoking much more intense and widespread government retaliation that eventually killed hundreds per week (Pileggi and Richter 2012).[6] It is unknown whether NATO's actions in spring 2011 – intervening on behalf of rebels in Libya, while ignoring non-violent protesters in Syria – were decisive in transforming Syria's uprising from peaceful to violent, and thereby magnifying the death toll. But the counter-factual is illuminating: if NATO had not intervened in Libya, and instead permitted Gaddafi to defeat the Libyan rebels in just six weeks, would Syria's peaceful protesters have been so eager to take up arms? At the least, NATO's intervention in Libya surely encouraged the militarization of Syria's uprising. Therefore, some portion of the death toll in Syria might be considered a consequence of NATO's intervention in Libya. Ironically, some original proponents of NATO's intervention in Libya had argued that such action was essential to sustain the momentum of the Arab Spring, following the peaceful uprisings in Tunisia and Egypt. In the event, NATO's action not only failed to spread peaceful revolution, it encouraged the militarization of Syria's uprising that has produced such tragic consequences.

Some proponents of the intervention claim that the removal of the infamous Gaddafi benefitted the region, but this is questionable, because the former Libyan leader had evolved into a relatively benign figure during his last decade. He had switched from supporting terrorists to providing intelligence against them, following the al-Qaeda attacks on the United States of 11 September 2011. He had voluntarily surrendered his weapons of mass destruction program after the US invasion of Iraq in 2003. And he had reduced aid to foreign rebels, instead sponsoring peace initiatives in conflicts such as Darfur. Indeed, it is difficult to identify any beneficial impact on the region from NATO's intervention in Libya, including from Gaddafi's demise.

Net humanitarian impact

Overall, NATO's intervention significantly worsened the humanitarian situation in Libya and its surrounding region. The only apparent benefit is that Libyans have been able to vote in democratic elections, but the elected government sadly has little authority in a country that is now controlled by dozens of tribal and religious militias accountable to no one (Hauslohner 2012). NATO's intervention increased the duration of Libya's civil war about six-fold, and its death toll by 7 to 27 times. Human rights conditions in post-intervention Libya – which include abuses 'so widespread and systematic that they may amount to crimes against humanity' (Human Rights Watch 2012) – are considerably worse than in the decade preceding the war (Amnesty International 2010).

Beyond Libya, NATO's intervention destabilized the previously peaceful and democratic Mali – giving rise to civil war, a coup, secession, displacement, a humanitarian emergency, a safe haven for radical Islamists and 'Mali's worst human rights situation in 50 years' (Amnesty International 2012). Violence and Islamic radicalism have also spread to Niger and Burkina Faso, and thousands of weapons ideal for shooting down civilian airliners have either gone missing or are in the hands of rebels or terrorists. Syria's peaceful protesters were encouraged to militarize, in hopes of attracting similar intervention, but their transformation to rebellion has only escalated the humanitarian toll there. It is possible that in the very long run, NATO's intervention will contribute indirectly to some beneficial consequences for Libya or its neighbours that cannot now be predicted or foreseen. But based on the humanitarian grounds originally invoked to justify it, NATO's intervention in Libya has been a disaster. If it is a 'model intervention', as US officials claim, it is a model of failure.

Lessons learned?

NATO's experience in Libya offers some important lessons for humanitarian intervention and R2P. First, potential interveners should be wary of both misinformation – resulting from inaccurate reporting or their own biased perceptions – and disinformation from concerted propaganda campaigns. Libya's initial uprising was not peaceful, nationwide and democratic – as reported and perceived in the West – but violent, regional and riven with tribalism and religious extremism. Gaddafi's response was not to slaughter peaceful protesters or bombard civilian areas indiscriminately, as reported in the West, but rather to target rebels and violent protesters relatively narrowly, to reduce collateral harm to non-combatants. By no means does this excuse the Libyan government's response, which may have included criminal acts. But the statistics, testimony and documentary evidence indicate that the Gaddafi regime committed no bloodbaths during the war, and had no intention of doing so. When NATO intervened, it misperceived the situation, believing that government forces already had slaughtered thousands of peaceful protesters and were about to perpetrate a bloodbath in Benghazi. If Western countries had accurately perceived Libya's conflict in late February and early March 2011, NATO would have been much less likely to launch the intervention that gravely exacerbated humanitarian suffering in Libya and its neighbours.

Such misperception had several causes, including *a priori* bias against Gaddafi stemming from his decades-old actions – including support for terrorism – and sensationalist and sloppy journalistic reporting. But the rebels' political wing also engaged in a concerted propaganda campaign that successfully introduced the meme of 'bloodbath'. Most prominently, on 14 March 2011, as the rebels faced imminent defeat, Soliman (aka Sliman) Bouchuiguir warned reporters in Geneva that if Gaddafi's forces were permitted to attack Benghazi, 'There will be a real bloodbath, a massacre like we saw in Rwanda' (Reuters 2011). Bouchuiguir was the political representative of the Libyan opposition's transitional council in Switzerland, where he also headed the Libyan League for Human Rights. In the week prior to his statement, Lexis/Nexis identifies only 19 news articles in English containing the words 'bloodbath' and 'Benghazi'. By contrast, in the week after his statement, the number of such articles jumps to 171 (Search terms: bloodbath and Benghazi; Source: All News (English); Dates: March 7–13, 2011 vs. March 15–21, 2011). Following the war, he was rewarded by being appointed Libyan ambassador to Switzerland (Cherif 2011).

A second lesson is that humanitarian intervention in a country may backfire by escalating rebellion there and elsewhere. It encourages substate groups to believe that by violently provoking state retaliation they can attract intervention to help achieve their political objectives, up to and including regime change. Typically, however, the escalation of rebellion magnifies the harm to civilians before intervention can protect them, if it ever does. As a result, the prospect of humanitarian intervention to protect civilians may perversely imperil them – a dynamic akin to moral hazard. NATO's intervention in Libya, for example, escalated and prolonged the rebellion and resultant civilian suffering not only in that country, but probably in Syria too. This problem can be addressed by modifying intervention in five ways (Kuperman 2009: 40–1). The most important of these is that humanitarian intervention should not aid rebels unless the state is responding to them by deliberately targeting noncombatants, because otherwise it will likely *increase* the harm to civilians. In Libya, for example, Gaddafi was not deliberately targeting civilians, so NATO's intervention actually endangered them by escalating and perpetuating the civil war, which is unjustifiable on humanitarian grounds. By contrast, in Rwanda during the genocide of 1994, civilians were targeted deliberately, so intervention could have reduced their endangerment and thus would have been justified on humanitarian grounds.

A third lesson is that intervention originally launched with the aim of protecting civilians is prone to evolve toward the goal of regime change, even if that magnifies the danger to civilians and thereby undermines the original intent. This is partly because intervening states, to justify their use of force to domestic and international audiences, tend to demonize the regime that they are targeting. Unfortunately, such demonization later inhibits the intervening states from considering a negotiated settlement that would permit the regime or its leaders to retain some power, which often would be the quickest way to end violence and protect civilians.[7] By demanding regime change, the interveners perversely encourage the regime to fight to the bitter end, which actually escalates and prolongs the war, maximizing the harm to civilians. In Libya, for example, Gaddafi repeatedly expressed a willingness to negotiate a ceasefire, beginning barely two weeks into the conflict. But the rebels refused to consider negotiations unless Gaddafi first stepped down, and NATO supported that intransigence. In this way, NATO's intervention, launched explicitly on humanitarian grounds, evolved within two weeks to the goal of regime change, thereby inhibiting even the exploration of a negotiated settlement that could have saved thousands of lives.

This evolutionary dynamic may pose a dilemma for those who support the principle of humanitarian intervention but oppose foreign-imposed regime change, if in practice one leads to the other. In 2011, this phenomenon occurred not just in Libya but also in Côte d'Ivoire, where a French-led intervention to protect civilians quickly evolved into helping rebels to oust the incumbent president.[8] Likewise, in Syria, the United States in August 2011 demanded on humanitarian grounds that president Bashar al-Assad leave office (McGreal and Chulov 2011) and then coordinated with its allies – Saudi Arabia, Qatar and Turkey – to arm the rebels (Englund 2012).

This dilemma does not arise where civilians are targeted intentionally, as in Rwanda's 1994 genocide, which justifies regime change. But such deliberate killing of civilians is rare in the civil conflicts that typically give rise to calls for intervention under R2P. Most cases are more like Libya, where non-combatants are caught in the cross-fire rather than being targeted. In such instances, international Samaritans may feel that intervention is justified to protect civilians but not to topple the regime. But if the former leads almost inevitably to the latter, it suggests yet another reason for restraint when contemplating humanitarian military intervention.

Notes

1. © 2012 by the author. Thanks to Mathew Smith for the bulk of the primary research, and Julieta Cuellar for preliminary research, while both were undergraduates at the University of Texas at Austin. Thanks also to the discussants

and audiences who provided helpful comments on earlier versions of this work at three venues: the Erasmus University International Institute of Social Studies in The Hague; the Oxford University Institute for Ethics, Law and Armed Conflict in the UK; and the annual convention of the Association for the Study of Nationalities at Columbia University. Funding to support this research was provided by the Policy Research Institute of the LBJ School of Public Affairs, University of Texas at Austin.

2. His statement also included the following excerpts: 'Whoever joins us, we the people, the liberator; whoever hands over his weapons, stays at home without any weapons, whatever he did previously, he will be pardoned, protected. We will pardon anyone in the streets. Throw away your rifle in the streets. Starting tomorrow, we will collect rifles from the streets – machine guns, ammunition. Anyone who throws away his weapon and stays at home peacefully will be pardoned no matter what he did in the past. He is protected. Throw away your rifle, you my son, and your family who are listening to me. I tell you get rid of your rifle, your automatic rifle and stay at home. But, if you enter any room with weapons, you'll be chased from room to room, and whoever is found with a weapon, it means he is an enemy . . . We will search only for Al-Zanadiqah [ancient term for unbelievers] and the traitors. We will have no mercy on them. We will remove the walls around them one by one in search of them. [Words indistinct] unless they flee. We have left the way open to them. Escape. Let those who escape go for ever. Let the dogs tear up their carcasses. Let them go to Egypt [words indistinct]. The search will be only for the traitors who [words indistinct] working for the United States and Britain, the colonialists.'
3. The number of wounded was estimated to be about 2,000 persons by this article and by the *Sydney Morning Herald* (2011), but the death toll estimate in the former was roughly twice that in the latter. The widely differing ratios of killed-to-wounded in these two reports suggests that at least one is inaccurate.
4. Regarding the violence in Tripoli, the International Criminal Court prosecutor alleged a somewhat higher death toll on those two days, plus smaller-scale killing on the three preceding days. See International Criminal Court (2011): 15–18. My thanks to Camille Sawak for this citation.
5. The executive summary released at the public presentation on 15 February 2012 states that 'in 12 months [sic] time 42% say they want a strong man (or men)'. This statistic was widely reported six weeks later in Kirkpatrick, (2012a). Although the statistic is correct, it overshadows that 54 per cent strongly agreed that Libya needed a single strong man immediately. I obtained a copy of the executive summary and full survey results from someone who attended the public presentation, which was held exactly one year after the start of the rebellion, at the Human Sciences Institute, the Pauling Centre, Oxford, UK.
6. This article includes a chart illustrating the acceleration of killing after Syria's uprising turned violent. For example, during the first 22 weeks, in mid-2011, when the uprising was mainly non-violent, about 2,000 were killed, or fewer than 100 per week. But during the final nine weeks of their data, in mid-2012, after the uprising had turned overwhelmingly violent, about 6,000 were killed, or nearly 700 per week.

7. Demonization does not always inhibit such a deal. To end war in Bosnia, for example, the United States negotiated the Dayton Accords of 1995 with Serbian leader Slobodan Milosevic, despite having previously demonized him. This was an exceptional case partly because Milosevic was not an official in Bosnia, but merely a foreign sponsor, so the United States demanded instead the removal of the leader of the Bosnian Serbs, Radovan Karadzic. See Holbrooke (1999).
8. The situation was not identical because international observers claimed that the incumbent president had lost a recent, disputed, election, which reignited the civil war. But it was similar in that intervention was initially justified on humanitarian grounds, to protect civilians, yet quickly evolved into an alliance with rebels to pursue regime change. See Crumley (2011); Lynch and Branigin (2011).

References

Abrahams, F. (2012) Personal communication with author, 15 April.

AFPTV (2011) 'French Doctor Gerard Buffet Recounts "Apocalyptic" Scenes in Libya', *AFPTV*, 25 February. Available online at: www.youtube.com/watch?v=JwHUqPflEPs [Accessed 25 September 2012].

Al Arabiya (2011) 'Qatar Admits It Had Boots on the Ground in Libya', *Al Arabiya*, 26 October. Available online at: www.alarabiya.net/articles/2011/10/26/173833.html [Accessed 25 September 2012].

Alive in Libya (2011) 'They Gave Us No Chance, Heavy Fire Like it was a War', Alive in Libya, 20 February. Available online at: http://alive.in/libya/2011/02/20/they-gave-us-no-chance-heavy-fire-like-it-was-a-war/?utm_campaign=libyatweet&utm_medium=twitter&utm_source=twitter [Accessed 25 September 2012].

Al Jazeera (2011) 'Gaddafi Accepts Chavez Talks Offer', *Al-Jazeera*, 3 March. Available online at: http://www.aljazeera.com/news/africa/2011/03/20113365739369754.html

Amnesty International (2010) 'Libya – Amnesty International Report 2010'. Available online at: www.amnesty.org/en/region/libya/report-2010 [Accessed 25 September 2012].

Amnesty International (2011) 'The Battle for Libya: Killings, Disappearances and Torture', Amnesty International, 8 September. Available online at: www.amnesty.org/en/library/asset/MDE19/025/2011/en/8f2e1c49-8f43-46d3-917d-383c17d36377/mde190252011en.pdf [Accessed 25 September 2012].

Amnesty International (2012) 'Mali's Worst Human Rights Situation in 50 Years', Amnesty International, 16 May. Available online at: www.amnesty.org.uk/news_details.asp?NewsID=20126 [Accessed 25 September 2012].

AP (2012) 'Burkina Faso: Deaths Reported in Clash', *AP*, 25 May.

BBC News (2011) 'Libya Protests: Second City Benghazi Hit by Violence', BBC News, 16 February. Available online at: http://www.bbc.co.uk/news/world-africa-12477275 [Accessed 25 September 2012].

BBC Monitoring Middle East (2011) 'Qadhafi Promises "No Mercy with Traitors" in Address to Benghazi, 17 March', *BBC Monitoring Middle East*, 19 March.

Birnbaum, M. (2011) 'France Sent Arms to Libyan Rebels', *Washington Post*, 29 June.
Black, I. (2011) 'Libyan Rebels Receiving Anti-tank Weapons from Qatar', *The Guardian*, 14 April. Available online at: www.guardian.co.uk/world/2011/apr/14/libya-rebels-weapons-qatar [Accessed 25 September 2012].
Cherif, M. (2011) 'We Have No Animosity towards the Swiss', *swissinfo.ch*, 13 October. Available online at: www.swissinfo.ch/eng/specials/the_arab_spring/We_have_no_animosity_towards_the_Swiss.html?cid=31333628 [Accessed 25 September 2012].
Chulov, M. (2011) 'Libyan Regime Makes Peace Offer that Sidelines Gaddafi', *The Guardian*, 26 May. Available online at: www.guardian.co.uk/world/2011/may/26/libyan-ceasefire-offer-sidelines-gaddafi [Accessed 25 September 2012].
Chulov, M., P. Curtis and A. Fallon (2011) '"SAS unit" captured in Libya', *guardian.co.uk*, 6 March. Available online at: www.guardian.co.uk/world/2011/mar/06/liam-fox-sas-unit-libya [Accessed 25 September 2012].
CNN (2011) 'Rebel Leader Calls for "Immediate Action" On No-fly Zone', *CNN*, 10 March. Available online at: http://edition.cnn.com/2011/WORLD/africa/03/09/libya.civil.war/index.html?eref=edition_world [Accessed 25 September 2012].
Cody, E. (2012) 'Restive Mali is Ripe for al-Qaeda', *Washington Post*, 8 June.
Crumley, B. (2011) 'Anatomy of an Intervention: Why France Joined the UN Action in Abidjan', *Time*, 6 April. Available online at: www.time.com/time/world/article/0,8599,2063613,00.html [Accessed 25 September 2012].
Daalder, I. H. and J. G. Stavridis (2012) 'NATO's Victory in Libya: The Right Way to Run an Intervention', *Foreign Affairs*, vol. 91, no. 2 (March/April), pp. 2–7.
Daily Telegraph (2011) 'Libyan Army Calls for Benghazi to Surrender as Saif Gaddafi Says Town Will Fall Within 48 Hours', *Daily Telegraph*, 16 March. Available online at: www.telegraph.co.uk/news/worldnews/africaandindianocean/libya/8385250/Libyan-army-calls-for-Benghazi-to-surrender-as-Saif-Gaddafi-says-town-will-fall-within-48-hours.html [Accessed 25 September 2012].
Douthat, R. (2012) 'Libya's Unintended Consequences', *New York Times*, 8 July.
Englund, W. (2012) 'Russia Sends Mission to Syria', *Washington Post*, 7 February.
Erlanger, S. (2011) 'By His Own Reckoning, One Man Made Libya a French Cause', *New York Times*, April 1. Available online at: www.nytimes.com/2011/04/02/world/africa/02levy.html?_r=3&pagewanted=all [Accessed 25 September 2012].
Fahim, K. (2011) 'Accused of Fighting for Qaddafi, a Libyan Town's Residents Face Reprisals', *New York Times*, 24 September.
Fahim, K. and D. D. Kirkpatrick (2011) 'Airstrikes Clear Way for Libyan Rebels' First Major Advance', *New York Times*, 27 March.
Hauslohner, A. (2012) 'Libya's Weak Government Leaves Perilous Void in East', *Washington Post*, 20 September.
Hauslohner, A. and E. Londono (2012) 'Security at Libya outpost faulted', *Washington Post*, 30 September.
Hendrix, S. (2012) 'Free from Gaddafi's Uniting Grip, Libya Confronts Its Diversity', *Washington Post*, 1 April.
Holbrooke, R. (1999) *To End a War* (New York: Knopf).
Hosenball, M. (2011) 'Obama Authorizes Secret Help for Libya Rebels', *Reuters*, 30 March. Available online at: www.reuters.com/article/2011/03/30/us-libya-usa-order-idUSTRE72T6H220110330 [Accessed 25 September 2012].

Human Rights Watch (2011a) 'Libya: Governments Should Demand End to Unlawful Killings: Death Toll Up to at Least 233 Over Four Days', 20 February. Available online at: www.hrw.org/news/2011/02/20/libya-governments-should-demand-end-unlawful-killings_[Accessed 25 September 2012].

Human Rights Watch (2011b) 'Libya: Government Attacks in Misrata Kill Civilians: Unlawful Strikes on Medical Clinic', 10 April. Available online at: www.hrw.org/news/2011/04/10/libya-government-attacks-misrata-kill-civilians [Accessed 25 September 2012].

Human Rights Watch (2012) 'Libya: Wake-up Call to Misrata's Leaders; Torture, Killings May Amount to Crimes against Humanity', 8 April. Available online at: www.hrw.org/news/2012/04/08/libya-wake-call-misrata-s-leaders [Accessed 25 September 2012].

Ignatius, D. (2012) 'Libyan Missiles on the Loose', *Washington Post*, 9 May.

International Criminal Court (2011a) 'First Report of the Prosecutor of the International Criminal Court to the UN Security Council Pursuant to UNSCR 1970', 4 May. Available online at: http://www.amicc.org/docs/UNSCLibyaRepo rtEng04052011.pdf [Accessed 25 September 2012].

International Criminal Court (2011b) 'Situation in the Libyan Arab Jamahiriya', ICC-01/11, 27 June.

International Crisis Group (2012) 'Divided We Stand: Libya's Enduring Conflicts', Middle East/North Africa Report No. 130, 14 September. Available online at: www.crisisgroup.org/en/regions/middle-east-north-africa/north-africa/libya/130-divided-we-stand-libyas-enduring-conflicts.aspx [Accessed 25 September 2012].

Kenyon, P. (2011) 'Libyan Rebels Reject AU Cease-Fire Plan', *NPR*, 11 April. Available online at: www.npr.org/2011/04/11/135324882/libyan-rebels-reject-au-ceasefire-plan [Accessed 25 September 2012].

Kirkpatrick, D. D. and K. Fahim (2011) 'Libyan Rebels March Toward Qaddafi Stronghold', *New York Times*, 28 March.

Kirkpatrick, D. D. (2012a) 'Libyan Militias Turn to Politics, A Volatile Mix', *New York Times*, 3 April.

Kirkpatrick, D. D. (2012b) 'Election Commission Offices in Eastern Libya Are Sacked', *New York Times*, 2 July.

Kirkpatrick, D. D. (2012c) 'Libya Results Seen to Break Islamist Wave', *New York Times*, 9 July.

Kirkpatrick, D. D. (2012d) 'Libya Dismisses Prime Minister, Widening a Power Vacuum', *New York Times*, 8 October.

Kirkpatrick, D. D., S. Ali Zway and K. Fahim (2012) 'Attack by Fringe Group Highlights the Problem of Libya's Militias', *New York Times*, 16 September.

Kuperman, A. J. (2008) 'The Moral Hazard of Humanitarian Intervention: Lessons from the Balkans', *International Studies Quarterly*, vol. 52, no. 1, pp. 49–80.

Kuperman, A. J. (2009) 'Rethinking the Responsibility to Protect', *Whitehead Journal of Diplomacy and International Relations*, vol. 10, no. 1, pp. 19–29.

Lambroschini, A. (2011) 'Kadhafi Says West after Libya's Oil as Rebels Pounded', *Sydney Morning Herald*, 9 March. Available online at: http://news.smh.com.au/breaking-news-world/kadhafi-says-west-after-libyas-oil-as-rebels-pounded-20110309-1bmrr.html [Accessed 25 September 2012].

Levinson, C. and M. Rosenberg (2011) 'Egypt Said to Arm Libya Rebels', *Wall Street Journal*, 17 March. Available online at: http://online.wsj.com/article/SB10001424052748704360404576206992835270906.html [Accessed 25 September 2012].

Lynch, C. (2012a) 'Report: Human Rights Abuses Continue in Libya', *Washington Post*, 3 March.

Lynch, C. (2012b) 'UN Panel Documents Military Shopping List that Helped Topple Qaddafi', 4 April. Available online at: http://turtlebay.foreignpolicy.com/posts/2012/04/04/un_panel_documents_military_shopping_list_that_helped_topple_qaddafi [Accessed 25 September 2012].

Lynch, C. and W. Branigin (2011) 'Ivory Coast Strongman Arrested after French Forces Intervene', *Washington Post*, 11 April. Available online at: www.washingtonpost.com/world/ivory-coast-strongman-arrested-after-french-forces-intervene/2011/04/11/AFOBaeKD_story.html [Accessed 25 September 2012].

Lyons, J. (2011) 'Libya's Rebels Take Revenge', *Weekend Australian*, 5 November.

Malye, F. (2011) 'Libye: "C'était un carnage absolu"', *Le Point*, 23 February.

McGreal, C. and M. Chulov (2011) 'Syria: Assad Must Resign, Says Obama', *The Guardian*, 18 August. Available online at: www.guardian.co.uk/world/2011/aug/18/syria-assad-must-resign-obama [Accessed 25 September 2012].

Miller, G. (2012) 'Assessing al-Qaeda a Year after bin Laden', *Washington Post*, 29 April.

Miller, G. and C. Whitlock (2012) 'Al-Qaeda in Africa Is Under Scrutiny', *Washington Post*, 2 October.

Milne, S. (2011) 'If the Libyan War Was about Saving Lives, It Was a Catastrophic Failure', *guardian.co.uk*, 26 October. Available online at: www.guardian.co.uk/commentisfree/2011/oct/26/libya-war-saving-lives-catastrophic-failure [Accessed 25 September 2012].

Nakhoul, S. (2011) 'Special Report: The Secret Plan to Take Tripoli', *Reuters*, 6 September. Available online at: www.reuters.com/article/2011/09/06/us-libya-endgame-idUSTRE7853C520110906 [Accessed 25 September 2012].

New York Times (2012) 'Antiaircraft Missile Is Fired From Gaza, Israeli Officials Say', *New York Times*, 17 October.

Nordland, R. and C. J. Chivers (2011) 'Heat-seeking Missiles Are Missing from Libyan Arms Stockpile', *New York Times*, 8 September.

Nossiter, A. (2012a) 'Qaddafi's Weapons, Taken by Old Allies, Reinvigorate an Insurgent Army in Mali', *New York Times*, 6 February.

Nossiter, A. (2012b) 'Jihadists' Fierce Justice Drives Thousands to Flee Mali', *New York Times*, 18 July.

O'Donnell, C. M. and J. Vaïsse (2011) 'Is Libya NATO's Final Bow?', Brookings Institution, 2 December. Available online at: www.brookings.edu/opinions/2011/1202_libya_odonnell_vaisse.aspx [Accessed 25 September 2012].

Oxford Research International (2012) 'First National Survey of Libya', Oxford Research International, in association with The Institute of Human Sciences, University of Oxford, and the University of Benghazi, based on fieldwork from 13 December 2011 to 1 January 2012, in author's possession.

Pelham, N. (2012) 'Libya's Restive Revolutionaries', Middle East Research and Information Project, 1 June. Available online at: http://www.merip.org/mero/mero060112 [Accessed 25 September 2012].

Pileggi, T. and E. D. Richter (2012) 'Butchers and Bystanders in Syria', *Times of Israel*, 26 July. Available online at: www.timesofisrael.com/butchers-and-bystanders-in-syria [Accessed 25 September 2012].
Raghavan, S. (2012) 'Niger Becomes Crossroads in Battle against Militants', *Washington Post*, 17 August.
Reuters (2011) 'Libya Jets Bomb Rebels, French Press for No-fly Zone', *Reuters*, 14 March.
Reuters (2012) 'Analyst Says Somali Pirates Have New Weapons from Libya', *Reuters*, 13 April.
Rossi, A. (2011) 'Libya: Rebels "May Use Force To Take Tripoli"', *Sky News*, 28 February. Available online at: http://news.sky.com/story/838903/libya-rebels-may-use-force-to-take-tripoli [Accessed 25 September 2012].
Stewart, S. (2012) 'The Continuing Threat of Libyan Missiles', *Stratfor*, 3 May.
Swami, P., R. Prince and T. Harnden (2011) 'Coalition Forces Strike Sirte; Leader's Home Town', *Daily Telegraph*, 28 March.
Tripoli Post (2011) 'At Least 30,000 Killed, 50,000 Wounded in Libyan Conflict', *Tripoli Post*, 8 September. Available online at: www.tripolipost.com/articledetail.asp?c=1&i=6862 [Accessed 25 September 2012].
UK Foreign and Commonwealth Office (2011) 'Foreign Secretary Speaks to General Abdul Fattah Younis al Obidi', 2 March. Available online at: www.fco.gov.uk/en/news/latest-news/?view=News&id=559394982 [Accessed 25 September 2012].
Umana, F. (2012) 'Is Libya Dissolving?', *Foreign Policy in Focus*, 30 March. Available online at: www.fpif.org/articles/is_libya_dissolving [Accessed 25 September 2012].
UN Human Rights Council (2012) 'Report of the International Commission of Inquiry on Libya', A/HRC/19/68, Advance Unedited Version, 2 March.
Urban, M. (2012) 'SAS on Ground during Libya Crisis', *BBC Newsnight*, 18 January. Available online at: www.bbc.co.uk/news/world-africa-16624401 [Accessed 25 September 2012].
Vaïsse, J. (2012) Personal communication with the author, 15 April.
Walt, V. (2011) 'Gaddafi Gets His Revenge: The Price of Rebellion', *Time*, 17 March. Available online at: www.time.com/time/world/article/0,8599,2059596,00.html#ixzz1rs50RJlA [Accessed 25 September 2012].
Wheeler, W. and A. Oghanna (2011) 'After Liberation, Nowhere to Run', *New York Times*, 30 October.
Wintour, P. and R. Norton-Taylor (2011) 'Libyan Opposition Leaders to Get Advice from UK Military', *The Guardian*, 4 March. Available online at: www.guardian.co.uk/world/2011/mar/04/libyan-opposition-leaders-advice [Accessed 25 September 2012].
Zoubir, Y. H. (2012) 'Qaddafi's Spawn: What the Dictator's Demise Unleashed in the Middle East', *Foreign Affairs*, July 24. Available online at: www.foreignaffairs.com/articles/137796/yahia-h-zoubir/qaddafis-spawn [Accessed 25 September 2012].

10
Conclusion: The Responsibility to Protect after Libya

Robert W. Murray

In 2010, Francis Deng, often credited as the first to articulate a 'responsibility' on the part of states to protect humanity in times of crisis, questioned whether the Responsibility to Protect doctrine actually presented anything 'new'. Since its first publication in 2001, the R2P doctrine has been one of the most debated, and perhaps overhyped, issues on the global agenda. Its champions maintain that human security is the way forward, and that states have begun to recognize the limitations of Westphalian sovereignty, while starting to comprehend their inherent responsibility towards their own citizens, and those of other states as well. Prior to Resolution 1973 and the UN mission in Libya, empirical cases to support the claims of R2P proponents were difficult to find. With Libya now under new leadership and the removal of a 40-year-long dictatorship, is R2P to credit for such success?

This book has attempted to engage this very issue, and has done so through varied lenses. It is difficult to deny that Libya represents a victory for humanitarian intervention, but this remains a far cry from R2P coming anywhere near fruition. Resolution 1973 was predicated on humanitarian protection, but vague references and hopeful connections are not enough to qualify the mission in Libya as an exercise of the R2P doctrine. In order for R2P to be used, the International Commission on Intervention and State Sovereignty highlighted a legitimate process that would need to be followed, and some of that process can be found in the time prior to physical intervention in Libya. That said, what often gets lost in debates about R2P is the reasoning for the doctrine that leads to action in the name of human security.

To define action as 'responsibility', especially in a system of self-interested states, is no small feat. Typically, states are 'responsible' for themselves, and the history of the state system has demonstrated this point time and again. Of course, we can always find examples of states acting in ways that do not clearly show how their interests will be met, but perfect information is impossible to attain. The commissioners on the ICISS made one point very clear in their 2001 report – that in order for R2P to work, states must see humanitarian protection for all human beings as a part of their own self-interest. The ICISS did not reject the suppositions about self-interested states, but rather, tried cleverly to argue that states can still act according to their natural inclinations, but those calculations should include human security.

History was not really on the side of R2P after the ICISS report was published. Very soon afterwards, the 9/11 attacks compelled all states and international institutions to reevaluate the world around them and how strategy would be made in a world of state and non-state threats. The NATO mission in Afghanistan, starting in late 2001, demonstrated how an R2P-like mission could work if it was ever approved – collective defence, pooling of resources and a long-term commitment to establishing a new regime that accepted democratic institution-building as a priority. Yet, if Afghanistan proved how such a deployment could work, only two years later did the US, UK and the rest of the 'Coalition of the Willing' absolutely destroy the early hopes of R2P advocates by perverting the use of human security as a justification for an illegal and illegitimate mission into Iraq. The Bush Doctrine posed a great challenge to the philosophical underpinnings of R2P by showing that great-power politics and preemption were still alive and well in the international system.

Since that initial articulation in 2001, and the series of events that followed, R2P has been interpreted, reinterpreted, misinterpreted and interpreted again and again by brilliant minds trying to find ways for R2P to survive. The 2005 World Summit Outcome Document made the interpretations of the United Nations very clear – that the R2P already existed in international law and convention, by narrowing the focus to include only instances of genocide, ethnic cleansing, crimes against humanity and war crimes. This returns us to Deng's 2010 question about what is truly 'new' about R2P, and whether it has contributed anything beyond scholarly debate to the world around us.

Lessons learned

This volume brings together some of the most powerful voices on intervention debates and effectively shows one thing – that while R2P may contribute to our aspirations in the future, it is by no means an effective doctrine today, nor did it found the basis for justification of an intervention into Libya in 2011.

Opponents of R2P are often characterized as simplistic or unable to see what 'ought to be' in world affairs. Make no mistake – the contributors to this book see what R2P is trying to do, they just do not think it has done it yet. Further, the chapters in the volume go well beyond the prototypical 'it is all about oil' polemic in their discussions of why interventions can take place without R2P influence.

One of the largest obstacles to any sort of true R2P mission highlighted in various chapters is the structure and conduct of the UN Security Council. Hehir (Chapter 3) makes it very clear that, in his mind, the Security Council is a 'perennial problem' affecting progress being made towards a coherent implementation strategy of R2P, or anything like it. Keating's chapter (8), exclusively focused on the Security Council, argues convincingly that the normative framework of R2P is contradictory to the way in which Security Council members make decisions, being solely for their national interests. Keating goes on to contend that the Security Council's actions and decisions actually do more to harm R2P than they do to promote its legitimacy. The ICISS identified the Security Council as the single most feasible body capable of operationalizing R2P, yet both Hehir and Keating demonstrate the major challenges facing such a thesis if the UN hopes to implement such a doctrine.

The rhetoric and insistence on R2P is also very much geographical. Naturally, much of the R2P discourse is focused on the African continent, with so many instances of human insecurity which continue to plague various African nations. De Waal's contribution (Chapter 4) compels us to ponder the responses of various African states and regional organizations, and whether there is truly a future for interventions when states on the African continent show such divergent understandings of human security and the legitimacy for intervention by Western states. Among the most important lessons we can learn from de Waal is that by interfering in the affairs of other states and regions, Western states, in this case NATO nations, actually harm R2P rather than promote its effective use in the future.

Canada has always been among the most prominent nations in R2P debates because it was the then Canadian Foreign Affairs Minister Lloyd Axworthy who assembled the ICISS. Since the first publication of its Report, various Canadian politicians have invoked the concept of R2P in some cases to claim ownership of the concept for Canada, and in other cases to distance Canadian foreign policy from R2P tenets. Nossal

(Chapter 6) examines whether the nation responsible for assembling the ICISS has implemented R2P, and finds its participation in the Libya mission to be a far cry from Axworthy's original vision. Instead, Nossal demonstrates how Canadian decision-makers are very careful to avoid mention of the doctrine in their justifications for such actions, in spite of the hopes of R2P proponents.

As noted previously, R2P advocates have done all they can to find ways that R2P might be justified or implemented. Some have moved from debating intervention to arguing that R2P is a doctrine of prevention; others have claimed that even a hint of R2P is enough to proclaim it as a victory; and lastly, some have turned to the regional thesis, in light of the UN's failures to use the doctrine in the face of humanitarian crisis. Reinold's chapter (5) dissects the regional theory, and shows that while Chapter VIII mandates may be an option in cases of human insecurity, a serious challenge facing R2P use is that no two regional organizations comprehend the doctrine in the same way. To demonstrate this hypothesis, Reinold applies her argument to the African Union and NATO during the Libya crisis, and though both were confronted with the same reality, strategies and understandings within both bodies were extremely different.

Kuperman (Chapter 9) adds even more to the discussion of regional organizations in his direct focus on NATO's role in the intervention. Among the most important contributions provided by Kuperman is the warning to regional organizations and Western states that misinformation and disinformation can severely impact the likelihood of success in an intervention situation. As a result, Kuperman argues that, rather than a triumphant demonstration of NATO's willingness to employ R2P, the mission in Libya was based on misperception and may have caused more harm to civilian populations than moral good. Further, Kuperman's contention that NATO involvement in the Libyan conflict both escalated and prolonged the rebellion and subsequent civilian suffering should serve as a warning in future cases, including the humanitarian crisis in Syria, that humanitarian intervention may negatively impact civil conflict more than it may help.

Beyond the empirical cases included in debates over R2P, Heinze and Steele (Chapter 7), Hehir (Chapter 3) and Murray (Chapter 2) engage with the theoretical underpinnings of R2P and why its use in Libya is doubtful. Heinze and Steele, through the use of generational analysis, show that humanitarian intervention has become incredibly difficult to apply and understand in the wake of the 1999 Kosovo mission. They contend that R2P has contributed to a streamlining of intervention debates since Bosnia and Kosovo, but has yet to come near transforming our thinking or willingness to act in the face of humanitarian crisis. According to their chapter, the 'illegal but legitimate' precedent created more questions about intervention practices than it did answers.

Hehir's scathing critique of R2P is based on his contentions that rather than the triumph of idealism, misinterpretations about R2P being used in Libya are based on hopeful musings about liberal hegemony. His discussions about the UN Security Council and historical examinations of interventionism since 1990 show a clear gap between the possible use of R2P and the realities of selective interventionism. Reference is also made to the impact of the 'unipolar moment' over the development of the R2P norm, and interventionism throughout the 1990s and 2000s. If, as Hehir argues, the international system is on the verge of a shift from unipolarity to multipolarity, he interestingly questions how this will alter state strategy towards any sort of mission grounded in humanitarianism.

What would it take for states to implement R2P as a coherent and consistent foreign and defence policy doctrine? The ICISS made the claim that states could integrate human security into their self-interest calculations and might then accept the notion of conditional sovereignty and R2P. In Chapter 2, Murray delves into what it means for an actor to be self-interested and how rational calculations about interest are made in foreign and defence policies. At the core of his contribution is a probing of whether states are even capable of acting as moral agents, or whether such an idea would be entirely contradictory to the rational decision-making processes of states. Ultimately, Murray argues that rather than 'responsibility', states have implemented a 'Rationality to Protect' doctrine, wherein they will act morally if it is rationally beneficial to do so.

Future outlook for R2P

When Colonel Gaddafi was ousted and NATO claimed victory for its mission in 2011, many thought this might be the first step towards a wider acceptance of interventionism in the name of humanity. Libya represented a milestone of sorts in world affairs, as states came together in the name of civilian protection and passed a resolution aimed at protecting them from a government massacring its own people. Yet, within a year, the world is wondering what happened to that spirit of humanitarianism as the people of Syria are suffering horrific realities at the hands of their own government. To date, sanctions and threats of intervention have yet to persuade the Syrian government to end its oppression, and there is no clear intention of any Libya-like mission to come forward anytime soon.

Syria, of course, is not the only ongoing example of humanitarian crisis in the world that would fall under the proposed auspices of R2P. We can easily look to the Democratic Republic of the Congo, Sudan and many other nations if questions surrounding the need for R2P are asked. There is, frankly, no need to wonder whether R2P is necessary, because the world has seen, and is seeing, so many stark examples of human atrocity that a solution is imperative. This being the case, what has become evident since 2001 is that states and international institutions do not see R2P as the framework through which to approach human insecurity.

Libya was by far the best opportunity for R2P to be used both in principle and in action because it posed absolutely no genuine strategic military threat to an intervening force and very few world leaders would lament the loss of Gaddafi's hold on power. Though he was consciously trying to reintegrate himself and Libya into the international political and economic landscape prior to 2011, Gaddafi's track record over 40-plus years was not going to disappear so quickly. The Arab Spring demonstrated that northern African states, and some in the Middle East, were ripe for change. These changes may not have been solely focused on democracy, but certainly showed people's discontent with oppression and strife. When Libyan citizens began to rise up against Gaddafi, and he reacted incredibly harshly, it was not a stretch to imagine that Western states would be interested in overthrowing his regime.

The problem that faced states and the institutions they comprise was whether this would be the first true opportunity to operationalize R2P. All of the elements were there and its use could be justified under both the 2001 version of the doctrine as well as the UN's 2005 interpretation. The Obama administration was using the rhetoric of R2P, meaning that one of the main obstacles to R2P implementation had been overcome. However, members of the P5, the UN more broadly and NATO ended up doing almost everything in their power not to mention or invoke R2P in their justifications for a mission into Libya. Naturally, it is fashionable to blame China and Russia for their respective reasons for opposing the doctrine, but these case studies have effectively shown that reluctance about R2P extends far beyond two states.

To put it bluntly, no state was so committed to R2P that it was going to be the deciding factor in whether intervention into Libya took place. Rather, it was almost as if states and institutions were relieved when R2P was removed from the equation. Why was this so?

R2P is inherently a doctrine of intervention, despite what some of its cleverest advocates say about prevention or normative development. There is a reason it was named the Responsibility to Protect, and not the Responsibility to Prevent or the Responsibility to Love. Protection, according to the tenets of the ICISS report, involves action and action is defined by intervention when it comes to the worst cases of humanitarian crisis. Important to note as well is that intervention can take various forms, whether it be political, economic or military in form. The R2P is a call for states to act when confronted with instances of atrocity, and if a crisis is occurring, clearly it is too late for the prevention argument.

States are not moral agents, nor have they ever been. States are concerned with themselves and their own interests, which at times can be combined with moral or ethical arguments for action. When the people of Libya were being massacred, the UN and NATO intervened. The Gaddafi regime was overthrown and a new era of political leadership has begun to emerge in Libya. The efforts of intervening states were noble and achieved the outcome desired by those who approved the mission, but this is not an admission on the part of states that they feel, or will act in the name of, 'responsibility'.

There is no denying the nobility of R2P, but the contributors to this volume deny the reality of R2P. Libya showed that states can act if they so choose, but this does not represent a transformation of strategic or normative interests for states. In fact, multiple authors in this book rightfully point out that all language and mention of R2P needed to be removed from national and international discourse before approval of the Libyan mission would take place. As we move forward, R2P advocates must contend with a globe full of crisis and strife, without any obvious solution in sight. The one thing we seem to know for sure is that states and institutions have said very clearly that R2P is not their preferred response.

Index

Page numbers in **bold** refer to figures, page numbers in *italic* refer to tables.

Printed and bound in Great Britain by
CPI Antony Rowe, Chippenham and Eastbourne